VOLUME II

The Big Picture

WHY THINGS ARE

VOLUME II

The Big Picture

Joel Achenbach

Illustrated by Richard Thompson

BALLANTINE BOOKS ■ NEW YORK

Copyright © 1993 by Joel Achenbach
Illustrations copyright © 1993 by Richard Thompson

The essays in this work were previously published in somewhat different form in the following newspapers:
The Miami Herald (1990) Copyright © 1990 by *The Miami Herald*
Washington Post (1990, 1991, 1992) Copyright © 1990, 1991, 1992 by the Washington Post Writers Group.

Library of Congress Catalog Card Number: 92-90409

ISBN: 0-345-37798-2

Cover design by Georgia Morrissey
Cover photo by Bill Wax

Manufactured in the United States of America
First Edition: April 1993
10 9 8 7 6 5 4 3 2 1

For Mary and Paris

ACKNOWLEDGMENTS

This book has only one weakness: It is fraudulent. The title of the book, the chapter headings, and the tone of the writing suggest that this is a definitive work by an omniscient author. The truth is that the author is kind of a dolt. Ignorance, in fact, is his only real virtue. I say it proudly: Stupidity is my strength. To be a good explainer, it helps to start from scratch, to have no illusions about one's own expertise, to be willing to say during an interview with a more knowledgeable source, "I'm sorry, I still don't understand why water is wet. Tell it to me one more time."

(Of course, when it comes time to write the stuff, one tries to sound like Aristotle.)

This book is made possible by the real, authentic experts, people who, for no money or glory, have remained on the line and retained a sense of humor even though someone they did not know called them late on a Friday afternoon and said something like, "Hi! I need to know why all the molecules in the air don't just fall to the ground—and I need to know *right now*." And then did not complain when their intellectual labors were reduced to a single paragraph, half of that devoted to a digression about, say, the color of phlegm. To them I say: Thanks. I'll be in touch. Probably this Friday, about a quarter to five.

I am indebted to my editor, Gene Weingarten of *The Washington Post*. (Literally—gambling losses at darts.) I also owe special thanks to Elizabeth Zack of Ballantine Books; Alan Shearer of The Washington Post Writers Group; and Tom Shroder of *The Miami Herald*. This book is not a festival of grammatical errors and misspelled words only because of the efforts of Pat Myers of *The Washington Post*, who faithfully polices my illiteracies and has managed to teach me the difference between "leach" and "leech." Though this material was originally written as perishable prose it has reached the bindery thanks to the efforts of my agent Michael Congdon.

I am also grateful to Mary Hadar, Bill Rose, Susan Olds and Brian Dickerson; to the staff of The Washington Post Writers Group; to Taki Telonidis of National Public Radio; to Dave Barry and Judith Martin for their encouragement; to the many news researchers at *The Washington Post* and *The Miami Herald*, especially Elisabeth Donovan; to my friends and colleagues, for putting up with my incessant Mr. Science routine; and to Mary Stapp, my lovely wife, faithful reader and editor of final authority.

CONTENTS

x ■ WHY THINGS ARE (VOLUME II): The Big Picture

VOLUME II

The Big Picture

THE ASTONISHING ADVENTURES OF PERCEPTIVEMAN

PerceptiveMan does not like to wake up. He recoils from consciousness. There is too much stimulation, too fast. When you are pathologically perceptive, the humble act of lying in bed and staring at the blank white ceiling—the mere condition of being—is brutally difficult work.

Because even before PerceptiveMan rises from the mattress he has to wonder why anything exists, and why, of all the things that exist, only humans lie in bed wondering why things exist, and why it is that he, personally, exists (to make money? to radiate merriment and glee? to convert food into waste?). Plus there's the underlying, freakish question of why he is he and not someone else. It seems so unlikely, to be a specific individual, to wake up in the same person's mind every day. Why doesn't he ever wake up as, say, Shirley MacLaine, or as Queenie, the lovable but mangy dog he had as a boy?

He budgets himself exactly three seconds to deal with these questions (because he's got so many other things to perceive, and because the questions are kind of stupid) and then slowly, heroically, lifts his torso from the mattress. Assuming a sitting posture on the edge of the bed, he registers, as he always does, the mysterious and strangely weak pull of the earth's gravity, as well as the electromagnetism that pervades the room, most noticeable in the wavelengths known as "light" (though for a moment he thinks: Jeez, there sure are a lot of radio waves in here). He listens to the sound of water dashing against a shower stall as his wife performs her morning ablutions; from the open window comes a faint clatter of birds and insects, fluttering and buzzing through their brilliantly engineered yet dishearteningly mechanistic existence.

Why are bugs and critters so strangely serene? The answer arrives instantly: Because they lack self-perception, and thus do not see themselves as actors in the grand and hideous spectacle of life.

As he stands, he detects the autonomic thumping of the muscle in his chest, the usual morning heaviness in the viscera, the new and distasteful colonies of bacteria in the mouth. He thinks: Why are some things "alive" and some things not? PerceptiveMan has the answer handy: Everything is made of the same stuff, the same generic subatomic particles and bland dime-store molecules, but some things are just so much better *organized*.

A woman appears. He recognizes her instantly as the person with whom he has sealed a marital covenant. She is scrubbed, well packaged, sensible; he is certain that by any objective measure she is a modern Venus.

"What's the matter," she says. "Are you pretending to be that thing again? What do you call him? Smartman? Mr. Smartypants?"

Incredibly, she doesn't realize her husband is PerceptiveMan. She doesn't realize that he has a *secret identity*. He often wishes he could reveal his amazing power—he would make analogies to the Green Lantern, The Flash, or perhaps one of the X-Men—but he feels that with such power comes the responsibility to conceal it.

He crosses the room toward the door, conscious that he is thrusting each leg alternately forward in a rhythmic motion that other people call "walking" and perform unconsciously. The major question of the morning is, will he achieve his objectives? The basic mission, before he goes off to his day job, is to cleanse himself, meet the dietary and hygienic needs of his infant child, converse in a meaningful fashion with his spouse, and read the morning paper.

Most of all, he wants his coffee. Even PerceptiveMan needs a dose of caffeine.

The air is suddenly filled with wailing. The offspring is awake!

Obediently he heads toward the nursery, peeks inside, and sees ... a tiny stubby-limbed creature with a huge head! It is a human child, the spawn of his loins. He thinks of her fondly as PerceptiveBaby. Her mere visage never ceases to astonish him, to invoke a primitive reaction; he knows he has been stricken by what Konrad Lorenz called "the cute response." With her oversized eyes, button nose, rounded features, and foreshortened limbs, the design is perfectly calculated to throw the levers of love within the observer. PerceptiveMan thinks: This is why those silly pandas are so popular at the National Zoo.

The infant girl is indeed awake, sitting upright, toying with something in her hands, as though she were a squirrel with an acorn. But no; the girl is toying with nothing, it turns out. It is merely her *hands* she is playing with. Why can't we all be so easily amused, PerceptiveMan thinks. For example, why are thumbs so bizarre? They look like transplanted big toes!

He sniffs, then his normal college-educated voice leaves him, replaced by something with a prepubescent pitch, and he says:

"Are we a poopy girl?"

Conscious of his infantile tone, he rationalizes it by noting that babies respond better to the higher frequencies of sound.

He changes the child, then takes her across the house to the kitchen. He can never enter the kitchen without encountering a machine-gun burst of mysteries: Why isn't salt colored? Why doesn't yeast die, even though it's dried up and packaged and put on grocery store shelves for weeks? Why does coffee taste so great? Why doesn't anyone make homemade cheese? He doesn't know all the answers, but that's okay: The secret to perception is not so much knowing the right answer as it is knowing the right question.

Indeed, there are questions so beautiful, so perfectly constructed, that they are inevitably superior to any possible answer. Like: Why is there something rather than nothing? The universe seems so unlikely a place! So darn big! So troublesome to create! What was there before? And before *that*? Does time recede infinitely into the past, or was there a true Beginning of it all?

He spoons a green mush into a pan, lights the fire under it, fills the tea kettle, grinds some coffee beans, searches for a filter, goes back to the mush and rescues it before it burns, loads the child into a high chair, searches for a baby spoon, can't find it, and calls out for the wife. She finds the spoon instantly and gives him a withering why-can't-men-find-things look. He mumbles, "I do The Big Picture, not the details."

In life it is better not to see everything. Sometimes when he is in a crowd of people he feels, for a brief agonizing moment, the collective pain of the species, the dominance of negative emotions over positive ones, the cruel evolutionary strategy that gives us hate, anxiety, fear, grief, remorse, jealousy and envy, and only a few unreliable palliatives, love and joy and hope. We are ruled by primitive forces, attuned to potential enemies, capable of shocking explosions of aggression, insidious low-voltage hostility, irrational prejudices, and self-destruction both gradual and precipitous.

He often wonders: Why does anything matter? Why should we try to figure things out? Why shouldn't we just let life happen to us and not ask questions? *Why bother?* He knows why: Because life is a gift, shrouded in mystery. We are given minds that have the power to penetrate that mystery, if not solve it outright. Human history is a grand piece of detective work, filled with blind alleys, red herrings, misbegotten conclusions, lies, deceits, cowardice, and, fortunately, courage and brilliance.

Contrary to common belief, science has not been a dehumanizing force in history, it hasn't reduced the significance of the species. We've seen much of the universe with our rockets and probes and telescopes, and so far there is nothing out there as poetic as what Shakespeare could turn out, even on one of his bad days.

The baby is occupied with the mush. Everything is going smoothly. PerceptiveMan sits down and looks at the newspaper and takes his first sip of coffee, which is throwing off lazy curls of steam. His wife eats a Pop Tart. Everyone is consuming something, processing fuel; a living thing is an open circuit, taking in, sending out. From green mush is constructed the cathedral of the human body.

The mush, suddenly, is airborne, signaling the termination of breakfast. He tries to siphon one last piece of information out of the newspaper, but suddenly it all seems pointless. Why do articles look so much more interesting from a distance, when someone else is holding the paper?

He sets the baby on the floor. She flashes those huge eyes at him. She wants something. He takes a scrap of bread and tosses it down to her, says, "There you go, sweet pea."

"Honey!" says the wife. "She's not a *dog*."

She is right, of course, and more amazing still, she knows these things even without having to think them through.

He picks up the child, and she returns the favor with a smile, a pure and guileless expression. How very of-the-moment! thinks PerceptiveMan. And suddenly, staring at the wee creature, his mind goes blank. He is utterly thoughtless. The sensation is so pleasant he almost drops the child.

But "drops" is an inappropriately active verb for what is essentially a passive act, he tells himself. The child is within the gravitational field of the earth and will accelerate toward the planet's core if his arms fail to support her.

"Perception," he whispers, pausing briefly to appreciate the human skill at forming consonants. "My power. My curse."

BAD HABITS

Why don't we say anything when the person we're talking to has a little blob of food on his face?

We're a nervous, worrying species, and perhaps our single greatest fear, even more terrifying than bankruptcy or divorce or nuclear war, is that we will be leaving a party, having presumed that we were charming and brilliant all night, only to discover that there is something on our nose that bears a strong resemblance to brie.

What's really strange is that we are also disturbed by encountering a blob on someone else's face. Indeed, it's the observer of this indecency who always suffers more than the perpetrator. The observer has to make a choice: Do I tell this poor loser that he has what looks like onion dip on his chin? Or do I fake a smile, pretend I hear my spouse calling my name, and flee toward the keg?

Judith Martin (a.k.a. "Miss Manners") has written that it is best to alert the victim in such a way as to raise doubt as to whether the problem even exists; she suggests you say, "Excuse me—I can't quite tell. Is there something on your tooth?" But this won't always work. You can't say, for example, "Excuse me—I can't quite tell. Is there roughly half a slice of pizza plastered to your chin? Like, with pepperoni and extra cheese?"

There is a reason for this outsized reaction to so small an event. If you acknowledge the blob, you shatter the entire structure of the social interface, as it were. Any social interaction is a carefully constructed piece of theater, and it requires a certain *suspension of candor*. To speak honestly of the blob is to ruin the performance. If one person is socially slimed, everyone feels slimed.

Erving Goffman talked about this situation in his book *Interaction Ritual: Essays on Face-to-Face Behavior*. You would assume that only the discredited person would feel shame and embarrassment, but Goffman writes, "The discreditor is just as guilty as the person he discredits—sometimes more so, for, if he has been posing as a tactful man, in destroying another's image he destroys his own."

So why, you ask, should a mere blob discredit a person? Margaret Visser, author of the book *The Rituals of Dinner*, explains that human beings are obsessed with the idea that they are sealed, self-contained, impermeable units. The blob violates our rules of boundaries. It reminds us of our "holes."

"Orifices must not be thought of," she said. "We are undermined by the thought of having orifices and gates where things can come in, or alternately where things can come out."

She said of the blob, "If it's a crumb, it's not so upsetting. We don't mind dry, hard things. We hate ooze and slime." The problem with slime, she said, is that it has lost the characteristics that give it definition, and Americans want everything separate and distinct, not mushed together.

These taboos vary from culture to culture. In India, it is considered loathsome to save handkerchiefs that are sullied, but this is acceptable in Western society. In ancient Europe, people would vomit before a meal, to make room. Gradually people learned a few manners, and by 1460, John Russell's *Boke of Nurture* laid down the new rules of etiquette, such as "Beware of blasting from thy hinder part as from a gun."

So the next time you go to a party, remember to check

the mirror every five minutes or so to make sure you're not wearing any hors d'oeuvres. Repeat to yourself, under your breath: The food goes in the mouth, not on the face.

And one other thing: Loosen up a little. No one likes a person who's too self-conscious.

Why do couples always quarrel as they drive to a party?

The central, overriding cruelty of our lives is that while we are biologically designed to form pair-bonds, we don't seem to be designed to get along with our mates. Men and women have different brains, different tools for communicating, different emotional and sexual needs. A "couple" is like a store-bought gadget that must be assembled at home, only the instructions have been lost and you are certain some of the parts are missing.

Going to a party is one of the key times to fight. Olivia Mellan, a Washington, D.C., psychotherapist, says, "Couples have problems with transitional phases." People always fight as they're leaving on vacation. They often fight going to work or coming home. And going to a party is a nightmare. All you can think about is how you will be perceived. Your image. And in such a moment, your partner, invariably, seems slightly *defective*.

"You're onto a real situation there," confirms Isaiah Zimmerman, a couples therapist in Washington. When a couple goes to a party, "each one wants the other one to fulfill an image of the couple," he explains. "So they're trying to program each other."

There are preparty instructions, he says: "Don't flirt. Or don't leave me alone. Or, when you're talking to other people, pay attention to me and include me in the conversation. Don't drink too much. Don't wander off."

(And we'd add: Don't blast from thy hinder part as from a gun.)

The key thing to realize is that none of this is abnormal or sick. Unfortunately, there is this nasty tendency among

would-be experts to turn every difficulty into a pathology, to see pain and suffering and discontent as unnatural and probably the result of faulty child-rearing by our parents. This is nonsense. There are simply some quirky aspects to our biological design. And, who knows, maybe some of the parts *are* missing.

Why do horrible songs like ''The Candy Man'' and ''Kung Fu Fighting'' get stuck in your head, until finally you want to throw yourself off a bridge (over Troubled Water)?

Other torturing tunes:
    ''I Write the Songs'' by Barry Manilow.
    ''Frosty the Snowman'' by Burl Ives.
''We Love to Fly and It Shows'' by Delta Air Lines.
These songs are auditory viruses. They invade the sys-

tem, replicate, and resist the brain's normal antibodies. They can strike anytime, anywhere. One second you are a normal, intelligent person, and the next, you hear yourself singing, "*Who* can make the sun riiiise. . . . "

And you can't stop! Your body has been seized by the spirit of Sammy Davis, Jr.!

". . . the Candy Man can!"

We have two thoughts on this, and together they may add up to something like an actual answer:

1. Humans are prone to addiction. The pleasure centers in the brain seize on something they like, and they are loath to let go. "It seems there's almost a tendency for the brain to become addicted to pleasurable pastimes, whatever they may be," says Dan Alkon, director of the Neural Systems Laboratory at the National Institutes of Health.

But now you might argue that the paradox here is that "The Candy Man" doesn't, in fact, make you happy. It makes you miserable. So how can that be called pleasurable? This brings us to:

2. Your brain does what it wants. You have less free will than you suppose.

We like to think that everything we do and everything we think is the product of our own volition (and cognition). Not so. If the brain is enjoying "The Candy Man," it will continue to hum that tune to itself unless you find a way to interrupt the proceedings. (The brain doesn't have bad taste, exactly. You also get "good" songs stuck there; they just don't annoy you as much.)

That song is stuck there for a reason. It's serving a function, not a malfunction. It's making the brain happy. What would you rather your brain be doing? Weighing the politics of the West Bank and Gaza? Calculating differential equations? "Those songs persist in your head because they constitute a satisfying state of affairs for you," says Isidore Gormezano, an experimental psychologist at the University of Iowa.

He says one reason some people have obsessive-compulsive disorders, such as washing their hands a hundred times a day, is that they are trying to eradicate disturbing thoughts that are stuck in their heads. They may suffer from recurring images of snakes, for example. "The only way they break it," he says, "is to engage in compulsive behaviors that break their thought processes."

So what can you do when "The Candy Man" strikes? There's a simple cure. Start singing "Frosty the Snowman."

Why do we procrastinate so much?

We had intended to answer this question in time to include it in the first *Why* book, but other things kept popping up, like the need to take naps.

Clinical psychologist Tom Petzel of Loyola University of Chicago told us that a procrastinator can be rooted out with a simple test. The suspected laggard is shown three anagrams and is told that one is easy, another moderately difficult, and the third very difficult. The procrastinators choose to do the easy one first, Petzel said.

Frankly, we don't quite buy this. It seems to us that a normal, sane person would start easy and get warmed up before tackling the harder anagrams. Moreover, we'd argue that procrastination has gotten a bad rap. True, letting dishes pile up in the sink is probably a mistake, but that's hardly neurotic, since doing the dishes is a drag. In fact, procrastination may actually be in your best interest. Through our own research in the Why bunker we've discovered that there are two direct benefits from postponing work until the last minute:

1. The no-time excuse. If you do a lousy job on something, you still can say, "Hey, considering that I wrote the entire story in fifteen minutes, it was practically literature." This is one reason why students cram at the last minute for tests—they can feel good with a B.

2. The dilation of time. If you procrastinate long enough, you can get yourself in such a jam that you have no choice but to perform at supraluminal speed with total concentration and magnificent brilliance. The net result is that a full day's work can be performed in, say, an hour. This is the definition of efficiency.

In fact, this entire book was written during a single Orange Bowl halftime show.

Why do men and women have distinct styles of handwriting?

In the days of Spencerian script, back when Tom Jefferson was inking the Declaration of Independence, men and women were instructed to write in distinctly masculine and feminine styles of handwriting. Each gender had its own set of squiggles, loops, garlands, tufts, knurls, jobbers, wangers, etc. This system was junked with the rise of public education, during the Industrial Revolution, when it seemed too much of a hassle to teach useless flourishes to the masses.

Now, the experts insist they can't tell the gender of a writer just from looking at script.

"I'm fooled all the time," says Ann Mahony, a handwriting analyst in San Francisco.

"If I were to show you a thousand samples of handwriting ... you'd miss on at least half," claims Kathryn K. Sackheim of KKS Grapho Consultants in Highland Park, Illinois.

Down in the bowels of the Why command bunker we jumped at that challenge. We figured that men would write with sharp, hostile, indecipherable letters and women's writing would be cleaner and softer and prettier and (no offense intended) loopier. So we conducted a thorough, highly scientific experiment in which we demanded handwriting samples from the first twelve people we bumped into. Then we roused two editor-types from their usual stupor and tested their ability to identify gender. They nailed eleven out of twelve.

But now we should note that they were guessing in several cases, and were absolutely sure in only one instance: an elegant, rounded, neat script that they figured to be a woman's. So let's issue our rule of handwriting, and the experts be damned: Women and men *tend* to have slightly different handwriting, because there are identifiably "feminine" and "masculine" writing traits, but don't wager your house and kids on any one given sample.

At least one expert agreed with us. "Technically, we say you can't tell a man's from a woman's," says handwriting analyst Nona Fried of Fort Lauderdale. "However, you can see yourself that it can be done. Men do write in a more angular, spread, sloppy fashion, whereas women write in a more rounded, smooth, flowing style."

Okay . . . but why's that?

Miami handwriting analyst Roxanne Lux suggests that it's brain-related. Men are more logical, linear-thinking, and women are more "pictorial," she says.

It might be wiser to assume that biological factors, if they exist at all, are overwhelmed by environmental ones—namely, that traditionally girls are taught to be pretty in every way, and thus have more decorative handwriting. Boys are trained as brutes.

Now let's talk about graphology. A fun profession. Check someone's handwriting and you can supposedly tell if he or she is happy, sad, a sniveling worm, a drooling geek, a cackling psychopath, and so on. "You can tell a person is likely to have committed a crime," says Lux. Criminals, for instance, have blotchy, smudgy, unclear, or threadlike handwriting, she notes. (Our advice to crooks: Type.)

You Analyze Handwriting, by Robert Holder, published in 1958, has all kinds of neat examples of his craft: If you write a small letter *f* with a sharp little deviation at the bottom, it denotes "a vindictive, revengeful disposition." If your *g* and your *y* have flourishes within the loops in the lower zone, it shows "a tendency toward moral weakness."

The book even contains a sample of Hitler's penmanship and says that the heavy strokes, fast writing pace, and *i* dots made like commas reveal a person who is "over-tense." (World War II: An example of what can happen after drinking too much coffee.)

We are inclined to agree with professional forgery-sniffer Dennis McGuire of Miami, that graphology is the slightest bit unscientific. "It's kind of an applied logic without a data set to back it up," he says.

Finally, a postscript: One particular deficit of the guy with his name on this book is his tendency toward a "wandering base line," to use Holder's phrase. This is where the script goes up and down in an unseemly fashion. Holder's interpretation: "Mentally ill and therefore cannot be trusted to follow a controlled standard of conduct. Unreliable but not dishonest."

We've heard worse.

Why do so many people like to smoke?

For a change, we'd like to see a pack of cigarettes that said, "The Surgeon General, who is no longer the guy with the weird beard who looks like a character out of a Stephen King novel, has determined that smoking doesn't look nearly as cool as it did in the original, Belmondo version of *Breathless*." Something like that.

Choosing to ignite a leafy vegetable and inhale its fumes seems sufficiently bizarre to demand a full explanation. It is not enough to dismiss this preference with the bland assertion that smoking is instigated by peer pressure and sustained by nicotine addiction. Something else is going on.

Smoking is a relatively modern phenomenon. The tobacco plant *(Nicotiana tabacum)* is native to the New World. Before the time of Columbus, Europeans had occasionally inhaled the smoke of dried cow dung for medicinal purposes—more evidence that living in the Dark Ages

was a bummer. After Sir Walter Raleigh popularized tobacco smoking in sixteenth-century England, King James I
banned the stuff, describing it as "lothesome to the eye,
hatefull to the Nose, harmfull to the braine, dangerous to
the Lungs, and in the blacke stinking fume thereof, neerest
resembling the horrible Stigian smoke of the pit that is
bottomelesse." (Okay, so maybe *that*'s what the Surgeon
General should say.)

Why would anyone want to inhale the aforesaid horrible
Stigian smoke of the pit? As you look through the literature,
the thing that pops out is that smokers and nonsmokers
are significantly different in personality, behavior, and even
biology. Smokers are measurably more extroverted. They
are also (not exactly paradoxically) more antisocial, defined
by one study as prone to "rebelliousness, belligerence, psychopathic deviance, misconduct, and disagreeableness."
They even get in more car accidents (from fiddling with the

lighter? Driving with one hand? More psychopathic deviance? It's not clear).

One matter of controversy is whether smokers have higher "orality." Some research says they are more likely to bite nails, chew pencils, drink lots of coffee, and engage in other "nonnutritional oral intake activities," as one study put it. Sigmund Freud also focused on orality, as you'd guess. To him cigars and cigarettes were loaded with symbolism. Smoking was an autoerotic reenactment of infant suckling, he thought. Freud himself smoked twenty cigars a day. He also had thirty-three operations for mouth cancer, according to one book we read. Killed him, eventually.

None of this, though, is an adequate explanation of why people smoke. What most explanations leave out is the fact that people *like* what the buzz of nicotine does for them. The flavor of tobacco is secondary; one study showed that only twenty percent of smokers cited flavor as the reason they smoke. What they do enjoy is the way smoking regulates their mood and mental alertness. Nicotine has dual effects on the brain: It can be either a stimulant or a relaxant, depending on your previous state (if you are stuporous, it perks you up). It measurably helps people stay alert, particularly in tedious jobs.

"The ease with which nicotine can produce rapid, reversible, biphasic effects over a small dose range is a remarkable characteristic which singles it out from most other drugs," writes Heather Ashton and Rob Stepney in the 1982 book *Smoking: Psychology and Pharmacology.* So ultimately, smoking is a form of nicotine self-administration. Nicotine is so powerful a drug that a single drop placed on the tongue of a dog will kill it within minutes. In lesser strength it's addictive; the Surgeon General reports that the "processes that determine tobacco addiction are similar to those that determine addiction to drugs such as heroin and cocaine."

Not so, says the Tobacco Institute, the Washington, D.C.-based lobbying group.

"I think we overuse the word 'addictive,'" Institute

spokeswoman Brennan Dawson said. But she added, "I think smoking can be a habit."

Maybe junkies should follow the same line of thought. You know: "I'm not addicted to heroin. It's just a habit of mine."

Why do so many Americans have a fanatical attachment to their guns?

There are about 200 million guns in the United States, plus another 5 million purchased every year, and . . . Wuh-oh! Statistics Alert! Have you noticed that no one can talk about guns without lapsing into stat-babble? Statistics have the remarkable ability to prove something that's not even remotely true (like, a single woman over thirty is less likely to get married than to be killed by a terrorist).

Let's avoid getting sucked into the Stat Wars and instead make an assertion that no one on either side of the gun debate denies: The United States has a "gun culture" unique on the planet. There is only one other country in the world that has a comparable number of guns per capita, according to Paul Blackman, research coordinator for the National Rifle Association:

"Afghanistan," he said, "is a fairly gunny sort of place."

We might also note that the Swiss have a lot of guns. They have virtually no standing army, so all males serve in the militia and are issued guns by the government. And not just puny handguns; they get machine guns. But remember, they're Swiss, so they're neutral about everything; the only danger they pose is that they might bore you to death.

So it's us, the Swiss, and the Afghans, brothers in arms. But why? Why are Americans so fond of guns even though we're famously peace-loving and kind and gentle—except for the occasional invasion of an annoying foreign country?

Our basic answer is that the proliferation of guns is precisely what America is all about.

There are twenty million hunters in this country, pardon the stat. The gun-loathers of the big city don't realize the depth and breadth of that hunting population. This passion for guns, which seems to sometimes reach levels of obsession, is an artifact of geography. America was founded as a racially hostile (specifically between whites and indigenous people) and relatively lawless frontier nation. It was an every-man-for-himself kind of place, where animals were killed not just because it's so much fun but also for food.

There was also, perhaps most importantly, no paramount ruler who wanted to keep folks in line by preventing them from owning guns (although slaves were not allowed to own guns, and in the northern colonies the Irish, Scots, and American Indians were barred from the militia). Thus America never developed the gun restrictions that are routine in other nations, like England, where, as a general rule, guns don't kill people. (*Soccer* kills people.)

Why do people hypnotically feed coins into slot machines over and over again even though they know they will probably lose a lot of money?

The way we usually answer questions is to hurl experts at the reader. There is always someone who can boast to be the final authority on, say, the digestive system of salamanders.

So surely there is someone who has studied slot machine hypnosis, and written papers about it, and given seminars with three or maybe even four people in attendance. But frankly, we don't care. This time, the Why Things Are staff is going to *hit the road*. Destination: Atlantic City.

First stop was the blackjack table. Ten-dollar minimum bet. Because we were feeling lucky, we bought not just ten dollars in chips but the big twenty. The dealer told us that, if we knew the correct strategy, we had a "point zero six" chance of coming out ahead, or maybe he said a "zero point

six" chance, but in any case we got the impression that a hundred bucks invested should turn into a hundred bucks and sixty cents. In other words, we'd be nuts not to heave the mortgage payment directly onto the table!

We didn't actually believe the dealer, though. The blackjack player has the disadvantage of taking a "hit" first. That means that if you bust, you lose, even if a moment later the dealer busts too. There's one other disadvantage that most players have: They don't actually know how to play the game. We had no clue whatsoever as to what it meant to "double down," or "split the cards," or "buy insurance." (And blackjack's easy. Have you played craps? You'd need to be a semiotician to figure it out. There's a big area marked COME. Is that a noun or a verb?)

Anyway, we were hoping to prove that gambling is irrational because the odds are that you will lose. What we didn't count on was . . . blind, glorious luck. Within mere minutes we were up by ninety-eight bucks. Gambling is fabulous! One minute we were Bozo, the next, James Bond.

So, then: Why were so many people over there with the slot machines, those silly one-armed bandits, gloomily wasting their savings on two-bit gadgets? The slots are known to return only about eighty-seven cents on the dollar. This is not a secret. So why would any rational, noncomatose person play the slots rather than the lucrative, can't lose, easily understood game of blackjack?

Four reasons:

1. Slot machines require no thought. They're brainless fun. Some people do not have an affinity for thinking.

2. It's cheap. Some machines still take quarters. So you lose, but you don't lose too much.

3. Winning at a slot machine is fabulously noisy. The lousy odds are the premium you pay for that one magical, rioutous moment of victory.

4. People believe in luck. "Luck" does not actually exist, of course, except in the sense that there is no reason why you couldn't hit JACKPOT every time you pulled the lever. But that kind of luck is randomly distributed and is not dependent on what kind of person you are, or whether you have a lucky rabbit's foot in your pocket. Luck is not even horoscope-linked. Yet it is superstition that keeps the gambling industry flush with cash. It's no coincidence that there are palm readers everywhere in Atlantic City; we even saw a phrenologist who charges fifty dollars to check the bumps on your head.

There is one other reason the slots are so popular:

5. The casinos offer retirees a roll of quarters to take a bus to Atlantic City. If it weren't for the retiree pipeline, Atlantic City would go under.

Why do we have a wider variety of negative emotions than positive emotions?

Not only are there a ridiculous number of negative emotions, say our sources, but the negative ones are much more intense than the positive ones. And the reason is: In a terrible world, negative emotions are more useful in the Darwinian competition for survival.

Here is an official list of emotions, provided by Richard

Lazarus, a Berkeley, California, psychologist and author of
Emotion and Adaptation:

Positive: Happiness, pride, relief, and love.
Negative: Anger, fright, anxiety, guilt, shame, sadness,
envy, jealousy, disgust, and love.

Yes, love is both positive and negative. If that's not obvious, you need to go take a long, reflective walk on a sandy
beach.

So you say, yeah, well, what about hope? Lazarus says
hope is one of those borderline emotions, because it often
is accompanied by some distress or unhappiness.

You could argue over the list forever. But let's proceed:
Why is life such a depressing affair?

"There are more dangers than opportunities; therefore
there are more negative emotions than positive emotions,"
is how Randolph Nesse, a psychiatrist at the University of
Michigan, puts it. By "opportunities" he means that, during most of human evolutionary history, there wasn't much
good that could happen out there on the savannah, at least
compared with all the nasty things (strangulation by
snakes, being devoured by jackals, getting ridiculed for bad
dental hygiene, etc.).

"Most animals are built to react more to danger than to
benign and positive circumstances," says Lazarus. "I
wouldn't want to suggest that positive emotions are not as
important, they're just not as acute in helping us to survive
and flourish."

For a good overview of some of these ideas, you might
check out Nesse's article in the November/December 1991
issue of *The Sciences*, titled "What Good Is Feeling Bad?"
He starts by describing a patient who wants a refill of an
antidepressant drug that takes away her anxieties. With
the drug, she's not shy at parties. With the drug, she never
feels anxious. The problem is, Nesse can't find any sign
that any of her worries in life are abnormal. "She was a
normal person whose normal feelings of distress were
blocked by the drug," he writes.

Another guy told him that he suffered from excessive

jealousy. Did he have reason to be jealous? Well, says the guy, my wife goes out several nights a week with another man, but she says they're just friends, and that if I don't stop being jealous she'll divorce me. Question: Does this guy have a problem? Answer: Yes. His *wife*.

Now, for an ancillary issue: We take our emotions for granted, and this is a habit we've gotta stop. If we see a shark's dorsal fin knifing through the water toward us, we feel an emotion called "fear" (or "fright"), and *no one questions that this should be so*. But here's the headline: We're scared of sharks not just because they're scary; we're scared because it's *useful* to be scared.

What is fear? It's both a physical reaction (heart racing, blood pumping to muscles, adrenal glands discharging) and also—perhaps more significantly—it's the experience of observing oneself being fearful. We watch ourselves undergo this emotion. So you should ask: Why wasn't life designed in such a way that we have only the physical manifestations of fear (the racing heart, etc.) without the emotional sensation of fear? Why do we have to get so *scared* when we behave fearfully?

Because emotions are part of another adaptive advantage we have: consciousness. Consciousness allows us to venture into the future, or into places where we've never been, and conduct imaginary experiments. Fantasizing—thinking about doing things, then calculating the consequences—is safer than actually doing those things. Like walloping the boss in the mouth.

So an evolutionist would say that consciousness has a "selective advantage" over unconsciousness.

The only downside is, when we get eaten by a ravenous sea creature, it's *really* frightening.

THE ARTS

Why do you never see parents in the comic strip "Peanuts"?

First we should note that, to his credit, Charles Schulz refused to kill the parents of his preteen stars. This is unusual in the world of TV and comic strips. Among the parents of child heroes, the mortality rate is shocking.

Nancy, the unprepossessing little girl created by Ernie Bushmiller, mysteriously lives with her Aunt Fritzi. Jody and Buffy of TV's "Family Affair" lost both parents in a plane crash or something terrible like that. Batman's teenage sidekick, Robin, lost both parents in a trapeze accident. Spider-Man alter ego Peter Parker committed himself to a life fighting crime after a burglar killed his Uncle Ben (note: he had been living with his aunt and uncle because of an unmentioned calamity that befell his parents). Opie Taylor lived with his widower father Andy and his aunt Bee. The kids on "My Three Sons" were also raised by their widower father, who was assisted by the cantankerous Uncle Charley. And, of course, the Brady Bunch came together thanks to a pair of dead spouses.

Why such carnage? Because parents are such a repressive, authoritarian force that, if not slain initially, they would prevent the prepubescent heroes from doing dangerous and dramatic stunts. So why, you might then ask, can't they simply be eliminated through the more common practice of divorce? It's a question of taste. Divorce is unseemly. *Death is nicer.*

Back to "Peanuts." We called the office of Charles Schulz in California and were given the official, traditional line: "Adults are never mentioned or shown because the readers are supposed to see the world through the eyes of children."

A bit unsatisfactory, we'd say. Why not show parents through the eyes of children? After all, parents are the major force in a child's life, and yet in "Peanuts" they barely exist. So let's float our own theory: The children in "Peanuts" don't need parents because they're not really children. They are proxies for everyone, of all ages. Listen to Peppermint Patty and Charlie Brown:

> *Patty:* Do you think I'm beautiful, Chuck?
> *C.B.:* Of course. You have what is sometimes called a "quiet beauty."
> *Patty:* You may be right, Chuck. I just wish it would speak up now and then.

Children don't talk that way. They aren't so tormented. Only adolescents and adults go through the kind of agony that routinely assails Charlie Brown. Although it's true that Charlie flies kites (ineptly) and plays hockey (ineptly) and manages his own neighborhood baseball team (ineptly), these strips aren't about childhood sports so much as about ineptitude, mediocrity, and perseverance.

Author Umberto Eco, in an article titled "The World of Charlie Brown," writes, "The tragedy is that Charlie Brown is not inferior. Worse: He is absolutely normal. He is like everybody else."

That said, it is true that in the early years of the strip, back in the fifties, the characters were distinctly more childlike, even infantile. Lucy Van Pelt was first seen in a high chair.

We probably should also note that some of the strips from the last couple of decades are cloyingly cute rather than timelessly profound. Still, the Peanuts strip comes up with surprising moments even after forty-plus years, like this strip from a few years ago when Charlie Brown is talking with Linus about Charlie's aging grandfather:

> *C.B.:* My grandfather says that after all these years he's beginning to forget the multiplication tables. The nines went first. Now the eights and sevens are going. It's very sad. I wish there were something I could say to him.
> *Linus:* Six times six is thirty-six.

Why are cartoon and comic strip characters often drawn with gigantic noses or some other disfiguring feature?

Check it out: Charlie Brown suffers from megacephalism. His head is a nearly hairless globe that's bigger than his torso. Andy Capp's nose is the size of a grapefruit. The King in "The Wizard of Id" has a nose the size of a watermelon. And Cathy has no nose whatsoever. Just a blank spot. No wonder she can't get dates!

Why do cartoonists distort their subjects?

Because otherwise they'd have Mary Worth on their hands. They'd have Rex Parker. Characters that look realistic lack the symbolic punch and nonliteral zap of the clownish freaks. Exaggeration is a potent form of communication. A caricature isn't a portrait, it's a device for delivering a message.

Caricaturist David Levine considers comic strips hieroglyphics. Levine, who draws for *The New York Review of Books*, noted that Leonardo da Vinci experimented with caricature as a way of imbuing his figures with some special menace or ugliness. Leonardo knew that a standard, symmetrical face is plain and meaningless.

We asked some other famous cartoonists for their thoughts.

Berkeley Breathed, creator of "Outland" and "Bloom County": "There's nothing that lends itself to stretching more than a nose sticking at a right angle out from a face, and invariably it keeps getting longer and longer." He said that when Opus the penguin had a nose job a while back, readers were furious. "Opus would not be Opus without a big nose. It leads him into trouble. It's where his brains are."

Paul Conrad, political cartoonist: "Quite unconsciously during the Nixon trauma, I started off with [Nixon's] head and shoulders about where they ought to be, and by the time I was finished [the shoulders] were way up in back of his head." Like? "The hunchback of Notre Dame."

Pat Oliphant, political cartoonist: "You look for features that are easily recognizable that you can stretch. You don't stretch just for the sake of stretching it. What you are trying to do is convey character, as you see it, by gaining a likeness which is more than a likeness. It's a reading of the person as well." He said that with George Bush he emphasized "thinness, meagerness."

Bill Clinton, we've noticed, is often depicted as being of bovine dimensions. We expect he will become increasingly cetaceous.

Why can Goofy drive, talk, wear clothes, and act like a human, while Pluto, the other Disney dog, can't?

Pluto can't do the things Goofy can do because Pluto is Mickey Mouse's pet dog. Thus Pluto is a lower order of cartoon figure. Rather than being a humanized animal, he is the *pet* of a humanized animal, and therefore his abilities must be limited, relative to his master, Mickey, and his master's pals, such as Donald Duck and Goofy.

Jennie Hendrickson of the Disney archives in Burbank, California, says that Pluto first appeared, unnamed, in *The Chain Gang* in 1930, then showed up again the same year as Rover in *The Picnic*, in which he was Minnie Mouse's dog. In *The Moose Hunt*, in 1931, he finally became Pluto. Since then he has occasionally spoken words, but basically he has been depicted as an inarticulate quadruped limited to miming jokes.

Why is *Citizen Kane* considered the greatest film of all time?

Not because of "Rosebud." That's the main thing you need to know. Critics think the sled was a mite corny.

No, *Kane* is atop the list not only for what is on the screen but also for how it was made: A young man arrives in Hollywood, having never worked at any length in the medium of film, and immediately cowrites, directs, produces, and stars in a masterpiece. Filmmaker François Truffaut said that of all the movies ever made, *Citizen Kane* is "probably the one that has started the largest number of filmmakers on their careers." But they don't make Orson Welleses anymore. Welles was a prodigy. At the age of ten he was giving public lectures on the history of art. At twenty-three he was one of the most famous radio personalities and actors in the country, making the cover of *Time* magazine after the notorious "War of the Worlds" broadcast in 1938. He drank a couple of bottles of whiskey a night, and preferred feasting to dining. Even his furniture was excessive: Because of its physical proportions it had to be lifted by a crane through the double windows of his apartment. (In his later years, Welles himself could have used such a crane.)

Twenty-four-year-old Welles went to Hollywood in 1939 on a much-publicized contract to write, direct, produce, and star in movies for RKO. After some false starts (he wanted to make a film of Joseph Conrad's *Heart of Darkness*) he produced *Citizen Kane* in 1941. Some reasons for the film's greatness:

1. Naivete was an asset. "It is one of the few films ever made inside a major studio in the United States *in free-*

dom—not merely in freedom from interference but in freedom from the routine methods of experienced directors," writes Pauline Kael in *The Citizen Kane Book*. Veteran film hands like cinematographer Gregg Toland were thrilled by the atmosphere of experimentation. Toland turned in a bravura technical performance, resulting in a film that is fascinating to watch, particularly in its deep-focus shots in which events are happening simultaneously in the foreground, middleground, and background.

2. It's wonderfully self-indulgent. There's nothing stuffy about it. Early on, we see the neon sign of the El Rancho cabaret, and then the camera slowly takes us across the dilapidated roof and down through the skylight to the interior, where the boozing Susan Alexander Kane is talking to a reporter. Later in the film, the shot is repeated in the same order, but this time when we reach the skylight we see that it is broken—by the camera earlier in the film, presumably. It's a gag! "Before Welles, Hollywood seemed only interested in telling the story as neatly organized as possible. With the advent of Welles, the process of how the story was told became almost equally as important," Frank Brady writes in *Citizen Welles*. Our colleague Hal Hinson, a film critic with *The Washington Post*, gave us the most concise explanation for *Kane*'s greatness:

"Perhaps no other film in history so fully exploits the possibilities of the medium, is more audaciously, playfully inventive, or more fun."

3. With only the thinnest of fictional veils, the movie is a devastating portrait of a powerful, then-living person: William Randolph Hearst, the tycoon of yellow journalism. Welles went so far as to show Kane's (a.k.a. Hearst's) lonely death at Xanadu (Hearst's castle, San Simeon).

Hearst, who was by no means deceased, was extremely influential in Hollywood and almost managed to stop the film's release. At one point movie mogul Louis B. Mayer, a friend of Hearst's, offered through an intermediary to buy the film from RKO, with a handsome profit margin included, so that it could be destroyed. That effort failed, but

Hearst's influence kept the movie from having a wider release and making any money. Never again was Welles given carte blanche to make a film. His second movie, *The Magnificent Ambersons*, was butchered in the editing room. He exiled himself to Europe and, despite a few triumphs, such as *Touch of Evil* (for our money a film nearly as good as *Kane*) and the recently restored *Othello*, eventually became known as a funny fat man on TV chat shows and pitchman for Paul Masson wine.

Why didn't Welles ever repeat his triumph? Perhaps he got lucky: Kael argues that *Kane* is largely the inspiration of Herman Mankiewicz, who wrote the original script and possibly should have had the sole writing credit rather than sharing it with Welles.

We have to wonder if the very characteristics that drive a person to greatness make him or her all the more susceptible to the damages of time and experience; a life led exceptionally is rarely stable.

Maybe the flaw is Hollywood: It could not handle true artistry. And maybe Welles's life would have gone differently had he chosen a less daunting subject for his first and most brilliant film.

Maybe he should have done *Heart of Darkness*.

Why are so many male movie stars kind of short, with big heads?

This is a Hollywood tradition. Ever since the silent film era, actors have had small bodies with large craniums. Gore Vidal, in his novel *Hollywood*, calls them "the little people, who were like dolls until properly lit and told to move about in that nine-foot-square area where the photo-play had its cramped limited life. . . ."

One theory we've heard is that big-headed people are more popular than people of normal dimensions. It may be that we are instinctively drawn to big-headed people. They have presence. At some primal Darwinian level, maybe we

Cineramus Megacephalus.   Some Nobody.

all want bigger heads. Just not so big that we look like Charlie Brown.

A more plausible theory, though, is that the camera loves a head that fills up the frame. It looks normal to the audience, and the attached body looks pleasingly slim. The rule that the camera adds fifteen pounds is too simple: It also *redistributes body mass*. It increases height and improves looks all around.

And yes, a lot of stars are short. "There seems to be an abundant number of rather tall leading ladies and a correlating number of relatively short leading men," says Jane Jenkins of the Casting Company. Another casting director, Mike Fenton, told us that there is a profusion of male stars between five feet seven and five feet nine and a half. "I think Sylvester Stallone is about five-eight. Chuck Norris is five-seven," he said. "The camera can make you look tall, depending on the lens you use and the angle at which you are shot."

Paul Newman is shorter in real life than on screen. So

are Mel Gibson and Robert De Niro and James Woods and Tom Cruise and Robert Redford. There is this rumor circulating (we've heard it several times) that Redford is somewhere in the neighborhood of five-eight, but someone once told us he looks no taller than five-five. (Any day now, *Variety* will break the story that Redford is no taller than Dr. Ruth Westheimer.)

Redford once told *Esquire* magazine, "I'm five feet ten and a half. I've been five-ten for a long, long time. That's why I'm not [perturbed] about all the stories wondering how tall I am. If I were some midget who had to have ditches dug for the actresses playing opposite me, if I were five feet two or something, then I would be [perturbed]."

After mulling this over we came upon the obvious truth of the situation: Movie stars are of normal height. For every Dustin Hoffman, there's a Gregory Peck. Clint Eastwood, Kevin Costner, Harrison Ford, and the *Terminator* fellow are not short. The average American male, according to the National Center for Health Statistics, is a mere five feet nine inches tall.

So even if Redford is fudging by an inch or two, that would make him about average height. The problem is with the audience: We expect more. We are biased. He's a leading man, so it's strange that he's not as tall as Geena Davis and Sigourney Weaver, who soar to about six feet.

Why is the copyright date of a film rendered in Roman numerals?

This is a truly obnoxious tradition. At two in the morning, when you're watching those night-owl movies on TV, it seems urgent to know when a movie was made, but the date flashes on the screen for only two-tenths of a second and it says XXLMMLXKGOOBERXXVVIII," or something like that. Why can't it just say "1937"?

The answer is: Because the movie people don't *want* you to know when the thing was made. That, at least, is the best guess of David L. Parker, a curator at the Library of

Congress film division. "The idea is that an old picture isn't as relevant," he says. "That's been given for years as the reason."

Especially back in the early days of film, there wasn't any magic in the concept of "old movies." Some films were made but not released for a couple of years; the Roman numerals just served as obfuscation. Even today, we see this practice in national magazines. Go to the newsstand in December and you can't buy the December issue of any magazine—they're all dated January or February, to improve the shelf life, just like milk or sour cream. And any issue of *Time* or *Newsweek* is preposterously postdated. Maybe newspapers should do this too. Thursday's paper should say Saturday. We need as many Saturdays in this life as we can get.

Why doesn't J.D. Salinger write anymore?

He does write. But he doesn't publish. Maybe he's written the ultimate modern novel, one step beyond Beckett: so minimalist no one even gets to read it.

Since *The Catcher in the Rye* came out in 1951, Salinger has published only a handful of stories, the last two in 1963. He has holed up in Cornish, New Hampshire, behind a high fence. His garage is connected to his house by a fifty-foot concrete tunnel guarded by dogs, so he can come and go without anyone spying on him from, say, a helicopter. He has, in the admiring words of John Updike, a tremendous "capacity for silence."

Salinger has long been attracted to Eastern mysticism and leads an appropriately monastic existence. One need only read of such mystics as Ramakrishna (1836–1886) to see the possible inspiration for Salinger's asceticism.

He did turn up in Manhattan in 1987 to give a deposition in a lawsuit he brought against biographer Ian Hamilton, who had tried to paraphrase many of Salinger's private letters. When Salinger was grilled by the opposing lawyer, he tried to be as vague as possible as to what he writes now.

"I just start writing fiction and see what happens to it," Salinger said.

"Would you tell me what your literary efforts have been in the field of fiction within the last twenty years?" the lawyer asked.

"Could I tell you or would I tell? . . . Just a work of fiction. That's all. That's the only description I can really give it. . . . It's almost impossible to define. I work with characters, and as they develop, I just go on from there."

There have been unconfirmed rumors that Salinger has submitted a number of short stories to *The New Yorker* during his long sabbatical from the public eye, only to have them rejected. *The New Yorker* won't talk about it.

Maybe Salinger is reluctant to endure a critical pounding. That's what happened the last time he published something, a two-story volume in 1963 called *Raise High the Roof Beam, Carpenters and Seymour: An Introduction.*

"Hopelessly prolix . . . they betray a loss of creative discipline, a surrender to cherished mannerisms," Irving Howe wrote in *The New York Times*. In 1972, during a rare interview with a *New York Times* reporter, Salinger said, "There is a marvelous peace in not publishing. It's peaceful. Still. Publishing is a terrible invasion of my privacy. I like to write. I love to write. But I write just for myself and my own pleasure."

Salinger shows signs of being unusually thin-skinned. He wrote a letter to biographer Hamilton saying, "I think I've borne all the exploitation and loss of privacy I can possibly bear in a single lifetime." This from a man who is adored, who has sold millions of books, and who, by modern standards of celebrity scrutiny, has been left alone.

We might speculate that Salinger has had trouble adjusting to the real world of mature adults. He had in life and in fiction a predilection for teenagers and children. As he aged, his fictional characters grew younger: Seymour was introduced in 1948 as an adult when, after a long and sweet talk with a delightful little girl, he blows his brains out; in 1959 Seymour reappears, having regressed into childhood. An interest in kids isn't abnormal unless it is exclusive of an interest in adults—such as the people in your family. Salinger's second wife sued him for divorce in 1967, saying his refusal to communicate injured her health and endangered her reason.

Whatever Salinger does, his place in the literary archives is secure. *The Catcher in the Rye* is still the greatest expression of teen wanderlust and colloquial writing, right from the get-go: "If you really want to hear about it, the first thing you'll probably want to know is where I was born, what my lousy childhood was like, and how my parents were occupied and all before they had me, and all that David Copperfield kind of crap, but I don't feel like going into it, if you want to know the truth."

Why are children more creative than adults?

Adults are creative, sometimes, but they aren't *pointlessly* creative the way children are. Children create for the sake of creation. They play make-believe games for no purpose other than to "make believe." They draw pictures for no reason other than to draw. Children just seem to be making things up as they go, as though life were a game, rather than (as we adults know) an endurance test of tediousness and pain relieved only by the hope that Ed McMahon may someday appear on our doorstep with a sweepstakes check.

Only gradually do their parents and teachers drum into their thick skulls the idea that art is a *product* and that they should feel bad if it's no good. And then we teach them that rather than playing like little kids they should engage in competitive sports, the better to learn how truly incompetent they are compared with other, larger, more talented, and ultimately more valuable children.

Eventually they turn into mature, purposeful adults who

have goals and aims and ambitions and daily lists of Things
To Do, filled with entries like:

  1. Make a list of Things to Do . . .
 27. Scrape grouting between bathroom tiles . . .
183. Learn Japanese.

It's not that adults aren't creative. But it's a different
kind of creativity, according to Brian Dorval of the Center
for Studies in Creativity at Buffalo State College. Adults
are more efficient when they create; their creativity is of a
more useful nature. The bad news is that as we get older
and more discerning about what is good and bad, we lose
the instinct for novelty, for open-ended experimentation,
for creativity for its own sake. Even our margin-of-memo
doodling becomes standardized!

"Children have a lot more of the novelty in them, because they haven't learned what works and what doesn't, because they haven't put up the screens on their imagination," Dorval says.

(Note the obvious analogy to Orson Welles and *Citizen Kane*—inexperience, we have to remember, is a great instigator of novelty.)

"The reason children are more creative than adults is they haven't learned to mistrust their instincts," says auxiliary Why staffer Anne Cushman, an editor at *Yoga Journal* and author of a widely reprinted essay on creativity. "School is designed to prepare you for a work force in which creativity is dangerous. I think there's a deep belief that creativity disturbs the status quo."

Adult society values creativity only with rigid limitations. Society values order; creativity is almost intrinsically disorderly. To take a simple example: Go into any office building and look at how men dress. They wear uniforms, basically. No one has purple hair.

It's certainly true that some kinds of creativity are rewarded, which is why there are many professional artists and musicians and many more struggling to make it. There is a market for creative ideas, funny scripts, beautiful paintings. But societal standards are discriminatory: We only value what's "good." Only good artists are supposed to make art. Only good writers are supposed to write. This is the orderly, hierarchical, capitalist way of running a society. So, unfortunately, we end up as passive consumers of someone else's creativity.

We listen to someone else's music. We look at someone else's art. We watch a lot of TV.

And we wonder why the shows are so bad.

Why don't characters on TV say goodbye when they hang up the phone?

Once you notice this phenomenon, it will drive you crazy the rest of your life. TV characters don't say goodbye! They just hang up.

There are other things you might notice too, particularly in half-hour situation comedies. No one ever fumbles for a front-door key, because the front doors are always unlocked. Neighbors barge in without knocking.

Until a few years ago TV heroes never buckled their seat belts. Since then the Buckle Up America campaign has tried to change that. Frankly, we can't picture Kojak buckling up. Kojak didn't even close his door, for crying out loud; he let the G-forces slam it shut as he accelerated away. (The verb for this is "to Kojak.")

"Personally, when people don't say goodbye on the telephone it annoys me," says Jennie Ayers, a Hollywood scriptwriter. But she adds, "I think most people don't notice it. I think writers notice."

One possible reason that TV characters don't say goodbye on the phone, and so on, is that there's no time for it. A sitcom lasts twenty-two minutes. Every line is supposed to set up a joke, be a joke, or advance the narrative.

The more important reason, though, is that jangling house keys or insipid telephone prattle would be a distraction from the story that's being told, not to mention boring.

"All that television *is* is a series of stories being told," says Ayers's writing partner, Susan Sebastian. "What's most important is what the characters are feeling."

In other words, these shows are not meant to be realistic, and the audience knows that intuitively. In real life, people don't face one direction all the time (away from the backdrop of the set) or speak with long enough pauses to allow for gales of canned laughter.

Though, come to think of it, that would be a great experiment for a week or two.

Why do TV commercials sound louder than the regular programs? And why doesn't the government put a stop to it?

There's a saying in the broadcast industry: Commercials aren't louder, they just sound that way.

This is not as stupid a saying as you might think. "Loudness" is not measured on a simple scale from silence to shouting, but rather is a multifaceted characteristic that can be easily exploited by advertisers through all sorts of electronic trickery.

Let's say a TV station wants to broadcast the Boston Pops. An orchestra doesn't play in a constant volume, you realize. The woodwinds are quiet, the trumpets earsplitting. This creates a problem for the TV station, as there is a maximum volume allowed by law. And if the station broadcasts the concert so that the trumpet blasts are at that maximum volume, the woodwinds would be impossible to hear. So the TV station uses a special amplifier that mutes the loud notes and simultaneously jacks up the volume on everything else.

This is called "volume compression." It smushes the sound together so there's less variation. The makers of TV commercials do the same thing, only more exaggeratedly.

Their motivation: to make it impossible *not* to listen. They speed up the commercial, take out the silent gaps between words and sounds, lop off the high points, and bring up all the "quiet" moments to the absolute limit. The peak volumes are no higher than allowed, but the average volume can pasteurize milk.

So, yes, you could say that commercials are louder.

This effect is often intensified by the frequent juxtaposition of a quiet, tender, "good night, John-Boy" scene in a TV program with a sudden commercial interruption for LICKING TOADS! THE NEW DRUG SCARE! ON THE NEXT GERALDO! Such juxtapositions cause us to perceive a commercial as being insanely loud.

The Federal Communications Commission has investigated the problem several times and keeps deciding to do nothing about it, on the grounds that loudness, as perceived by listeners, is too complex and subjective to be measured. In 1965, when commercials were in the Golden Age of Annoyance, the FCC put forth some general guidelines, like the dictate that "loud, rapid and strident" material "is to be avoided." (Is that a command? A prediction? Or just a cop-out?)

In 1975, the FCC reminded all licensed TV stations that "they have an affirmative obligation to see that objectionably loud commercials are not broadcast." When the government uses language like "affirmative obligation," you know you can get away with murder.

Why are aliens from space usually described by eyewitnesses as bald?

Because they are bald. How obvious! It is such a joy to live in a world of logic.

We made "contact" with four ufologists, all of whom said that the description of aliens in recent years has been impressively consistent. In fact, that's how they tell a real alien sighting from a bogus one: Does it match previous descriptions? Specifically, the alien should have a bald, egg-shaped head; ear holes but no external ears; huge black eyes that look sort of like wraparound sunglasses; skinny limbs; four fingers with some webbing; and gray skin. Also, he/she/it should be short. Like four feet six inches high. A half-pint. (We know what you're thinking: They're hairless versions of movie stars.)

The term "little green men" is now completely passe. Today, when the UFO crowd talks about people from outer space, they often refer to "the Grays."

"The generally accepted description of a Gray has only been around for about ten years," notes Bruce Maccabee, chairman of the Fund for UFO Research. "One doesn't know if these things are seen naked or in a suit. They do not have the proportions of human beings. The feature

Hair Club for Martians

that's most universally reported around the world by abductees is large black eyes."

Bob Bletchman, a spokesman for the Mutual UFO Network (MUFON), says these hirsutically challenged aliens aren't imaginary: "It's not the collective meanderings of a population gone bonkers. It's based on empirical stuff. This is what very sober persons have witnessed."

Evidently sobriety is the first thing the experts want to check out in a serious UFO investigation. ("Exactly how many beers did you consume, sir, before your pickup truck was beamed into the starship Googaloog?")

Philip Klass, who has made a career out of debunking UFO reports, says that almost all the sightings of strange objects in the sky come from straightforward, honest, clearheaded people, while almost all the reports of actual alien encounters come from people with psychological problems. One in every six UFO sightings, he says, is provoked by a plane pulling an electronic advertising banner, like those used above football stadiums at night. One in three nighttime UFO sightings are caused by nothing more than a bright star or planet, he says.

There's a logical reason, he says, why people always describe aliens as short and bald: because otherwise they won't be believed by ufologists.

Still, where did this image originate? No doubt within our own egos. Aliens "R" Us. Only they're us in the future. The idea that other intelligent species would be anthropoid is not entirely unreasonable considering our own terrestrial phenomenon of "convergent evolution," in which far-flung species developed similar characteristics independently. Still, it's presumptuous on our part.

The question becomes, then, what will we look like down the road? H. G. Wells speculated that human beings would evolve into creatures with large heads and little bodies. The hairlessness is an obvious extension of this evolutionary process—as we get balder, we're less like apes.

Why is Superman able to fly even though he lacks any visible means of propulsion?

Obnoxiously, Superman has never provided any reasonable explanation for his ability to fly. You might quickly retort that he's just a hero in a comic book, and so who cares what the reason is. But comic books, like science fiction, usually try to provide some vaguely plausible explanation for unusual phenomena. They distort reality, not reject it.

Look at other heroes. Iron Man has jets in his boots. The Sub-Mariner has winglets on his ankles. The Silver Surfer rides a magic surfboard. Thor throws his hammer and, niftily defying Newtonian physics, gets dragged along by the wrist strap. Superman? He just goes up, up, and away. It's absurd!

What we have here is the phenomenon known as Inflation of Superpower. Over time, heroes inexorably get stronger, faster, trickier. Superman is the most conspicuous example, because originally he couldn't fly. He could merely jump! That's why they brag that he can "leap tall buildings in a single bound."

When the Supester, as he is affectionately called around the Why bunker, first appeared in Action Comics in 1938, he was a humanoid of exaggerated, but not supernatural, abilities.

He could run about 100 miles per hour, bend steel with his hands, and withstand ordinary gunfire. There was, by comic book standards, a reasonable "scientific" basis for those powers: He was from another planet, Krypton, where the gravity was several hundred times that of Earth's. You needed super-strength (relative to earthlings) just to stand on Krypton.

Superman quickly became a phenomenal success, a mini-industry, and within a few years there were several Superman comics operating at once, plus a radio show, a series of animated cartoons, and a daily newspaper strip, all produced independently and, unfortunately, incoherently. The varying writers tried to top one another with tall tales of Superman's powers.

According to the book *Superman at Fifty: The Persistence of a Legend*, there are some people who think that Superman first began to fly in animated cartoons that played in movie houses. But Superman's cocreator, Joe Shuster, says Superman first flew—sort of—in the magazine: "There were cases where he would leap off a tall building or swoop down, and at that point he would look like he was flying, I suppose."

The inflation of Superman's superpowers culminated in the late 1950s when he blew out a star with his Superbreath. When it comes to violating the laws of physics, the man is a recidivist felon.

MIND AND BRAIN

Why does time speed up as you get older?

This really happens. You may have noticed lately that time is in overdrive. You spend what seems like forever in grade school, and five minutes later you're in your forties and worried about gum disease. Entire years go by faster than individual episodes of "The Beverly Hillbillies" in 1966.

No laws of physics prevent this from happening. Time isn't an objectively existing thing, but, rather, a dimension by which we try to take the measure of the world.

As we are taking this subjective measurement, two things are happening at once: We are receiving input, and are comparing that input to the rest of our memories. Over time, this means life becomes less "impressive," because each bit of stimuli has to compete with a greater amount of memory. Life gets duller, when compared to what it is like for a six-year-old.

Time is just another casualty of this. A year doesn't seem as long anymore because each passing year becomes an ever smaller fraction of our memory. Smaller is perceived

as shorter. But we know a full year has passed, so we can only conclude, reasonably, that time has speeded up.

Why do we use only 10 percent of our brains?

If you believe this, then you probably also believe that the Great Wall of China is visible from the moon. Or that alligators live in the sewers of New York City.

These are Fun Factoids that have the annoying characteristic of not being true. People love 'em just the same, though, because they seem to contain a message that's worth embracing. If we use only 10 percent of our brain, then obviously we're much smarter than we ever realized.

We're not dumb, we're just a bunch of underachievers! The next time some wiseacre tries to say something clever, *whoa*, baby, we'll fire back with some of them *snappy rejoinders*.

Richard Restak, a Washington neurologist who has written several popular books on the brain, says the 10 percent myth dates to the nineteenth century, when experiments showed that stimulation of small areas of the brain could have dramatic results. Touch a tiny part of brain tissue and you might be able to induce the patient (or laboratory rat) to extend a limb. There was an easy, if unscientific, extrapolation: If a small percentage of the brain could do so much, then obviously most of the brain was unused.

In reality, most of the brain mass *is* used for thinking. Any small-brained creature can extend limbs or see what's across the room, but it takes a big brain to handle the wiring necessary for a profound and abstract thought, such as, "I stink, therefore I am."

Today it is possible to watch brain activity through positron emission tomograms, or PET scans, which show electrical firing among billions of brain cells. Not every cell is involved in every thought or nerve impulse, but there is no evidence that any gray matter is superfluous. The brain has no unused parts, no equivalent of the appendix.

In fact, the moral of the story should be turned upside down: It's stupid to use too many brain cells to do your thinking. Restak describes a study in which two people, one with high intelligence (according to a standard written IQ test) and the other with mediocre intelligence, were examined using PET scans. Both were then given another IQ test. The result: The smarter person showed less brain activity than the dumber one.

Thoughtlessness, in other words, is a sign of intelligence.

Why hasn't anybody designed a computer that's conscious and has emotions, like "Hal" in the movie *2001: A Space Odyssey*?

We know exactly what would happen if we let computers think like humans: *They'd turn on us.* In every science fiction movie, machines are double-crossers. Give a computer an ounce of emotion and the next thing you know, it's Norman Bates.

There's also a more fundamental problem: We don't know what consciousness is, precisely. We can only define it in abstract terms. It's what allows us to notice that we are thinking about consciousness, and to notice that we are thinking about ourselves thinking about consciousness. What we can't do is understand how consciousness emerges from the hardware, from that big gloppy gray thing in the skull.

"When will computers be like human beings? I don't know," says Ramesh Jain, director of the Artificial Intelligence Lab at the University of Michigan. "The problem is, we know very little about human beings—how we see things, how we hear things, how we react to different things. The day we know human beings better, we'll be able to design computers like human beings."

Seventeenth-century philosopher René Descartes, no doubt confused by the fact that he had a woman's name, articulated the idea that the body is a kind of machine but the mind is a separate, immaterial essence. How did the mind interact with the body? Through the pineal gland, he said. (The *pineal* gland?! It's amazing how people used to be able to get famous by saying stupid things.)

Nowadays the idea of "mind" no longer meets the standards of scientific inquiry. We look in the head and see nothing but a brain. A chunk of matter. The prevalent view is that the brain is a kind of computer. Even things like love are supposedly merely the result of a certain pattern of electrochemical interactions among neurons. Marriage is what happens when two machines interface. When we get passionate it's just our way of showing off the hard drive. You get the picture.

The corollary is that we should be able to design computers that have humanlike intelligence. One major problem is that the human brain has about a hundred billion neurons, each firing at various moments. Even if this could be modeled in a computer program, it's hard to see how the computer ever would learn to be self-referential, to stand apart from its computations and discern itself as an entity. One famous dictum is that the huge electronic billboard at Times Square may be able to flick its lights on and off in innumerable patterns but never really will "know" what its message is.

Among the defenders of the old Cartesian view of the mind is Roger Penrose, author of *The Emperor's New Mind*, in which he contends that principles of quantum mechanics apply to mental processes. All readers of the Why column know that it's in our contract that we don't do quantum mechanics. So we'll summarize the situation: Since events at the subatomic level are really weird—electrons are kind of mystical little things, for example, lacking a fixed position or velocity—then perhaps those same kinds of spooky, indeterminate forces allow our brains to think in a way that machines could not.

The Penrose argument isn't likely to carry the day. The magazine *The Sciences* said of the Penrose book, "What seems at first a daunting piece of intellectual architecture turns out to be a teetering superstructure built atop a gut-level feeling that there simply cannot be a computer running inside Roger Penrose's head."

We managed to reach Mr. Artificial Intelligence himself, Douglas Hofstadter, author of the classic science book/doorstopper *Gödel, Escher, Bach*. He emphasized that there is no major difference between organic and inorganic matter. Therefore, in principle, a computer with advanced intelligence *could* be designed. Life—and human thinking—is merely the result of a highly organized set of molecules.

"I certainly feel that in principle, theoretically, it's

possible for humans to design a system that is very, very complex and that has its own personality," Hofstadter says. "I even hesitate at that point to call it a computer. The connotations of the word 'computer' are very strong in people's minds." He refers to such a computer program as "a synthetic entity."

Perhaps computer intelligence will simply emerge by itself. After all, that's how we think human intelligence appeared: It evolved from an earlier, brutish state. We needed about a couple of million years. Computers may need only a few decades before they can utter a collective gasp and realize they are living entities, albeit synthetic.

And then, suddenly, the 24-hour tellers will stop dispensing cash—and we'll know we're doomed.

Why aren't people with surgically severed hemispheres of the brain considered to be two separate human beings?

Because the right side ain't human.

Scoff not, thou cynic! This is a serious issue. As far back as the nineteenth century, German psychologist Gustav Fechner proposed that by splitting the hemispheres you could create two separate human beings. Such surgery had never been tried.

Fechner's argument outraged William McDougall, founder of the British Psychological Society, who thought that consciousness was not dependent on the continuity of the nervous system. He even volunteered to have an operation to sever his own hemispheres . . . should he ever develop an incurable disease.

As it turned out, such surgery—called commissurotomy, because the "commissures" between the hemispheres, particularly the large connective tissue called the corpus callosum, are cut—was first conducted on humans in the early 1940s. It was intended to treat epilepsy, and in some cases it worked.

Amazingly, this radical treatment didn't cause drastic

changes in the patient's behavior or personality. While patients had some memory loss or perceptual problems, otherwise they were normal. Today the surgery is still done in rare cases; at the moment there are about three hundred commissurotomy patients in the United States, says Mike Gazzaniga, a professor of neuroscience at Dartmouth Medical School.

But in split-brain patients, the two hemispheres have no way of communicating with each other. This allows for some neat experiments with bizarre implications. One common technique is to show the patient visual images that can be seen by only one eye at a time. For example:

A patient, N.G., was shown a picture of a spoon, but only to her left eye. (Because the brain and body are cross-wired, only the right half of the brain could see what was on the patient's left.) N.G. was asked what she saw. She said, "Nothing."

She wasn't lying: The language center of the brain, the part that allows us to translate what we see into words, is in the left hemisphere—and that part couldn't see the spoon. So the left brain answered for itself; it saw nothing. The right brain, which did see the spoon, had no way to communicate.

Then, N.G. was shown a picture of a naked woman, again to her left eye only. She giggled and blushed. She was asked what she saw. "Nothing," she said again. She was asked why she was giggling. She said merely, "Oh, doctor, you have some machine."

An analysis of this experiment is in *Left Brain, Right Brain*, by Sally Springer and Georg Deutsch. They write: "Her right hemisphere saw the picture and processed it sufficiently to evoke a general, nonverbal reaction—the giggling and blushing. The left hemisphere, meanwhile, did not 'know' what the right had seen, although its comment about 'some machine' seems to be a sign that it was aware of the bodily reactions induced by the right hemisphere."

Now then: You've got two hemispheres; they don't communicate; they are essentially autonomous. Why isn't that two "human beings"? Some people, like Nobel laureate neurobiologist Roger Sperry, have argued that it is. But the counterargument is that the right side cannot truly think.

There's a distinction, says Australian physiologist Sir John Eccles, between "mere consciousness"—which your average dog or cat has—and the kind of language, thought, and culture that denote human consciousness (we will ignore the humans vs. apes issue for now). Language, thought, and culture reside in the left brain. (There are exceptions: about 1 percent of right-handers and 40 percent of left-handers have right-brain dominance. Another 20 percent of left-handers are of mixed dominance.)

"The right side is a very stupid hemisphere. It's a very minor cognitive system. I don't even know if you could assign it the attribute of having an attitude. It might have some conditioned responses to things," says Gazzaniga.

That said, he had one unusual split-brain patient who was able to manipulate Scrabble letters with his left hand, and thus communicate from his right brain. When the left brain was asked what job he would most like, it said, "Draftsman." When the right brain was asked the same question, it said, rather cryptically, "Automobile race."

Why do we stare into space when we daydream?

Hmmm?
Oh, yeah. Right. We stare into space, obviously enough, because we don't want to focus on anything. To focus on something tangible and real is to be distracted from the deeper metaphysical mystery of existence.

The real question, which we would have asked initially were we not so slavishly devoted to the Why format, is, how far into space are we staring when we daydream, on average? It varies, depending on whether you are nearsighted or farsighted. For the average person, it's about one meter. That is, if someone stuck his hand in the air one meter from your glazed expression, the hand would be in perfect focus. This information should keep you busy the rest of the day.

Why can't we control what's happening in our dreams?

Frankly, we're so very, very sick and tired of showing up for work without any clothes on. And discovering that our spouse is, for some inexplicable reason, the person who fixes the Xerox machine at work. And showing up for a final exam, only to find that the subject is not "super conductors" but "superconductors."

Why are dreams so out of control? Why do dreams just happen to us, unlike real life, which at the very least has the superficial appearance of being slightly under our direction?

The key thing to understand is that dreaming is a *primitive* activity. It's not exclusive to humans. Dogs dream. Bats dream. Rats dream. Almost all mammals dream. And like humans, they have muscular atonia (paralysis) when they dream, to prevent them from acting out the hallucination. This means something: that dreams are an ancient evolutionary adaptation, predating the arrival on the scene of the human species.

Dreams may have first appeared in living creatures some 140 million years ago, says Jonathan Winson, a neuroscientist at Rockefeller University, and that is "way, way before language, consciousness, and human control."

In other words, you can't control your dreams for the same reason that dogs can't convert their feelings into coherent speech: The mental process is too primitive.

You might even think of dreaming as a return to the animal brand of consciousness. This is your life as a dog: You are the protagonist in a drama, things happen to you, you react, you are happy or sad, you are content or fearful. Yet something is missing. Thoughts! You don't really *reason* when you dream. Sure, you might have some abstract

thoughts once in a while, but in general a dream is strangely self-centered and action-oriented.

Why? Why are dreams so dramatic, rather than conceptual? Why do you dream that you are lost in a hallway at school and can't find the examination room, instead of simply dreaming the words "I am anxious about my upcoming test"?

Theories about this are plentiful. After decades in which Freudian psychoanalysis reigned, dreams recently came into disrepute after some neuroscientists argued that they are just mental junk, stuff produced by random electrical activity in the brain. But Winson argues that Freud was fundamentally correct, that dreams really are a "royal road to the unconscious."

Winson's theory is that dreams are a type of filing system. They are the mechanism by which the unconscious brain (human or otherwise) transfers experiences into memory. And since this mechanism is so biologically ancient, the "language" of dreams must necessarily be experiential, like a movie. A dog can't store an idea like "I get wet if I go out in the rain" because he has no dog language with which to express this thought; instead, he stores the entire cinematic spectacle, full of sound and fury, of venturing into the rain and getting wet. "We inherited this from a lower species that didn't have language," Winson says.

Another question: Why are we usually unaware that we're dreaming, even though absurd things are happening to us?

"We're conned by our unconscious," says Rosalind Cartwright, a psychologist at Rush Presbyterian St. Luke's Medical Center in Chicago. "Our most critical powers are very high-level frontal lobe activity, and that's not what's involved in dreaming. We're really down in our middle brain and lower stem, the primitive parts of our mental apparatus. It's very much the emotional side."

Some people can learn to control their dreams. This is called "lucid dreaming," but Cartwright says it's a difficult skill to learn if it doesn't come naturally.

"You can develop some control. For example, people with nightmaring, with really bad, unpleasant experiences, can abort a bad dream, recognize that a bad dream is happening, and pop their eyes open," she says.

Now if we could only find a similar trick that works when we're awake.

BABIES AND BIOLOGY

(In which the author tries to salvage the quaint notion of parenting.)

abies who aren't cuddled don't grow. They fail to "thrive," as doctors put it. Everyone knows this. It's one of those reassuring True Science Facts. The lesson is that parenting, not merely food and water and oxygen, is what injects life into a child. That we are more than machines. That love matters.

Alas, it's untrue! I have here in my hands *The World of the Newborn*, a wonderfully unsentimental and scientific book by Daphne and Charles Maurer, and they report that the response to fondling is far more "mechanical" than emotional. For example, premature babies grow more quickly "when they are merely massaged regularly but quite impersonally by the gloved hands of an unseen technician."

Lovely stuff! Our presumption that a baby responds to a mother's love is further shaken by the discovery that rat pups also need the stroking of a mother's ratty little tongue—presumably an act of rat instinct, not emotion. Write the Maurers, "Indeed, rat pups resemble human babies so closely in their need for stimulation that researchers have been able to switch back and forth between study-ing rats and studying babies, to work out some of the phys-iological mechanisms involved."

Humans, vermin, it's all the same.

Here's another charming thing I've just learned: My ba-by's laughter is fake. When I blow on her belly or give her a long kiss to the cheek she laughs and squeals, and until now I had assumed this was because Daddy is such a hoot. But according to the Maurers, a small baby's laughter is "without humor" and "is merely a reflex at the level of the knee jerk."

It gets worse. She doesn't even know I'm alive! She doesn't yet perceive the world as a series of discrete ob-jects and individuals; just as she lacks knowledge of her-self as an independent entity, so too am I denied that condition. I'm no more alive than the educational mobile or the wind-up fuzzy lamb. All those sweet smiles, they're just reflex. She gives the same smile to the pizza man! Ac-cording to the Maurers, "Real attachment cannot develop before seven to eight months, for the baby must under-stand that things exist before he can form attachments to them, and he must be able to recollect things that are not in front of him to be able to maintain those attachments from one moment to the next."

Here's another delightful science fact: *Babies aren't cute.* This is hard for a new parent to accept, particularly those of us with babies that are so "cute" that we fear we will be unable to love our subsequent and presumably less at-tractive offspring. I require friends, associates, and total strangers at the zoo to comment on her surpassing beauty if they want to remain in her presence. (Fortunately, ev-eryone obliges, because as a social species, relying on re-lations between extended kinship groups, we develop rules that we call "etiquette," which prevent someone from say-ing, for example, "Excuse me, but I can't help but notice that your child looks like the spawn of a grouper.")

The problem with "cute" is that it has no objective re-ality, no trustworthy unit of measurement. It is not like the speed of light or the diameter of an electron. According to anthropologist Donald Symons, the belief in cuteness is just a trick that we play on ourselves, an evolutionary adaptation that makes us perceive a certain set of visual images (silky hair, symmetrical face, big eyes, soft skin, puffy cheeks) as an objectively existing phenomenon worthy of adjectival description ("a cute baby").

Says Symons, "The cuteness is an adaptation of the beholder, just like beauty or anything else. There's no such thing as cute out there in the environment."

Someone should put that on a Hallmark card.

Biology, biology, biology: It is the science of the nineties. It's getting downright oppressive. We seem to be entering a new and disturbing phase in the history of science, an era of biological totalitarianism, when all the foibles and glories of human existence turn out to be predetermined by genes. The secret agents of civilization, we are now told, have nothing to do with the CIA or FBI; they are protein sequences on strands of DNA. The decisions we thought were made with free will are but the dictates of the biological thought police.

Everything in life—love, hatred, aggression, anxiety—has been reduced to some biological imperative, some survival mechanism that dates to our tenure on the savannah.

Male philandering? That's a statistically based strategy for optimizing sperm distribution.

Female intuition? Women have more connective tissue in the corpus callosum, linking the hemispheres of the brain.

Male impotence? That's merely an insufficiency of nitric oxide.

Hardly a week passes without some story in the newspaper announcing that researchers are smacking their foreheads and saying, Whoa! We were wrong all along! It's just a gene thing! On December 17, 1991, *The Washington Post* reported that scientists studying homosexuality among brothers concluded that it must have a strong genetic component, results that "appear to contradict the widely held perception that sexual orientation is largely determined by a child's early influences, conditioning and environment."

Biology has been booming for about fifteen years, following roughly half a century in which a favorite parlor
game was arguing over Nature vs. Nurture. That battle is
just about over. Nature won.

The question now is, if we're mostly mechanistic, what's
left for Mom and Dad to do? Have we been marginalized
by biology? Are we just supposed to stand by and clap
while the little computers boot up and display their preprogrammed precociousness?

Do parents matter anymore?

Does love?

I look to my kid for an answer, and the first thing I notice is: *Damn*, she's cute.

My job requires me to talk to experts, to get answers to
things. Like, why do little boys go "pow-pow" with sticks
if they can't get their hands on an actual toy gun? Twenty
years ago, the experts would have cited "culture" as the
reason. Boys are programmed to be monstrously aggressive. They are forced to emulate G.I. Joe. Little girls are
channeled into nurturing roles. Blue rooms, pink rooms.

Today, that's like believing in the flat earth. Only an old
guard still clings to the culture explanation. The new theory—so obvious to every parent—is that boys are just that
way.

This change in scientific opinion has just now percolated
through the protective filters of conventional wisdom and
reached the mass public. These things become official when
they reach the cover of *Time* magazine, and a new issue
asks, "Why Are Men and Women Different?" The answer,
of course, is biology.

The cynics will say it's just political fashion. That this
is part of the conservative swing in America. Science,
truly, has always been political, and just as surely biology
has been used as a weapon against women, blacks, Jews,
the Irish, the Poles, and on and on. Even today the people
you hear talking about biology most vehemently, most
passionately, tend to be radical racists like David Duke
and Leonard Jeffries. Biology is a science that makes
trouble. It's politically suspect. Talk about biology at a

cocktail party and you'll be left alone with the chips and dip.

Forget facts and empiricism; people still communicate at the emotional level. The biology rap sounds hostile. It intrudes upon one's comfort zone.

Consider the reaction to the report in 1991 that certain cells in the hypothalamus are larger in heterosexual men than in homosexual men or in women. I spoke at the time to John P. De Cecco, a professor of psychology at San Francisco State University and editor of the *Journal of Homosexuality*. He was incensed by the report—never mind that the author of the study, Simon LeVay, was openly gay himself.

"What this man is claiming is that gay men have malformed brains," De Cecco said. "I'm unwilling to buy gay liberation at the price of being considered abnormal. I think the whole thing is insulting."

He blasted the biology boom in general: "It's reductionist research. It tries to reduce human beings pretty much to the level of rat behavior. It simply is ignoring the fact that we're thinking animals, that we have a whole cortex, and out of that cortex arises a whole civilization over years, and we're no longer just responsive to our animal makeup."

I got a totally different reaction from G. Luther Whitington, an editor for *The Advocate*, a gay and lesbian news magazine. Whitington said the LeVay study came as a great relief. He had always felt gay. His closest friends had always felt gay too. The old-fashioned psychoanalytic theories (i.e., domineering mother/absent father) didn't apply to his circle of friends. The LeVay study implied that their homosexuality was natural—that God had made them that way.

"I was very excited," he said. "I feel like, in the long run, this type of an argument, or this type of scientific proof, is exactly what the gay and lesbian movement needs to fight right-wing homophobes, to show that being gay or lesbian is not like being Methodist or Presbyterian, it's not a choice."

Even the language of the gay community has changed in recent years. No longer should one say "sexual preference." That's verboten. Now, you say "sexual orientation."

The Nature vs. Nurture debate first broke out back in the 1920s. Before then, Nature ruled. Nature, it was thought, justified European imperialism, racial discrimination, etc. The facts suddenly intruded: Tests showed that theories of intelligence were wrong, that economic status (environment)—not race or ethnicity or gender—seemed the prime predictor of IQ test performance. The Nature/Nurture debate was resolved, temporarily, with the sensible conclusion that both are major factors in shaping human society.

But starting in the 1930s, and for decades thereafter, social scientists increasingly ignored "the biological side of the compromise," according to Carl Degler in his recent book *In Search of Human Nature.*

Margaret Mead, the great anthropologist, instigated much of the shift toward Nurture. In 1935, after studying several primitive societies in New Guinea, she wrote, "We are forced to conclude that human nature is almost unbelievably malleable, responding accurately and contrastingly to contrasting cultural conditions." The sexes had virtually no innate differences, she said: "We may say that many, if not all, of the personality traits which we have called masculine or feminine are as lightly linked to sex as are the clothing, the manners, and the form of headdress that a society at a given period assigns to either sex."

There developed a belief in "cultural determinism." The radicals in the Nuture camp argued that humans were limitlessly plastic, that you could take a baby and make it into a killer, or take the same baby and make it into a saint. It was an intoxicating thought. People could be changed! If human nature were plastic, unfixed, it could be reshaped and manipulated into something better. We could re-create humankind. Patriarchy could be overthrown. Imperialism could be reversed. What a brave new world it would be!

In 1954, anthropologist Ashley Montagu said that a human "has no instincts, because everything he is and has become he has learned, acquired, from his culture, from the man-made part of the environment, from other human beings."

There was one major problem: Reality wouldn't behave. Babies refused to adhere to the theories expounded in classrooms. Around the world, newly progressive parents were stunned when their gender-neutral childrearing resulted, damn it all, in aggressive boys and sweet-natured girls. These kids just wouldn't learn.

Then came E. O. Wilson. This Harvard professor is probably the single person most responsible for the resurgence of Nature as a valid explanation of human behavior. His groundbreaking 1975 book *Sociobiology* was, as it happens, about bees and ants. Only in the last chapter did he address humans, and he made the not-too-unreasonable assertion that relatively small genetic differences between human groups might predispose human societies toward cultural differences.

The academic community was shocked, shocked!

Wilson's own colleagues ganged up on him. Harvard biologist Richard Lewontin—who had said in a 1973 interview that "nothing we can know about the genetics of human behavior can have any implications for human society"—was one of a number of Boston scientists who formed the Science for the People Sociobiology Study Group. The group all but labeled Wilson a Nazi. Such sociobiological theories, the group said, helped inspire "the eugenics politics which led to the establishment of gas chambers in Nazi Germany."

I spoke to Lewontin last year and he remains a critic of Wilson and all these other newfangled biological theories. Lewontin's argument is that these theories simply haven't been proven, that the science is flimsy.

"I think it's the same bull it always was," he said. "It amounts to a large amount of fanciful storytelling with no really solid genetic basis at all."

He does not, however, absolutely reject the role of biology in human society. "Look, some of it's probably right."

When I spoke to Wilson, he said Nature didn't defeat Nurture, exactly; Nature merely regained permission to be part of the equation. "The Nurture view," he said, "was more ideological. It was insisted upon by people who thought that was the necessary view, the prerequisite view, for an egalitarian political philosophy."

Egalitarianism isn't dead. But sameness is. Egalitarianism must now promote itself without gambling everything on the belief that every human being is an identical, mass-produced, blank unit, waiting for Mommy and Daddy and Society to transform it into a winner or a loser, a victor or a victim.

There's consolation in biology for all of us. Our problems—substance abuse, depression, anger, impotence, sexual deviance—are probably not the fault of our parents. They may not even be the fault of our character (though this line of argument can obviously be taken too far). They may not even be faults at all. If my child turns out to be a drug addict, or a manic depressive, or a ne'er-do-well, I won't immediately assume it was my fault. (And if she turns out to be a hero? Well, come on, that's the sign of a great father.)

Anyone convinced that parenting is the crucial determinant of how a child grows up need merely look at the studies of identical twins raised apart. One of the most celebrated cases was that of Jerry Levey and Mark Newman, once united in a single fertilized cell, separated as newborns, reunited at the age of thirty. Both had similar mustaches and hairstyles, wore aviator glasses and big belt buckles, and carried oversized, industrial-looking key rings. Both were captains with their local volunteer fire departments. Both made their living installing safety equipment.

Both drank Budweiser, and held the bottle with the pinkie finger stretched along the bottom. If it was a can, they crushed it.

Levey and Newman were the subjects of research by Thomas Bouchard, Jr., a University of Minnesota psychologist. Bouchard's work is perhaps the most dramatic evidence yet of what biology dictates. There was, to take another example, the celebrated case of Jack Yufe and Oscar Stohr, identical twins born in 1933 and separated after a few months, the first raised as a Jew, the second as a Nazi. When they met in 1979 for the first time, they slowly realized they had peculiar traits in common: flushing the toilet before using it, keeping rubber bands encircled around their wrists, dipping buttered toast into coffee, issuing loud fake sneezes in elevators to shake people up—weird stuff!

Bouchard's study of twins concluded that, in a standard middle-class home, genes are responsible for 70 percent of the difference in intelligence among people, 50 percent of the difference in personality, and 40 percent of the difference in job preference.

Bouchard told me, "I was raised and trained as a psychologist at Berkeley from an entirely environmental point of view. Ninety-eight percent of my graduate education was from a environmental point of view. . . . I didn't perceive it as an orthodoxy. I thought these were the facts."

Then one day he came across evidence that schizophrenia has a genetic basis. He spoke about it in class. He was virtually shouted down.

"I can remember how vehement the other graduate students in the seminar were. It was really quite incredible. I was surprised. That was the point in time when I could see that there was an orthodoxy and I was attacking it."

My guess is that someday the Nurture argument may seem as old-fashioned as the idea that God is an old dude with a high forehead, a white beard, and a hair-trigger temper. In both cases the promoters of the belief are engaging in self-importance, putting themselves in the power position, in the role of Creator. The gall! Babies are unimaginably sophisticated organisms by the time they emerge from the womb, and it's presumptuous to think that this genetic code, which can design something as marvelous as a functioning eyeball, cannot also design at least the rudiments of a personality.

There's only so much Nature I can take.

A while back I asked a researcher why guys watch so much football on TV. She floated a theory: In prehistoric times, men spent a lot of time in the bushes, watching animals. They watched wildebeests, let's say. They figured out which wildebeest was the slowest, then ran out and stabbed it.

Hence, Monday Night Football.

I have to take issue also with a line in *Brain Sex*, by Anne Moir and David Jessel, that states that marriage "is profoundly unnatural to the biology of the male." They later write, "The very fact that marriage is, for humans, the norm throughout the world—when, as we know, men are naturally disposed against the institution—represents a remarkable triumph of the female brain, and will. It is a truly stunning victory for female power and control over the naturally promiscuous biology of the male. In starkly sexual, and evolutionary, terms, there is nothing in marriage for men, given their rooster desire for novelty and the widest possible distribution of their seed."

This is absurd. Men get married because it is natural for them to pair-bond. It's a classic case of Darwinian natural selection. Children who have caring fathers are more likely to survive and prosper and pass on their genetic code, half of which comes from Daddy; thus, over millions of years, natural selection rewards men who resist their rooster impulse.

The real horror of the situation emerges when you realize how twisted is Nature's sense of humor. Daddy is a victim of his own perverse biology: Sure, he wants to stay at home with the wife and kids, it feels natural to him, but at the same time he is fascinated by . . . the Swedish Bikini Team! Blonde airheads with giant hooters!

Mommy will never, in her entire life, understand this. She too has urges—Helen Fisher of the American Museum of Natural History points out that for every man committing adultery, there's a woman committing adultery with him—but women are much choosier in their licentiousness. They aren't so cheap. Sex isn't divorced from emotion.

Donald Symons, the anthropologist, says men suffer from a "roving eye" that is genetically driven. Biology dictates that women have a greater investment in their offspring, and have to be more selective about their mates, while a man can theoretically sire thousands of children. Figure it out logically, he says: "If you got two men, they're both married, they're both investing in their wives and in their children, and one man has a roving eye, and the other doesn't—one man is disposed to capitalize on low-risk opportunities and the other isn't—which one's genes do you think will predominate in the next generation? Wouldn't you expect that a roving eye will win out over a 'lack of roving eye'? Being a loving father and having a roving eye are not incompatible psychological characteristics."

This is a really ill-advised line of thought to pursue over the dinner table. And my tip to guys out there is that it's not a license to cheat. The danger with taking the biology line too far is that it suggests that people aren't in control of themselves, that we are slaves to some unseen genetic code, that we are mere automata. Humans have choices that rats don't have; humans can say no. As Symons points out: "It's like any other desire. The desire exists, but human beings, a choice-making animal, can choose to do or not do things."

Nature, it seems, is structurally paradoxical. Men and women aren't made for each other. Genes, rather, are selfish things that created men and women in precisely the right way so as to pass themselves (the genes) along most efficiently. We are all victims of the tortuous logic of DNA.

Since this is the new golden age of biology, the burden is to get comfortable with it. I find a few general thoughts helpful, things we know today but were rejected a century ago: the fact that there is no hierarchy in nature; that there is no such thing as "inferiority" or "superiority";

that "races" are the arbitrary inventions of the colonialist era; that women are not "the weaker sex."

And finally: Truth is important for its own sake, regardless of whether it makes us feel good or bad.

I do not doubt that women love their babies more than men. My wife had a subverbal bond with the baby that I could never penetrate. In fact, I didn't really love my child at first, at least compared with how I feel now. Initially she was just a strange, fascinating object. That my bond to this child has deepened is something I can thank culture for: Culture taught me that fatherhood is good. Friends and family were encouraging. People told me, one way or another, that I was supposed to love my kid. "It's the most wonderful thing that will ever happen to you!" they said. So as I changed diapers, studying the subtleties of poop, wondering why it starts out green for a week or so and then becomes mustard yellow, I would tell myself, "This is the most wonderful thing that has ever happened to me!"

And there were the TV ads. On TV, professional men carry babies around as props. Babies connote status. A baby in a backpack is the Rolex of the nineties.

My favorite ad is for McDonald's. A young guy is wandering around a playground at dawn. He then goes into a McDonald's and orders an Egg McMuffin. The pretty young woman behind the counter asks, "Is that for here or to go?" She smiles flirtatiously. We are trained by years of TV watching to assume that these two young people will, at some point, have sex. Instead, the guy says, "To go. I'm meeting my daughter for breakfast." Cut to a hospital room, a sleeping woman, a baby in a bassinet. The guy is beaming. He's a hero! Because he's a dad! The wife is irrelevant, of course: She merely screamed in agony for about eighteen hours, but *he* gave up a chance to make it with the cute babe at the McDonald's.

The genes that will turn my baby into a human being haven't quite kicked in. What makes humans special, scientists say, is the ability to manipulate language, and perhaps even consciousness, the perception of oneself in time and space. The baby, by these criteria, is still basically a lower order of primate. She has the language skills of your average lemur. She and the cat are just now bonding; I think it's because they both like to shred toilet paper and occasionally vomit in a sudden theatrical fashion.

I sometimes wonder: Is she merely *similar* to a subhuman creature at this stage, or is she *literally* a subhuman creature? In the womb she had a tail at one point, and you couldn't say that she merely *resembled* a creature with a tail. She *had a tail*! True fact! So I don't see why she couldn't literally be a lemur, only less furry.

But of course, a lemur—and I must confess that I don't really know what a lemur is, other than a monkeylike thing—would not be so helpless. Humans emerge in a strangely fetal condition, unable to so much as lift the head or roll over, and the entirety of childhood is absurdly long. Complete maturity takes a couple of decades, including the bizarre postpubescent period we call "adolescence" that no other animal experiences and which, quite frankly, may be some kind of factory error. The teenage period is so awful that, if humans were cars, they'd be recalled.

Biology makes mistakes. Just because it's natural doesn't mean it's good. There are species of insects in which the mother literally explodes because her offspring are genetically designed to erupt from the viscera without the more delicate procedure of birth. From my standpoint, much of the food chain looks morally indefensible. Think of all the creatures that find themselves being eaten alive. Chewed up. The screams. A world of agony. Can't there be a better way? Like, everything comes from a store in a package?

On the other hand you have to applaud the subtle brilliance of human design. When my baby falls backward she doesn't plummet like a tree but neatly folds at the knee and quickly sits on her diaper-padded rump, the head never leaving the vertical. One generation away, my wife when pregnant developed a powerful aversion to cigarettes, car exhaust, sausage, and any other unhealthy food; the theory now is that morning sickness is actually good for you, a control mechanism to ensure a bland and healthy diet and prevent the introduction of toxins. This is the new biology—don't fight it, accept it.

We are machines, this I don't doubt. The baby is never more like a machine than in the middle of the night. The baby's cry is obviously designed for maximum listener discomfort. Her decibel-to-pound ratio is astonishing, but the real genius is in the pitch, the tone, the treble, which is the auditory equivalent of a blinding flash of light. Is it something in her vocal cords, her trachea, her supralaryngeal structure? Or is it all in the listener's head, a special receptor for baby screams, like the gadget up there that detects yawns even over the telephone and induces an immediate counteryawn?

Anyway, I'm staggering around in the dark, careening off dressers and door jambs, arms outstretched like The Mummy, and my one goal in life is to get the little critter to stop crying. It's a mission exactly like fixing a flat tire on the side of the road, or changing a light bulb, or realigning a bike chain. A mechanical procedure. My tools are fresh diapers and baby formula. Or does she need decongestant? Whatever it takes to shut her up, that's what I want to do, to find that knob in there that needs a quarter-turn to the left.

Inevitably I end up carrying her around the apartment, trying to lull her back to sleep, pacing, bobbing up and down, squinting at the green digits on the VCR informing me that it is 3:24 A.M., and as the sleep fog recedes it is replaced by a rush of love. It's counterintuitive. I should be mad. Perhaps the positive feelings come from knowing that I can satisfy this little girl's needs through nothing more than my love and attention; there's an efficacy, a power in that. Maybe any parent, and maybe a man in particular, enjoys the sense of having conquered mortality, of passing on the genes, a fairly competitive and aggressive thought in a way, but happily coinciding with good parenting.

Or maybe she's just lovable.

Am I really a marginal part of her life? Not at 3:30 A.M.

At that hour, her daddy is more than just a 30 percent factor in some gene-dominated equation. The answer to my original question is "no": Parents haven't been marginalized. Parenting is still the job it has always been. Parents matter.

Rather, it is biology—all this science stuff, this never ending Nature vs. Nurture philosophizing, this endless explication of the subcellular machinery that turns a microscopic zygote into a functioning human being—that ultimately is meaningless.

Because you have to love them just the same.

THOSE DAFFY
CRITTERS

Why did the passenger pigeon become extinct, but not the kind of pigeons that poop on statues in front of the court-house?

You know the basic story of the passenger pigeon: Man killed them. All of them. What makes this extinction all the more monstrous and baffling is that there were once more passenger pigeons than any other type of bird on the planet. It is commonly estimated that two of every five birds in North America in the early 1800s were passenger pigeons. Incredible? Not so incredible when you read descriptions of these pigeons from that time period.

For example, in 1813, ornithologist John James Audubon saw a column of migrating pigeons so thick that the "light of the noonday sun was obscured as by an eclipse." They kept flying overhead for hours, and Audubon guessed that he had seen at least a billion birds. Another ornithologist, Alexander Wilson, visited a pigeon breeding ground in Kentucky in 1806 and guessed that it held 2,230,272,000 birds. (Had he rounded it to the nearest million, that would have been precise enough for us.)

But they were edible and so people ate them. Their

feathers made good pillows. They were so densely packed that killing them was as easy as shooting fish in a barrel. Naturally, you couldn't gun down thousands of birds at once: It would take too long and cost too much. So the professional hunters used large nets. To get the birds into the net, they used a "stool pigeon," which was a live pigeon with its eyes sewn shut and feet attached to a post, or stool. The pigeon would act agitated—understandably—and attract all the other birds.

The last great nesting group was tracked down in 1896 near Bowling Green, Ohio. Of the 250,000 birds, only about 5,000 escaped. The ones that were harvested went to waste: The train carrying the carcasses derailed, and the entire load putrefied in the heat.

So why didn't the 5,000 escapees seek refuge somewhere? Couldn't they have lived on top of government buildings? The problem was multifold: A female passenger pigeon lays only one egg per reproductive cycle, so they don't reproduce quickly. Rather, the huge number of birds was largely a testament to how long each bird lives—up to twenty-five years. Another problem was that the birds tended to congregate in a central spot, making them easy to track, particularly once the telegraph and locomotive made communication and travel throughout the United States possible. Deforestation also destroyed much of their habitat.

And finally—the real problem—they didn't reproduce in pairs. They showed no interest. They were not sexually programmed to mate and bear offspring like a bird version of Ozzie and Harriet Nelson (or even like those feral pigeons at the courthouse). To get their juices going, they needed the incessant, thunderous backbeat of a million flapping wings. Like New York's Studio 54 crowd of the 1970s, these pigeons needed a critical mass to survive.

The last passenger pigeon, named Martha, died in 1914 at the Cincinnati Zoo.

Why don't we eat insects even though they probably don't taste that bad and undoubtedly build strong bodies twelve ways?

Because we are wimps. Bugs are delicious! Really. Take, for example, a wax moth larva. Drop it in a fat fryer for forty-five seconds, then sprinkle it with salt. "It tastes just like bacon," says Gene DeFoliart, who should know. As professor of entomology at the University of Wisconsin, and editor of *The Food Insects Newsletter*—yes, *every good idea has already been taken*—he has frequently eaten bugs on the seminar circuit.

Only in the Western world do humans eschew insects. "What we define as food is really sort of a cultural concept," says George Armelagos, chairman of anthropology at the University of Florida and coauthor of *Consuming Passions: The Anthropology of Eating.* He says that the rise of agriculture may have instilled in Western society a grudge against insects. Because they devour crops, bugs are the enemy. The Pilgrims who settled in Massachusetts supposedly wouldn't eat lobsters because they looked so much like insects. So if you're planning a meal for a foreign visitor, remember that every country has its own taboos and dislikes. Certain Africans will be nauseated by shellfish. And don't serve cheese fondue to a Chinese guest—the Chinese are lactose-intolerant and can't properly digest milk products. The result can be explosive.

Cultures that still forage have no such compunction about eating insects. In Africa, caterpillars, grasshoppers, locusts, termites, and grub worms are eaten happily. In Thailand, you can buy giant water bugs at any market. In Mexico City, ants are served at many of the finer restaurants (but the males must wear jackets).

We might note that bugs can be a culinary hassle. If you want to eat a locust—admirably, 75 percent protein and 20 percent fat in its dried state—you have to pick off the wings, the short legs, and the terminal portion of the stiff, prickly hind legs. Otherwise you might suffer intestinal blockage, a plight known to beset certain careless cooks of

East Africa. Nonetheless, locusts historically have been eaten in all manner of ways, including roasted (Navajos and Greeks), boiled (Vietnamese), in dumplings (Chinese), and dried and served with milk, like breakfast cereal (Arabs in North Africa). Moses himself declared four varieties of locust to be kosher.

DeFoliart, the bug eater, says insects have been described as tasting like nuts, sunflower seeds, shrimp, and pork rinds. (We are relieved to hear that they don't taste like chicken. It gets tiring, how everything in nature from frog legs to fried gator tastes like chicken. Why does it? Because the meat of wild game, like that of a chicken, is lean and therefore rather bland—it is the fat that gives meat most of its flavor. When we say it tastes like chicken, we mean it needs barbecue sauce.)

As protein sources, insects equal soybeans in value. Anyhow, we had to ask DeFoliart: Would he dare to dine on poached roach? "That's where I would draw the line," he says, but he gives a purely scientific reason: "A roach, for one thing, can transmit organisms. They're also one of the few insects that have been reported to cause allergies if you eat them."

Excuses, excuses.

Why do gnats go for your eyes?

Despicable creatures that they are, gnats—specifically, "eye gnats" of the family *Chloropidae*—drink eye juice. They also go for open cuts and other moist parts.

"They feed on sweat or secretions from the eye. That would have things in it they wouldn't get from just water," says Al Norrbom, research entomologist for the U.S. Department of Agriculture.

(The real question is, why is there a *g* in gnat? See page 150.)

(Not Endangered)

Why is there no multi-talented creature that can fly, swim, run really fast, inflict poisonous bites, stink horribly like a skunk, and so on?

We posed this question to Stephen Jay Gould, the Harvard paleobiologist and one of the world's foremost theorists of evolution. (That's a bit like calling up the president of the United States and asking him what's the capital of South Dakota.)

Why doesn't evolution cause creatures to develop more and more survival mechanisms? Wouldn't a porcupine that also stank like a skunk have greater evolutionary success? Why don't gorillas have wings? Why don't humans have huge mouths that can strain krill from the ocean?

"It costs energy and time to build structures," Gould told us. "Evolution isn't an optimizing principle."

That sums it up pretty well. We all tend to think of evolution as a progression in which slime gradually turns into bacteria, which then gradually turn into bugs, which then turn into rats, which then become monkeys, which then become Neanderthal people, until finally we reach the evolutionary zenith, a creature who spends one hour a day hunting and gathering and the remainder trying to set the clock on the VCR. But if that were so, why are there still mollusks that live in mud at the bottom of the ocean? What about fleas and ticks? Colonic parasites? *Where is their ambition?*

As Gould said, evolution isn't optimizing. It operates more on the theory of "If it ain't broke, don't fix it." Colonic parasites have a great life. They eat. They poop. They reproduce. As far as nature is concerned, that's a life every bit the equal of Ben Franklin's.

It certainly happens that new traits evolve, but they tend to streamline a creature's design, to make it better suited for one particular environment—to become, in essence, a more parasitical parasite—rather than add on all kinds of additional expensive new features and options as though it were the new luxury model of the Honda Accord.

Why do fish generally bite at dawn and at dusk?

Fish that are active at the twilight hours are called "crepuscular" (although not directly to their faces).

First, we should note that one reason anglers do well at both dawn and dusk is that it's the marine rush hour. The fish population is undergoing a shift change, which is the same reason a police station is so crowded at three in the afternoon. The day shift is going and the night shift is coming in.

But why are many fish so rambunctious at twilight? Because dimly lit water is perfect for predation.

Look at the alternative. Let's say you're a big fish living just off the Florida Keys on one of the coral reefs not yet ground to powder by wayward tankers or poisoned by fertilizer runoff. It's high noon. The water is brilliant. You're cruising along, hungry, grouchy, vaguely annoyed that you are a mere fish and not something more exciting, like a mammal, and suddenly a school of snapper flashes by. You love snapper. Preferably broiled in garlic butter. You lunge wildly forward and . . . fall flat on your face. Why? Because you were blinded. Your sensitive eyes aren't ideally designed for nabbing prey in bright light. To prosper as a fish, you need to be able to navigate the waters during those hectic happy hours at dawn and at dusk.

The moment the sun gets low in the sky, water gets dim, and then it gets exceedingly dim, until finally it's lights out. In contrast, in the middle of the day the water is permeated with a white haze of water-scattered sunlight. But that's only the half of it. Instead of camouflaging themselves in dark, drab colors, fish take the opposite approach: They take advantage of the predators' sun blindness and hide themselves in the dazzling light by reflecting it with silvery scales. These are the fish equivalent of sequins and rhinestones.

This "countershading" is even more effective when the fish hang out in schools. In fact, that's why they hang out in schools. They make for a confusing target, and the predator can't easily focus on a lone victim. (Other reasons for schooling: It's easier for a fish to swim in the vortex created by a fish just ahead; it's easier to attack prey from a group formation; and there are plenty of dating opportunities.)

Now, being logical, you say: If fish bite when the light is gentler, shouldn't they also bite more when it's overcast? The answer is: Yes. They do. Case closed.

Why is there something as ridiculous as a seventeen-year-cicada, which spends seventeen years as a larva under the ground and then finally emerges to briefly reproduce?

Because we are sensitive, nature-loving people, we instantly grasp the concept that critters fill every environmental niche. The deep ocean. Air-conditioning ducts. Really ugly suburban tract house neighborhoods.

Nonetheless, isn't a seventeen-year cicada (*Magicicada sep-temdecim*, a.k.a. the "seventeen-year locust") something of an absurdity? Is there really a seventeen-year niche that needs to be scratched?

The answer is that this is a great survival mechanism, right up there with skunk scent. The seventeen-year cicadas employ the simple trick of outliving most of their potential predators within a specific brood's region. (Incidentally, there are at least twenty-three broods operating in different regions of the United States and on different cycles.) By the time they emerge and start swarming, after all those years sucking roots, there's nothing nearby that has any memory of cicadas, except for humans, elephants, some very feeble dogs, etc. Thus there is nothing that is specifically adapted to eating these annoying beasts, which is why they are such a plague.

But there's a second reason a seventeen-year life span is clever. Consider the fact that in the Southern and Southwestern United States, some cicada broods are on a thirteen-year cycle. The numbers 17 and 13 are prime. (A prime number is divisible only by itself and 1.) This makes it all the harder for any other creature to get in sync with the cicada's life cycle. If the cicadas were on cycles of, say, twelve years and eighteen years, they might be more vulnerable to creatures who live for six years and become used to having a cicada dessert every second or third generation.

Now, if only American high school students knew as much about math as your average locust.

Why do birds fly in formation?

You might think that it would be smart for them to fly single-file, "drafting" behind one another like race car drivers. Instead, they prefer the V shape, though sometimes one side of the V is only slightly realized or completely absent.

Formation flying has a distinct aeronautical advantage: As the lead bird flaps its wings, it creates a vortex out near the wing tip, and the trailing bird rests its own wings on the updraft. Thus it's easier for the trailing bird to stay aloft, and so on down the line. The birds take turns being the leader. But you'll notice that only large birds fly in formation: geese, seagulls, pelicans, and so on. That's because only large birds can exploit the aerodynamics of their own beating wings.

A 1970 study published in *Science* magazine stated that a flock of twenty-five birds can extend their flight range by 70 percent by flying in formation. (This is not to be confused with flying information, which is what you find on an airplane in the seat pocket directly in front of you.)

Why do we think squirrels are cute and rats hideous, when the only major different in their appearance is in the tail?

You might incorrectly suppose that this is simply a matter of preference for furry animals—squirrels, monkeys, pandas, whatever—combined with the well-founded association of rats with disease and poverty. The real answer is more complicated and far more interesting: We respond, as observers, to certain physical characteristics, many of them subtle, that remind us of human babies.

Obviously a squirrel isn't very babylike—but it is when compared with a rat. A squirrel, for one thing, will sit back on its haunches and manipulate an acorn or some other object in the same way that a baby will sit upright and fondle a rattle or perhaps a rusty nail. Rats can sit up, but they rarely do so, invariably because they're too busy behaving in a detestably verminous manner and spreading the Black Death and so on.

"They're both rodents," says Bill Xanten, associate curator of mammals at the National Zoo in Washington, D.C., but he adds that there are distinct differences between rats

and squirrels. "Rats have got a very sharp, long, pointed snout and a naked tail, which does not necessarily denote a pleasing look. Even though squirrels have kind of a pointed nose too, it's a much shorter muzzle, the eyes are bigger, and they have a fluffy tail."

Eye size and nose length are crucial to inciting the "cute response" in humans. Human babies have large heads, big eyes, button noses, and stubby limbs. Because we are genetically programmed to respond to these features, we also respond to animals that have analogous physiognomy. National Zoo spokesman Bill Hoage says puppies are cuter than full-grown dogs not just because they're smaller, but because their snouts are flatter, eyes larger, etc. Mickey Mouse, likewise, has seen his nose grow shorter and his face rounder since his original incarnation half a century ago.

Why do possums "play possum"?

The American opossum is generally called the "possum," since "opossum" sounds like something sold in a fast-food joint, as in, "I'll take the jumbo fries and the bag-o-possum." When attacked, the possum snaps and snarls, but when it starts to lose the fight it suddenly goes stiff and acts dead. It's as though it goes into a trance. Keep in mind that it does this when already *in* the mouth of some carnivorous predator. Wouldn't that make the possum all the more easily eaten? How could natural selection allow such a thing to develop?

The answer is because many predators don't want to eat something that isn't writhing and screaming. That's the solution provided by Desmond Morris in *Animalwatching*. The idea is that, deep within the low-wattage brain of a meat eater, a warning light flashes when meat doesn't squirm. The meat might be spoiled. Laden with gross bacteria.

The question we can't answer is why human beings don't have the same prejudice. (Waiter: "How would you like that steak?" Customer: "Thrashing and whimpering.")

Why don't we like the smell of skunks?

Because skunks stink. But do they stink because they secrete a noxious odor, or because human beings have developed a culture in which the smell of skunk is considered noxious? This is actually a subject of academic debate. One Yale University psychologist has insisted that with enough effort, you could make a child grow up to savor *parfum de skunk*.

This is in keeping with the broader theory that "hedonic reactions" to odors—whether you like 'em or not—are learned, not genetically predetermined.

There is evidence for this theory: Newborns don't show signs of liking "nice" smells and disliking "bad" smells. Babies put nasty things in their mouths.

Nonetheless, a new study by psychologist Hilary J. Schmidt of the Monell Chemical Senses Center in Philadelphia shows that as early as nine months of age, babies prefer to play with rattles with a scent deemed pleasant to adults.

In the experiment, Schmidt used three rattles. One rattle had no smell, one smelled of wintergreen, and one smelled of nasty cheese. Wintergreen won. Schmidt adds a cautionary note. Wintergreen is common in toothpaste, and maybe the babies were reacting to something that smelled like their mother's breath. As for the bad odor, it was caused by butyric acid, also found in vomit. Babies throw up a fair bit and they probably don't like it, particularly when the parents start shrieking.

"The reactions we have may possibly be genetic," Schmidt says. "If learning is what determines our preferences, it's going on very early in life."

We must hastily add that it is quite reasonable to think that natural selection would favor humans who disliked the smell of skunk and any other odor that's remotely similar to rancid food. Spoiled food can kill you.

Besides, skunks wouldn't have survived as a species if the scent of their effluent was based solely on the cultural prissiness of other species.

Why are there thousands of species of beetles and sparrows and whatnot, but all dogs are considered part of the same species?

Speciation isn't defined by appearance. All that matters is whether under natural conditions, you can make children who are themselves fertile. (Not you personally. Living things in general.)

A Great Dane is the same species as a dachshund because the two can mate and produce an offspring, though we shudder to contemplate what this would look like. (Ross Perot, maybe?)

Why do dogs come in all shapes and sizes? For one thing, some species of animals are simply more genetically variable than others. The one with the most variety is the human species. Second is dogs. (Cats are somewhere down the line, and eventually you get to the beetles and such.) Dogs may appear to vary more than humans, but that's because humans wanted it that way. Humans began domesticating wolves in Southern Europe and Asia Minor about fourteen thousand years ago. Dogs ended up looking funny because they became victims of inbreeding.

See, throughout history the human tribes didn't allow their new, domesticated dogs to mate with wild wolves—if they could help it. So the gene pool was small. Inbreeding causes peculiarities. Also, different tribes may have had different ideas of what a dog should look like, and so they bred toward that end. After a few thousand years, poof, you've got (unfortunately) a poodle.

Why do you never see wild hamsters?

Keep in mind that hamster lore, hamster trivia, hamster biological data, and true hamster facts of any kind can be a powerful secret weapon during conversation lulls at a cocktail party. Don't just stand there in silence, looking like an idiot, when you can knock 'em dead with something like, "Say, did you know that a hamster can hoard up to a hundred pounds of food for its winter store?" Trust us, you won't go home alone.

It turns out that there is a single good reason why you never see wild hamsters in the United States: The hamsters that are sold in pet shops and tormented by millions of kids are called Syrian golden hamsters and are native to only a small piece of desert in Syria, around the town of Aleppo. The only hamsters at large in a place like Kansas are the ones that have somehow escaped from their masters, and even if they could adapt to the conditions and find some grain to eat, it wouldn't be easy for them to run into another such hamster and start a family.

There is a creature called the common black-bellied hamster that lives in Europe, but these are pests, not pets. (Say that ten times fast: "Pests, not pets.") They breed like mad and erupt in veritable plagues of hamsters, inciting farmers to hamster massacres.

The Syrian golden hamster is a recent biological discovery. The first such hamster was described in 1797 by Alexander Russell, a biologist who lived in Aleppo. He didn't quite grasp how important his discovery was, so the credit for naming the species went to a British naturalist named George Robert Waterhouse, who presented a dead specimen to his colleagues at a meeting in 1839.

That was the last mention of the hamster until 1930, when a zoologist named Israel Aharoni captured a female and eleven pups on a farm near Aleppo. Unfortunately, the mother became so freaked out that she killed one of her own young. One of Aharoni's fellow hamster hunters then became so enraged by this that he submerged the mother in a bottle of cyanide. (This whole saga would make a charming bedtime story.) Aharoni had to nurse by hand the still-blind, nearly hairless pups and, although several of them escaped, he managed, thanks to hamster fecundity, to raise 150 of the suckers within a year. They turned out to be easily adapted to captivity and ideally suited for laboratory experiments.

In 1938 the first batch arrived in the United States, and

after World War II the home hamster market boomed. For years thereafter every pet hamster in America, without exception, was descended from the one that had died in that bottle of cyanide.

LOVE AND SEX

(Not necessarily in that order)

Why aren't there three sexes? Or a hundred sexes? Why are there just two sexes?

Let's go back to basics. What exactly is a "male," anyway? Other than an organism that takes out the garbage and picks its nose while driving? The answer is: an organism with lots of tiny, motile gametes.

That's right! Men have incredibly small gametes, not that they'd ever admit to it. A female produces *large* gametes—eggs, basically. (Gametes are sex cells.) A human female is born with a couple of million gametes, but during her lifetime only about four hundred of them come into play. A male produces billions of usable gametes (sperm). This pattern—one sex producing a few big sex cells, the other producing zillions of small ones—exists all throughout the biological world. Bugs. Plants. You name it. Evolution has rewarded a kind of extremism in which one sex uses a strategy of quantity and the other goes for quality. Moderation doesn't work here.

The reason there's not a third sex (with, who knows, a

billion medium-size, only slightly lethargic gametes) is that two sexes are more than enough to make life complicated. When we say "make life complicated," we are making a low-grade joke (your head nods backward, as though gently pushed, but no sound emerges from the thorax) and also referring to the scientific fact that sexual reproduction on the planet seems to be designed to mix up genes and recombine them. This variability allows the process of natural selection to sort through genes, reward the well adapted, punish the geeks, and keep evolution cranking.

There's no technical reason why a species couldn't employ three sexes, each contributing genetic material to the offspring. It just hasn't happened. Maybe on some other planet. Here, the situation has stabilized at two sexes. You can get an almost infinite combination of genes through two sexes, so there's no advantage to having a third sex. Think of a binary computer: You can write any number with some combination of the digits 0 and 1. (So we have been told, though to be honest we've never actually tried.)

That said, scientists still aren't satisfied with their understanding of why sex exists.

"We haven't done a very good job of finding out why sex is so common," says Jim Bull, a professor of zoology at the University of Texas. Sex, he says, is "a very pervasive phenomenon that cries out for an explanation."

Is sex necessary? No. Some species have only one sex and reproduce just fine by parthenogenesis. The mothers spit out daughters that are genetic duplicates—clones. One advantage of this strategy is that a critter can invade new turf without having to bring along a cumbersome male and keep him amused. An aphid, for example, can start an infestation of your garden all by itself; it reproduces by cloning. Some types of geckos employ parthenogenesis too. (Parents who are squeamish about telling their kids where babies come from should just talk about "the geckos and the aphids.")

Cloning doesn't allow for much genetic variety, so sex is

After years of frustration in the bar scene, parthenogenesis seemed to solve my relationship problems.

Yeah same here.

Gecko & Aphid

a more common way to reproduce. But now ask yourself: Why do we need two people to have two sexes? We don't. In fact, many species are hermaphroditic. They are both male and female. Many flowering plants are hermaphrodites. They fertilize each other with wild abandon. So why aren't we all hermaphroditic? Wouldn't that be a lot less of a hassle? True, you'd probably spend a lot of time arguing at the mirror—"You left hair in the tub!" "Yeah? At least I *bathe* once in a while!"—but it would seem more efficient than the current two-person form of sex.

The answer is: to prevent "inbreeding depression." If you possess both sexual characteristics, sometimes you will fertilize yourself. Right, just like the famous insult. This self-fertilization can create genetic defects. As it is, all of us carry at least one or two of the couple thousand genes that cause birth defects, but they are recessive and don't show up unless we are paired with someone else with the same recessive gene.

"You can pay a severe penalty for self-fertilization" is the warning from Brian Charlesworth, a professor of ecology and evolution at the University of Chicago.

So be careful what you do with yourself. You could go blind.

Why can't humans interbreed with other animals?

Because it would be wrong. Also there are, for the moment, two major biological obstacles that keep different species from begetting children.

1. Finding the egg. We have to remember that sperm have no eyeballs. So how do they find that dang egg? They have no guidance system. They just wriggle and twist and juke their way through those mysterious passageways until finally some truly heroic commando of a sperm collides with the egg and sticks. The genius of the system is that a human sperm will bind only to a human egg. If a human sperm makes contact with, say, a sheep egg—and we are not passing judgment here on the people of Texas—the sperm doesn't recognize it, and keeps on truckin'.

2. Matching DNA. It's like building a zipper: you have to get all those teeth to interlock. Humans have twenty-three pairs of chromosomes, one half contributed by Mom and the other by Dad, or perhaps the milkman. If Dad tries to offer his twenty-three to a creature that has only fifteen, they won't fit together correctly, and, moreover, if the cell starts to divide, the chromosomes will get mixed up in all the wrong proportions, so that the child cells will carry wildly diverging genetic instructions. Instead of gradually growing into a living, coherently structured creature, it will remain a small abstract blob, like something Jackson Pollock would have designed.

Now, let's talk about something really creepy: Genetic engineering makes it theoretically possible to circumvent Nature's plan. The myths of antiquity about such exotic half-human creatures as Minotaurs and mermaids may someday seem like prophecy.

There is a long-term project under way in the United States to map all three billion parts of the human genetic blueprint, and there are similar studies on other species. The good news is that this has already enabled us to correlate certain genes with specific traits, such as the ability to produce insulin and the tendency to be alcoholic. The bad news is that there are all kinds of scary possibilities that arise from this knowledge, ranging from old-fashioned Nazi-style eugenics to what we are talking about here, mixing genes among creatures that Nature wanted to keep apart.

Could we make a Minotaur? No. A Minotaur has a man's head and a bull's body, and genes don't work that way. There's not a section that says "bull's body." Genes are way more complicated than that. Mix a big chunk of man with a big chunk of bull and you'd get another Pollock masterpiece. We couldn't even make a man with a dog's nose. "There's just too many steps that are involved in making a dog's nose versus a human's nose," says University of Miami cell biologist Nevis Fregien.

Eventually, though, we might be able to find the gene that causes hairiness in dogs, and insert that into the chromosomes of a fertilized human egg. Says UM biologist Peter Lutz, "In principle what you could produce is a human with a nice shiny coat and maybe a damp nose."

Or perhaps a dog that worries about the Visa bill.

Why do people kiss?

Go to the mirror sometime and closely scrutinize this thing in the lower region of your face. It is a slime pit. The hole has a nifty valve in the form of two "lips," beyond which are some bony protuberances and then a wriggly muscle. Everything is coated in what is called "mucus." Incredibly, you expect another person to be willing to affix his or her slime pit to yours.

The fancy word for this is "osculation." Next time you tongue-wrassle, remind yourself that you are merely engaging in osculatory behavior. That will boost the romantic yield, no doubt.

Is kissing an instinct? Or a cultural artifact?

The answer is a little complicated: Kissing is instinctive, but not quite universal among humans. Some prefer the rubbing, nuzzling, or sniffing of the face. There are a few scattered peoples who find kissing disgusting. When Europeans kissed in front of some Thonga tribesmen in Africa, one reportedly said, "Look at them, they eat each other's saliva and dirt."

That said, the bottom line is that kissing is common just about everywhere, including among aboriginal cultures.

"Despite the fact that people think that kissing is recent, and kissing is Western, it is neither," says Helen Fisher, an anthropologist at the American Museum of Natural History in New York City.

Critters kiss too. Chimpanzees are known to throw their arms around each other and French kiss. Sea lions rub mouths, dolphins nibble faces, wolves lick lips, dogs lap their owners' faces, and so on.

Some people might object and say that not all of this is kissing, per se. That's the wrong attitude: Kissing encompasses all manner of hijinks with the mouth. The *Kama Sutra* describes twenty kisses, like the Throbbing Kiss (the lower lip trembles), the Clasping Kiss (clamp the lips between your teeth), the Column Kiss (do it up against a column), and the Pressed Kiss, which is sort of like the old-fashioned Hollywood movie kiss that required the two stars to mash their faces together as though they had a walnut pinned in there and were trying to crack it.

(The sticky matter of what to do with the tongue has always perplexed polite society. Alfred E. Crawley, an anthropologist, wrote early in this century that in "abnormal forms" of kissing, "some use of the tongue occurs.")

So anyway, why has this kissing business evolved? There is a simple, but wrong, answer: "Because it feels good." Kissing is sensual, to be sure, but the mouth is not actually one of your erogenous zones. Those are to the south. The erotic voltage of a kiss comes not from the nerves in your mouth but from the mind. At the rational level you are getting intensely close to someone. But more importantly, at the subconscious level you are recreating your behavior as a suckling infant.

Babies are built for osculation. The sensitivity and elaborate musculature of the mouth enables babies to eat more easily. A three-month-old baby's lips and tongue are designed not only for breast sucking, but also for rooting around in the mother's mouth for food. In pre-Gerber days, the mother would have to chew the food and then pass it to the infant. This practice continues in some cultures around the world.

We spoke to Sylvia Shipp, a student at the University of California at Santa Barbara who recently experimented with feeding babies this way. She chewed up some food, opened her mouth, and waited to see what the babies would do.

"It worked," Shipp reports. "They'll take it right out of your mouth."

The more general point is that many of the things we do as adults are psychic returns to the pleasures of infancy.

"For a lot of things people do in courtship, male to female, there's a parent–child model for it," says David Givens, an anthropologist and spokesman for the American Anthropological Association. (That was the Official Expert Quote so our editors don't think we make this stuff up.)

A kiss, contrary to what the song says, is not "just a kiss." It's a psychological compulsion. (A sigh, however, is just a sigh.)

Why isn't there a huge black market in testosterone, for use as an aphrodisiac?

Testosterone determines sexual desire in both men and women. But it has a funny quality: So long as you have enough, more won't do anything. Except maybe harm you. Hair will shoot out of your warts or something. Your internal organs will turn into chicken giblets.

Actually, steroids containing testosterone are a controlled substance because, although they can radically improve some athletic performance, the harm to internal organs can be life-threatening. You really don't want a testosterone boost unless for some reason (and we prefer not to visualize such a reason) your body isn't capable of producing sufficient testosterone for a normal sexual drive.

"I'm sure if it was available people would buy it like mad. But it would be a mistake. If you have a lack of testosterone, you can go to the doctor and the doctor will give you the drug," says Julian Davidson, a physiologist at Stanford University who studies hormones.

Let's put it this way: Once you get some gas in your tank, it doesn't matter how much more gas you add; the car won't go any faster.

Why do sexual turn-ons vary so greatly from person to person?

One of the big lies in our society is that most people have "normal" sexual desires, and everyone else is some kind of weirdo or pervert. The fact is, eroticism within the human species is highly diverse. Go into any "adult bookstore" and see how balkanized the material is. (Note to readers: This is not, as one angry caller from Croatia believed, a reference to the sexual habits of people in the Balkans.) On the shelves, the specific has replaced the general; you got your chest-oriented magazines, your face-oriented magazines, etc. (Note the world's quickest and most cowardly use of "etc.")

Fantasyland, 5:00 p.m.

You would think, based on the Darwinian logic of survival of the species, that every human being would be aroused by similar thoughts of straightforward, heterosexual intercourse. We should be sexual robots. Like sheep. ("Hey, it's springtime! You must be in heat! Waiter, the check!") Instead, the psychic pleasure button varies significantly from one person to another.

The traditional binary breakdown of heterosexual and homosexual is too simplistic; there are innumerable subcategories, plus a plethora of bizarre "paraphilia," such as transvestism, self-asphyxiation, acrotomophilia (so you don't call us, it has to do with amputated limbs), klismaphilia (enemas), and so forth into absurdity. We are told that some men spend thousands of dollars building gigantic cribs in their bedrooms in order to pretend they are infants, sometimes forcing their wives to dress them in diapers and feed them bottles and so forth—all toward the goal of flipping an impossibly remote erotic switch.

But don't pay too much attention to the extreme

cases. Everyone has some predilection, if not an outright fetish.

Why such variation? Our first thought was that erotic variation is an evolutionary trait that offers some adaptive advantage to the species. For example, if people have divergent tastes, then nobody is going to be deemed undesirable and left out in the cold. No matter how physically repulsive you are, there's someone who thinks you're dishy!

"Evolution looks for variety," says James H. Geer, a Louisiana State University psychologist and coauthor of *Theories of Sexuality*.

The problem is, many sexual turn-ons are completely disassociated from the act of mating—they might not involve another person, even in fantasy.

For help we turned to John Money, a professor emeritus of medical psychology and pediatrics at Johns Hopkins University and Hospital, and author of *Lovemaps*. In his book, Money says that no one has formulated an indisputable hypothesis for the "kinky and paraphilic embellishments" that enter the erotic program, but he offers his own speculation:

"Diversity may be an inevitable evolutionary trade-off—the price paid for the freeing of the primate brain to develop its uniquely human genesis of syntactical speech and creative intelligence."

This rings true: What makes humans unique, as we have noted elsewhere in this book, is the capacity to create and manipulate complex language. The brain is genetically designed to handle diverse sounds and images and turn them into the language of speech and conscious thought. Dr. Money is saying that erotic variability is not itself an adaptive trait, but rather the *side effect* of an adaptive trait, the development of the linguistic brain.

He told us, "The freeing up of the brain to make it a linguistic organ automatically freed it up to become an erotic organ."

Just as you learn, through what you hear, to speak a language, so too do you learn, through sight and touch, what is erotic. You've got many years of childhood to put together your "lovemap." Unfortunately, society likes to pretend that children are asexual, and punishes any behavior that provides evidence to the contrary. Children are vulnerable to all kinds of lovemap vandalism, Money argues, often by well-meaning but misguided parents.

This, then, is a case of Nurture being more important than Nature. How refreshing! And it helps us understand why sexual tastes vary from culture to culture (think: Chinese foot binding).

So, the next time you think someone has perverse desires, keep in mind that those cravings are as explicable and as human as any others. Sallie Tisdale put it well in an essay in *Harper's*: "I want never to forget the bell curve of human desire, or that few of us have much say about where on the curve we land."

Why aren't porn stars embarrassed?

Don't porn stars worry that their parents will see them? Don't they have any shame?

Intrepidly, we called up several adult-film stars, and we can report that they sounded anything but demented. They seemed . . . normal. Proud of their work. Like any other professionals. They gave three basic reasons why some people have sex on camera.

1. Money. "There are certain people, male and female, who will do anything for money," said actress Porsche Lynn.

But she and her colleagues say this is a minor consideration, in part because there's not much money to be made. The business is saturated with "product," and even a big star might make only thirty thousand dollars in a year—not exactly Hollywood wages.

2. Sex. A few actors and actresses simply wanted to be in an environment where they could have sex more often.

They have libidos from outer space. Jerry Butler, a major male star, reports in his autobiography, *Raw Talent*, that he wants to have six or seven orgasms a day. His colleagues say he's not exaggerating. Someone needs to expose this guy to kryptonite.

3. Expression. "I'm an exhibitionist," actress Nina Hartley said: "When I go to work I like to have sex in public . . . I look at every scene I do as potentially educational." Candida Royalle, a former star whose company, Femme Distribution, Inc., sells adult videos targeted at married couples, said, "I was of a rebellious nature, I was politically progressive, and I felt that I shouldn't be embarrassed. But on the other hand, I know that there was a part of me that was embarrassed. It was not because what I was doing was so shameful, but rather that I was indoctrinated by a very sex-negative culture that says I should be ashamed. We live in a culture that is based on the madonna–whore mythology."

Okay, but still. A lot of people are rebellious and politically progressive and they don't drop their trousers for the rest of the country. The fact is, every porn star has a history, a reason for becoming an exhibitionist by trade if not psychologically.

For instance, Jerry Butler's father sold porn movies, and Butler watched them continuously when he was seven and eight years old. He later became alienated from his parents—a common phenomenon in the business.

"A lot of the talent comes from a really Catholic upbringing. I think some of it is rebellion, maybe some of them are living out what they perceive themselves to be—bad," says Royalle.

What do the parents say? Usually they don't know, at first. Nina Hartley was in video stores around the country for three years before her parents found out. They thought she was a cocktail waitress. "They're not real happy with what I do, but they have accepted it, and they understand I am happy." She's married, by the way. With a mistress. They're all swingers.

"My husband and my girlfriend are very supportive of what I do," she said.

Is there anything these people are reluctant to do in public? Yes—they don't like to kiss.

"Very few people kiss passionately in porno," Butler writes in his autobiography. "Sure, sometimes there's a quick peck to get things started, but that's about it. Kissing is a very private thing."

Why are private parts private? Why isn't your mouth a private part? Why not the nose?

You may have noticed that dogs don't understand the concept of private parts. You can train a dog to do a lot of things, but he will never, ever grasp the idea that there are certain stunts inappropriate for high tea.

Only humans, of all the animals, have a sense of modesty about their sexual organs. Why did this idea evolve?

The basic answer is that primitive humans realized that the genitals (as opposed to the mouth or nose) were a unique resource. They had value. You could barter with them. Trade. Negotiate. You didn't let just anyone have access to them, says Rutgers University anthropologist Lionel Tiger.

For example, virginity has always been valued in human societies, particularly in females, which are the "main reproductive resource," says Tiger. In primitive cultures, a virgin girl had great value to her kinship group, which could engage in exogamy, marrying the girl to a boy or a man in a different kinship group in a ritual that would be far more political and economic than romantic. The marriage ritual would ensure peace and cooperation.

"Genital modesty is one rather straightforward and simple feature of this whole process of complex sexual negotiation and marital arrangement," Tiger says.

The curious thing is that, although almost every culture has some rule about genital modesty, the rules vary dra-

matically. Robert Carneiro, an ethnologist at the American Museum of Natural History in New York, notes the case of the Amahuaca people of central Brazil. An Amahuaca man goes about naked except for a broad bark belt, under which he tucks the tip of his penis, which otherwise is utterly exposed. If the penis slips out and dangles for a moment, the Amahuaca man will become extremely embarrassed.

Another nearby group, the Chonibo, wear cotton garments like nightshirts. The Amahuaca think the Chonibo are bawdy, says Carneiro. "They sort of guffaw" when the Chonibo are mentioned, he says, "because they're letting their penises hang free."

If they saw American hospital gowns, the Amahuaca would be appalled.

Why does love have to be so difficult?

The irony of life is that the thing we crave the most also causes us the most pain. Love and pain are inextricably wed. Why? Why can't it just be *dreamy*? Why does love make us worry, fret, argue, despair? Why is it that the most toxic poisons are synthesized within what is supposed to be a love relationship?

Here are the principal reasons:

1. Love is an addiction. According to Robert J. Sternberg, a psychologist at Yale University, people in love display the characteristics of drug addicts: "At times, when you're not getting your fix, you experience a feeling of withdrawal." He means this in the medical sense. Like a junkie going cold turkey, you can become profoundly unhappy, irritable, depressed, anxious.

2. We fight in order to make up. A smooth, easy relationship may fail to produce the emotional intensity we associate with "being in love." Lovers want love to sweep them off their feet, to be a revolutionary force. But you can't have a revolution without the occasional pitched battle. Many people intentionally seek a fight solely to keep their emotions boiling, knowing the cauldron will eventually bubble back to something more pleasurable than a knock-down-drag-out. "In order to keep generating the feelings of closeness, you need some hot sauce," says Sternberg.

3. Childhood fears. Our love partner has replaced our parents as the object of our dependence. When there is any problem, long-forgotten emotions kick in, like the panic every child feels when he or she is temporarily lost and feeling abandoned. Growing up doesn't end our vulnerability.

But as the official arbiters of truth, we'd have to say that the most compelling reason that love goes hand in hand with pain is:

4. This is an impermanent life. Everything dies eventually. Even in our moments of supreme happiness there is the inner dread that it cannot last forever. We are the only creatures on this planet with a grasp of the future, and so we suffer the pain of our mortality. Says Stanley Charnofsky, a psychologist at California State University at Northridge, "All joy is tainted by pain, because there is the promise of the loss of it."

Why do some women think they are making themselves more attractive to men by ripping out their eyebrows and drawing new ones higher up?

This is a relatively mild form of self-mutilation in the name of beauty when compared with such cross-cultural reference points as lip disks, neck-stretching rings, scarification, Dolly Partonization, and so forth. But plucked and repenciled eyebrows seem particularly strange today, in an era when the fashion totems have decreed that bushy female brows are beautiful (or are the simpleminded Why Things Are staffers two years behind New York and Milan, as always?).

Back in the thirties, when reality was such a downer that people were willing to invest what little they had in fantasy, Hollywood obliged. Designers and scriptwriters stylized and idealized everything they got their hands on, including women's faces. It was a black-and-white kind of thinking: Facial hair was masculine; therefore, the lack of it was feminine. The eyebrows were innocent bystanders. Since five o'clock eye shadow wouldn't cut it, the big starlets of the day took to plucking out their eyebrows and replacing them with stencils.

Millions of glamour-starved women followed their example. It was fashionable. And if it ever went out of style, they could always just let the real brows grow back in, right?

Wrong. Unfortunately, says Miami dermatologist Richard Feinstein, constant plucking can damage the hair follicles and prevent the eyebrow from growing back. So the brow must be penciled on forever. The result of this fashion fling half a century ago is that Miguel Pacheco, resident makeup artist at the Georgette Klinger beauty salon in Bal Harbour, Florida, sees a lot of 2-D eyebrows on his older clients. "They have no choice now," Pacheco says. "It's pencil or nothing."

And speaking of not-entirely-successful attempts to compensate for depilation:

Why do some men think they are making themselves more attractive to women by allowing hair to grow extra long on one side, and then combing it over the bald spot in the middle?

The thing about comb-overs is that there is exactly one angle from which they appear to be anything but a pathetic attempt to hide baldness: looking straight ahead, plumb level, out of the wind, directly into a mirror. Self-delusion in its most public form. Now that the comb-over has become standard fare for humorists, how can so many persist in thinking it is a tonsorial plus?

We began our search for understanding and, yes, compassion, at Pete's Suniland Barber Shop in South Miami, because it is not the kind of place where they do "pre-interviews" about "style options." It is a guy's kind of place, and a guy has no secrets from the man who cuts his hair. When that comb-over lock flops down past the chin, you can't just ignore it.

"They make all kinds of excuses," says Louis Kings, who has been cutting men's hair "all my life." "Some say it's to keep the sun off their head. Some say their face is too round without it. Most of them know deep down it doesn't fool anyone, but it's like they just can't walk into a fancy restaurant with no shirt on. Everybody else has got a shirt. They feel naked without it."

The technical term is denial. To many men, loss of hair is psychically equal to loss of virility, or even worse, impending mortality. Rather than facing the truth, they grasp at straws—or, in this case, a few hair strands—in a desperate attempt to deny the obvious: Baldness means no hair on the head. Look! Hair on my head! Ergo, I am not bald.

THE BODY

Why don't we rot, even though we are exposed to the air and are basically large chunks of raw meat?

We do rot. Constantly. No doubt you have noticed that some people smell a little more rotten than others. They seem to have . . . spoiled.

The polite thing to do when you encounter a person with an unfortunate corona of unpleasant odor is to say, "Pardon me, but I believe that you have 'gone bad,' so to speak."

"Rot" is not a scientific word, but it connotes a scientific concept. When we put a piece of meat on the table and leave it for a few days, something very obvious happens to it: we call this "rotting."

"What that really means," says Greg Francis, a microbiologist at the University of Maryland, "is that microorganisms from the air have landed on the piece of meat and have begun to digest it. What you smell are the by-products of the microorganisms. There are things like butyric acid, and butyric acid has a very overpowering rotten smell to it."

The key thing to realize is that these little bacteria can digest something whether it's alive or dead. They don't discriminate.

"We have a certain number of bacteria that live in our bodies, so theoretically we are subject to the same digestive processes that this piece of meat on the table is. However, we also have an immune system that is keeping the bacteria in our bodies in check," Francis says.

Notice he says "in check." In other words, we are being digested by scummy little creatures, but not *fatally*. There are jillions of the tiny beasts inside us, and so to help prevent rotting, our bodies slough off dead cells and bacterial by-products. Sadly, as the years pass by, our bodily renewal procedures work less and less efficiently. Also, when we get sick, the rot can take hold. Look in the mirror the next time you get strep throat—your tonsils back there are literally rotting away, at least until the immune system can deal with the situation.

"A lot of time, if you smell the breath of someone who is very ill, you will get an aroma that is tantamount to rotting meat," Francis says. (Excuse us if we don't try to verify this through experimentation.)

As long as we are delving into these gummy, goopy details, we should note that people who don't ventilate their skin or who don't shower very often will also suffer the fate of dead meat. Soap destroys the cell walls of bacteria and the water rinses the crud away. Air, though full of bacteria, also has lots of oxygen, which helps the chemistry of our skin. So you can oxidize the rot away.

Now then: Last one into the shower is a rotten egg.

Why do you never see a partially gray hair? Why isn't it ever gray at the root and dark at the tip?

Gray hairs have this mysterious way of arriving full-blown on your head, neatly interspersed among dark ones. It is as though the follicle emits some kind of fiendish secretion that, overnight, travels the length of the hair and dyes it gray or white.

The truth is, you just aren't sufficiently perceptive. The

B.O. Frankenstein
Meets
S. Sontag

pigment in a given follicle—the juice that makes your hair black, brown, red, orange, or yellow—is slowly diluted as a person gets older, the exact timing being a function primarily of heredity. There is no sudden cutoff of pigment, and so no hair goes abruptly from black to white. But the transition is usually too subtle to notice unless you're really vain and you're always checking yourself out.

If you are—"You should be able to see a hair that has both dark and light in it," says Andrew Atton, a dermatologist at the Johns Hopkins School of Medicine.

Hey, what about Marie Antoinette, who supposedly went gray overnight as she awaited execution? What about people whose hair has suddenly turned white from fear? How does that happen?

The famous cases may be apocryphal; Marie Antoinette was locked up for a while and may have just run out of her artificial hair coloring. (We're not sure what they used back then—pig's blood, maybe?) In the more credible cases, what may have happened is that the pigmented hairs fell out over the course of a couple of weeks, leaving the white or gray hairs that already were there. According to the textbook *Diseases of the Hair and Scalp*, by Arthur Rook and Rodney Dawber, this may be a quirky result of the hair follicle disease *alopecia areata*. Though no one knows why sometimes only the dark hairs are affected enough to drop out.

It's more fun to think Marie Antoinette was just scared pigmentless.

Why do tapeworms make you lose weight even though the tapeworm presumably is getting bigger and bigger?

You would think that the tapeworm, which sits in your gut and steals your food, would gain weight in exact proportion to the weight you lose, so that there would be no net change when you stand on the bathroom scale. Isn't that logical? And don't you think about this quandary every day?

Yes, it's true that the parasite is in direct competition with the human for the nutrients in the intestines, and if the worm did nothing but grow larger and larger, there would be no change in the sum of the weight of the person and the worm. But if you were to uncoil one of these worms, it wouldn't be much longer than about fifteen feet (except in the occasional event of an eighty-foot monster) and that's only about half a pound's worth of worm. The rest of the energy that's metabolized goes into making eggs, and these are "sloughed off," to use one of our least favorite expressions, and they pass from the body. Also, there are dead segments of worms that break off and . . . look, it's a nasty business; do we *have* to talk about it?

Fact is, weight loss from a tapeworm is not dramatic, and to the extent that it does occur it is not due so much to the competition for nutrients as it is to the side effects of being occupied by a parasite—essentially, your insides are so grossed out, you lose your appetite.

Our advice is to cook your food and kill these damn things. Avoid becoming part of some other creature's life cycle.

An afterthought: The tapeworm question reminds us of a puzzle we heard recently. Let's say you crunch your ex's car into a cube about one foot on each side. Then you take it on a boat out into a really small lake. You drop the car cube into the water. Does the water level rise, drop, or stay the same on the shoreline? You make the call.

. . . The "Jeopardy!" theme song plays while you figure it out. . . .

Okay, we're back. The water level *drops*.

It's a question of density: We can presume that the car cube would be denser than the equivalent volume of water. When the cube is on the boat, the *weight* of the cube is the critical factor in displacing the water of the lake, via the hull of the boat. But when the cube is thrown overboard, the weight no longer matters (because the lake is no longer holding the cube up), and instead the *volume* of the cube is the factor that determines how much water is displaced. Since the cube has a relatively high weight but low volume—and is denser than water—it displaces more water when it is up on the boat.

Why does beer give you a beer belly, and not, say, a beer butt?

We thought that maybe it was the carbonation, all those bubbles accumulating in the gut. Nah. Wine can give you a beer belly too. So can chocolate cake. Calories are calories. Lots of beer drinkers don't get beer bellies; it just depends on who you are, your personal body composition, and whether you are prone to abdominal weight gain. Some people become apple-shaped, some pear-shaped.

The strange thing is that there is evidence that people with heavy abdominal fat tend to have more heart trouble than those who bulk up elsewhere. We could swear that they also tend to smoke, wear white undershirts around the house, watch bowling tournaments on TV, emit wheezing noises, and never move except to wield a flyswatter, but we've got no evidence.

Why, when we gain weight, do some parts of our body remain the same size?

The ears don't get any bigger. Nor do noses. Nor eyes nor mouths nor teeth. You only gain weight in your "fat pads." These cover much of the body, serving to protect, insulate, and store all those yummy calories. The fat pads are absent in certain essential organs that might be encumbered by excessive flesh.

No doubt many heavy men have rued the unfairness of it all.

Why is some cholesterol good for you?

You have to love those bags of junk food that boast "low cholesterol," as though we're supposed to believe that Nacho Cheese Doritos are, at the molecular level, the same thing as bean sprouts.

Honest to gosh, we went into a doughnut shop recently and there was a big sign, right there by the jelly doughnuts and the chocolate-glazed crullers and the sugar-slathered cinnamon rolls, saying NO CHOLESTEROL. We ordered an extra dozen of the jelly-filled, because *you can never be too cautious about heart disease.*

Cholesterol phobia reached a peak a couple of years ago, when innumerable scary nutrition articles and TV spots convinced the public that even a smidgen of this stuff

Good Cholesterol   Bad Cholesterol

would cause your arteries to clog up like those see-through drainage pipes featured in Drano commercials. Lately, things have gotten more complicated, because now there's a new, improved concept, that of Good Cholesterol versus Bad Cholesterol.

What's the difference? Is it in their physical properties? Is some cholesterol green and some yellow? Nope.

"Cholesterol's all the same," explains Eddie Rubin, a molecular biologist at Lawrence Berkeley Laboratory in California. Cholesterol is a type of fat, a "lipid," and it's important for some bodily functions, like building cell membranes. But there is a big difference in how cholesterol *gets around*. There's Hyundai cholesterol and there's Cadillac cholesterol.

"It's transported through the bloodstream on different particles. When we talk about good cholesterol we're talking about cholesterol that's carried on high-density lipoproteins. Bad cholesterol is carried on low-density lipoproteins," he said.

It's quite obvious that low-density lipoproteins are disgusting. Would you want your lipoprotein density to be *low*? Not if you had some pride.

Cholesterol at a
Moral Crossroads

The reason that some lipoproteins are low-density is that they're mostly wads of fat, and fats are low in density compared with proteins. You can tell a fatty lipoprotein on sight, because it floats more easily to the surface of your blood. Think: a pudgy guy on his back in the ocean.

When these fat-laden lipoproteins circulate through the body, they can't dump all their excess fatty baggage, and it winds up getting stuck inside the cells along the walls of your arteries. This is bad. You get all caulked up.

So don't get fooled by "no cholesterol" labels. If food is full of saturated fat, it can contribute to excessive production of low-density lipoproteins and thus to a dangerous cholesterol level. The fact is, your body can make its own cholesterol from scratch.

Eventually they'll probably come up with another dichotomy: good zits and bad zits.

Why do we—excuse us, why does *our partner*—snore?

When they dream, their body goes into a state something like paralysis. It's called *atonia*. Their muscles become flaccid. In their throat, the uvula (that nasty stalactite back there) and the soft palate get saggy, restricting the air passage, causing them to snore. When they're awake, or when they're asleep but not dreaming, the tissue is all firmed up. They also snore when they go to bed drunk, because the tissue is all sloppy.

People who are overweight have extra loads of tissue back there and thus are more prone to snoring. One way this is treated, with limited success, is through an operation called a uvulopalatopharyngoplasty. Sounds pretty bloody.

If we did have muscle tone when dreaming, says Suzan Norman, the clinical director of the Sleep Disorders Center at Mount Sinai Medical Center in Miami Beach, "we'd be up acting out our dreams. . . . The inhibition of tone is actually a safety valve so we can fantasize all these dreams while still staying in bed."

(In other words, were it not for atonia, when you dreamed about showing up at work without any clothes on, you actually would show up at work without any clothes on.)

Why do left-handed people die nine years younger than righties?

When we first heard this factoid, we immediately wondered: Are scissors designed for right-handed people *that dangerous*? Are lefties somehow finding a way to fall victim to can openers? Automobile stick shifts? *Gravy ladles?* You can imagine the freakiest accidents. ("What happened, Officer, was that Marge here accidentally ladled the gravy directly into the blow-dryer, and . . .")

The lefties-die-younger story caused headlines in 1991, when two researchers announced in *The New England Journal of Medicine* that they had reviewed thousands of deaths in California and discovered that the lefties had died, on average, at age sixty-six, while righties lasted to the ripe old age of seventy-five.

"We were concerned that our colleagues were going to look at us as though we just descended from flying saucers with deely-boppers on our heads," recalls one of the researchers, Stanley Coren, a professor of psychology at the University of British Columbia and author of *The Left-Hander Syndrome*. He has a special interest in the topic: His son is left-handed. Not that he's worried. "Obviously it's difficult to make predictions for any one individual," he says.

He gave us two possible reasons for why lefties die younger:

1. Accidents. "Left-handers are five times more likely to die of accidental injuries," says Coren. Unfortunately, he doesn't know why. He offered some speculation: Elderly lefties are more likely to cut themselves (like on gardening shears) and develop a fatal infection. But that's a lot of fatal gardening accidents!

2. Left-handedness often is a side effect of some other neuropathology. Babies from difficult pregnancies or stressed births are more likely to be left-handed. Lefties tend to mature more slowly and suffer from learning disabilities. Most important, lefties often have sluggish or dysfunctional immune systems.

Is Coren right? Not even close, say his critics, and there are many of them. They offer a third explanation for the discrepancy in life span:

3. The statistics are skewed by the prejudice against left-handedness that existed sixty or seventy years ago.

This argument was raised in a series of letters to *The New England Journal of Medicine*. The critics of Coren and co-researcher Diane Halpern say that many years ago, children were forced to be right-handed even if they were naturally left-handed. As a result, there aren't very many seventy-five-year-old left-handers, compared with, say, the number of twenty-five-year-old left-handers. This, in turn, creates a quirky situation: Lefties, being younger than righties on average, can appear to have a lower average age of death even though their risk of dying isn't any lower.

It's a simple mathematical proposition: All these eighty-five-year-old righties and pseudo-righties that are wandering around are skewing the numbers on behalf of right-handedness. It might be true that righties, on average, live longer—but only because there are so many old righties!

"Using the same approach as Halpern and Coren, one would conclude that nursery school is more dangerous than paratrooper training, since the mean age at death of children in nursery school is much lower than that of paratrooper trainers," epidemiologist Kenneth Rothman of Boston said in a letter to the journal.

Coren and Halpern, in the same letters column, reply that the alleged historical bias against left-handedness isn't documented, and they offer statistics to support their contention that sinistrality has been fairly constant since early in the century. Thus, they write, "an analysis based on the mean age at death is completely justified." Plus, they say their critics can't refute their observation that left-handers are far more likely to die of accident-related injuries.

So, who's right? Hard to say. The data are likely to fuel a prolonged argument among the experts. The key will be to find out, conclusively, whether there are a lot of switched-over right-handers in the elderly population. But this gets even more complicated because there are ten separate indicators of "handedness," and they don't all point in the same direction (a person, for instance, might write as a lefty but throw a ball as a righty).

For the time being we'll take the word of Marcel E. Salive, an epidemiologist at the National Institute on Aging, who told us, "The evidence points to right- and left-handed people having the same risk of death at any age."

In any case, southpaws shouldn't feel inferior, says Steven Schachter, a neurologist at Harvard University. Left-handers, he says, are better at spatial perception than right-handers, have superior physical skills, and are unusually creative: "They're actually overrepresented at both ends of the IQ scale," he says.

Dave Barry, the famous sinistral funnyman, told us that lefties die younger intentionally, because they're smarter: "They just realize at some point in their life that the whole world is pointless anyway, while right-handed people keep plodding along waiting for something meaningful."

Why don't we see the world upside down, since the image is flipped upside down by the lenses of our eyeballs?

Check any anatomy textbook. The lens of the eyeball inverts the entering light, so the image of the world is projected upside down on the back of the retina. If you are walking down the street, the image of the sidewalk shines on the top of the retina, and the image of the clouds overhead shines on the bottom of the retina.

So why do we see the world right side up? One ophthalmologist told us rather feebly that the brain readjusts the image. This is not so. In fact, this is precisely the kind of nonsense that *Why Things Are* has been trying to surgically extract from the public consciousness. Trust us: Your brain makes no correction whatsoever. The fact is, you *do* see the world as being "upside down," you just don't realize it.

We define "up" as that which hits the bottom of our retina, and "down" as that which hits the top. Moreover, down and up are merely social conventions that we learn as we grow up. We are told, as children, that down is the direction of gravitational pull. If we were told instead that gravity pulled us *up* to the ground, then we'd be content with that too. This is because there is no up and down in nature.

Confused? Try this: Pretend you are, in fact, upside down. Pretend the world around you is constructed on the underside of a table that is accelerating through space in the direction of your head, creating the equivalent of gravity at your feet. What do you notice? That nothing is different.

Now, let's go to the scientific literature. There have been several experiments in which people wore funny goggles equipped with inverting prisms, causing the ground to hit the lower part of the retina and the sky to hit the upper part. The goggle wearers were initially discombobulated. They didn't feel upside down, exactly, because all their visual cues were still lined up correctly—and gravity still pulled them toward the ground at their feet. But they still had a sense of unreality. A Japanese study in 1980, published in *Kyushu Neuro-psychiatry*, stated that over the course of a week, two goggle wearers gradually adjusted to the inverted world but never became completely comfortable. They never managed to read and write, and they lacked dexterity. A similar study by the Soviets, published in the September 1974 issue of the journal *Voprosy Psikhologii*, said it took eight days for the subjects to become accustomed to the inverted world. When the prisms were removed, it took another couple of days to set things straight again.

The experiments indicate that, over time, it doesn't matter whether the light is inverted when it hits the retina, because the right-side-up nature of the world is something we learn, not an objective reality. It doesn't matter whether you are dispatched to the North Pole or the South Pole, you will feel right side up either way.

Though we'd prefer the North Pole, just in case.

Why don't people die after they stop producing offspring, the way queen bees and tomatoes do?

We don't sit around for hours trying to think up offensive questions, they come to us naturally. Why the heck do the elderly *exist*?

Consider the rest of nature. Pacific salmon swim thousands of miles upstream, spawn, then die. Bamboo grows for a hundred years, flowers, and dies. Mayflies live a few hours, mate, and die.

Bean plants give themselves a death hormone after they go to seed.

When a male praying mantis mates, he's eaten alive by the female.

When a queen bee stops cranking out eggs, she's murdered by the workers.

Look around and the cold-hearted message is ubiquitous: Make babies and then get the heck outta Dodge.

Fortunately, we are social mammals, and we get to break the rules. Postmenopausal pilot whales still breast-feed young whales. Among baboons, a male will sometimes try to attack his son, due to a perceived threat of sexual rivalry, but will be stopped by the grandmother. And among humans, the elderly are typically the leaders of society. So, let's content ourselves with a simple, feel-good answer: The elderly exist because we are social creatures, and they enforce our socialization.

That, however, leads us to a more complicated question:

Why don't we live to be a thousand years old, other than for the fact that Social Security would go bankrupt?

For some reason, we're wired to live to about 115, at most. Why do we deteriorate and die?

The short answer is that no one knows. One theory that the Why staff enjoys, for purely aesthetic reasons, is that oxygen is toxic. Oxygen atoms have a tendency to run around as free radicals, meaning they are highly reactive and tend to scuff up our cells and break things. So we just get banged up by random oxygen impacts.

The problem with the oxygen theory is that all species have such precise maximum life spans that we have to conclude that death isn't random, but rather a scheduled event, a genetic prescription. It appears that we are programmed to rust and die.

The strange thing is that our cells don't gradually wither up and croak—not at all. In fact, a person of ninety makes new red blood cells as well as a nine-year-old. What usually kills us is some larger systemic problem like cancer or heart disease. These diseases are not by any means an inevitable part of being alive; the Pacific rockfish, for example, doesn't get cancer or heart disease and can live to be a hundred or more years old. Pacific rockfish die from random accidents, as far as we can tell. Only the law of probability keeps the rockfish from living to be a thousand. It's quite likely that the rockfish is simply lucky; the genes causing cancer and heart disease have never entered the fish's gene pool. No such luck with us.

"During the evolution of mammals, they acquired sets of genes that cause high risk for blood vessel disease and cancer with aging," says Caleb Finch, a neurobiologist at the University of Southern California.

Why would evolution allow such a horrible thing to happen?

The answer is rather shocking: because cancer, heart disease, and other ailments of old age have no significant effect on human reproduction, and therefore are sort of irrelevant to the processes of evolution. Bad things that crop up in old age can't be mitigated by evolutionary pressures; natural selection works only on breeding populations.

So it's not a cheery situation. We die because we get diseases in old age, and we get those diseases because Nature doesn't care much about us anymore.

Why do some people spontaneously combust, leaving only a pile of ashes in their wake?

Over the centuries there have been about two hundred alleged cases of SHC—spontaneous human combustion. In the classic scenario, the body of a person who had been lonely and depressed is found incinerated, all external tissues reduced to black ash. There is no obvious source of fire, and nearby flammable objects—and perhaps even the person's clothes—are untouched.

One of the most famous cases was that of Mary Reeser, a St. Petersburg, Florida, widow who burned to death on July 1, 1951. There was almost nothing left of her but a slippered foot. The chair underneath her had burned down to the springs, but only a small circular area on the floor was charred. Investigators were baffled. For the body to have been destroyed so extensively, there had to have been intense heat, but there was little evidence of a major blaze.

The explanations for SHC range from ball lightning to microwave bursts that cook the human being but leave the wrapper intact.

This is nonsense, naturally.

"It doesn't exist," says Roger Mittleman of the Dade County Medical Examiner's Office in Miami. "Usually what it means is that the death investigation has not been adequate. Bodies do not just spontaneously ignite."

Take the Reeser case. She had last been seen smoking while sitting in the stuffed chair. She had taken two sleeping tablets. She obviously nodded off and dropped the cigarette. The stuffed chair provided plenty of fuel. That's the thing about SHC cases: They're only mysterious because people have grotesque imaginations. As for human flesh . . .

"It's quite burnable," says Mittleman.

Terrific.

Why are we all about five or six feet tall, instead of, say, five or six inches tall, or fifty or sixty feet tall?

Don't be daft. There are only so many calories of energy in the environment. If we were huge, we'd be constantly hungry, unless we were extremely sluggish, in which case we'd be hunted down by ants and devoured like unsupervised luncheon meat.

If, on the other hand, we were small, we'd have pea brains and wouldn't know how to operate farm equipment, like automatic balers and corn shuckers. Think of the tragic dialogue:

"Honey, the worst thing happened . . ."

"No! No!"

"Yep. I shucked Junior."

Why is AIDS so hard to cure?

People have a paradoxical attitude toward science: On the one hand, we are annoyed by the know-it-all attitude of physicists, biologists, psychologists—by their arrogance, their smugness, their impersonal delivery of information—and yet we insist that they solve every last medical problem that might strike us down. We have unlimited faith in medical science. Surely there is nothing that can't be figured out eventually, with enough money and gumption.

People figure, hey, they came up with a polio vaccine, they ought to be able to make an AIDS vaccine. It's caused by a virus, after all, and we imagine viruses as very tiny bugs that can be rooted out and exterminated.

The truth is that no virus has ever been "cured." Some have been successfully counterattacked or repulsed through vaccines, though even polio is still around. In any case, the human immunodeficiency virus is much harder to attack than the polio virus. It is quite possible that a broadly applicable vaccine will never be found. The virus, says Dr. Nava Sarver of the AIDS division of the National Institute of Allergy and Infectious Diseases, "is probably the most difficult [virus] the scientific community has ever encountered."

Here are a few of the reasons why stopping HIV is so difficult:

1. The virus changes. Even within one person, the virus can mutate in a matter of hours. This is partly because the virus is sloppy at reproducing itself and makes inaccurate copies. These errors work to the virus's advantage—it is a moving, shifting target for the body's immune system and for any potential vaccine.

"It may be like the cold virus in that we may never get a vaccine that works," says Bob Rubin, a cell biologist at the University of Miami, which has an extensive program in AIDS research. Like HIV, cold viruses change constantly. So too with the flu virus—every year it undergoes a slight alteration, called a genetic drift, and roughly every tenth year it changes more drastically, a genetic shift. (Why? According to immunologist Parker Small of the University of Florida, this shift may occur when someone already infected with flu is coughed on by an animal with a different strain of the virus. The two viruses then fuse, in a sense, to form a new and more lethal strain of flu.)

2. HIV, unlike most viruses, is able to become part of the genetic code of a cell, to integrate itself into the very brain of a cell's operation, the DNA. So you have to kill the cell in order to save it. Polio, by contrast, remains outside the cell's genetic machinery and is easier to target.

The reason you can't simply try to kill all the HIV-infected cells is:

3. HIV infects the entire body. If it were just in the blood, you might be able to clean it out. "But the virus is also present in the tissue, in the brain, in the pancreas, in the lungs. . . . You can't get to it very easily; it's not accessible," says Sarver.

These are not insurmountable obstacles. We notice that almost every week there is a new announcement of progress in finding a vaccine for the simian version of the virus. There are also techniques being developed that might provide immunity for specific individuals, though they are so costly they can't be widely (or fairly) used.

More importantly, drug therapy has succeeded in slowing down the progress of the disease in many patients. Over time, a multi-pronged attack against HIV may neutralize it to the point that it does not radically alter the normal life expectancy of an infected person. This is where many researchers are looking: not for a miracle cure, but for a relentless counterattack.

"I don't think it's going to be cured, but I think we're going to find a treatment for it, a very good treatment," says Sarver.

And we trust her on this. She's a scientist, after all.

Why is the shape of the human ear so strange, so—let's be frank—hideous?

Ears are our most tragic appendage. They are not merely ugly, they are illogical. The design has no obvious function.

They're stiff, first of all, so you can't aim them toward the source of a noise, as can a deer or a cat. (There are two tiny muscles attached to the ear that in most people are dysfunctional; some people, however, can use these muscles to wiggle their auricles. This, however, is a drunken party stunt, not a survival mechanism.)

If ears were merely supposed to capture and funnel sound, you'd expect them to be much bigger, like elephant ears. Or Prince Charles's. And you'd think the design would more closely resemble the sugar cone into which we place scoops of ice cream. Instead, they are horribly twisted, folded, flapped, and lobed.

Is it just a terrible mistake? Of course not, you silly

goose. One major reason ears are designed the way they are is to let us know whether a sound came from in front of us or in back of us. We have obtained this astonishing revelation from Dixon Ward, a professor of otolaryngology at the University of Minnesota.

Think about what would happen if, instead of those ungainly cartilaginous ears, you just had little holes in the sides of your head. You would be able to hear just fine, but a sound coming from behind you would sound exactly like one coming from in front of you.

The shape of our ear, however, affects the timbre of sound, particularly the highest frequencies, the squeaks and clicks and snaps, up there around 4,000 hertz. The protruding ear slightly blocks those high frequencies if they are coming from behind us, and amplifies that a little bit if they are coming from the front. As infants we learn, subconsciously, to recognize how this slight impedance affects sounds.

According to Michael S. Morris, an ear specialist at Georgetown University Medical Center, the design of the ear can affect the resonance frequency of sound in the same way that a bottle half-filled with liquid sounds different, when you blow across the mouth, from a bottle three-quarters filled. Our ears help funnel sound to the eardrum at frequencies we can easily register.

We have our own theory for the purpose of ears: holding pencils. If you look at the pinna (the external, cartilaginous portion of the ear), you will see that the top flange (the helix) is folded outward and downward, and just below that is another fold (the anthelix), which thrusts the helix back toward the skull to prevent unsightly ear jutting and simultaneously creates a slot between the ear and the skull that is ideal for inserting a pencil.

Ears are also great for holding up eyeglasses, which brings up another little mystery:

Why don't we have eyes on the sides of our heads so we can see in every direction at once?

Humans are innately nervous, on account of not having eyes in back of their head. You hear a sound behind you and you wonder: Is it something innocuous? Or is it a PSYCHOTIC CLEAVER-WIELDING BUTCHER?

The evolutionary defect of one-direction vision has one plus side, though: With our eyes close together, we see in stereo. 3-D. This is so we can reach out and grab branches as we swing through the trees.

So there you have it—two eyes in front, two ears on the sides. Picasso notwithstanding.

Why do some people sneeze so much more violently than others?

Everyone has a signature sneeze. A person who sneezes violently doesn't typically have, in his or her repertoire, a modest, low-voltage sneeze. Likewise, someone who issues a polite "ca-choo" is unlikely to erupt in a floorboard-shaking, china-cabinet-rattling, vermin-frightening ARR-FGGGNN-EWGBRGEEWW! type of sneeze.

So a sneeze is like a handshake, something that's fairly consistent from day to day for any given person and yet highly variable throughout the general population. And, as with our handshake, we have limited knowledge of how others perceive it; for all you know, when other people refer to you they say, "You know—the one with the posthumous handshake and the hydrogen bomb sneeze."

Why do sneezes vary so much? No one knows. Robert Naclerio, an associate professor of otolaryngology at Johns Hopkins University, says there are two obstacles to finding an answer: First, sneezes are complex, multi-step physical reactions, and no one has isolated any particular influence that corresponds to the violence of the sneeze. For example, we know that a person with hay fever will sneeze when exposed to pollen. But the vehemence of the sneeze doesn't correlate with the quantity of pollen in the air, or the number of pollen-detecting antibodies in the nose, or the amount of the chemical histamine secreted by cells when alerted to the presence of pollen by the antibodies.

Second, and probably more important, there's no unit of sneeze measurement. "We don't have any objective measures other than *counting* sneezes," says Philip Fireman, director of the Asthma and Allergic Disease Center at the University of Pittsburgh.

Naclerio says it best: "There's not, like, a Richter scale of sneezing."

Why do we get the dry heaves when there's no food in our stomach?

This is officially known as "retching," which is not the same thing as "vomiting." To vomit you have to actually expel something, but you can retch away for entire geologic epochs even if your belly is empty.

We spoke to Mark Feldman, an expert on vomiting at the University of Texas Southwestern Medical School in Dallas (he also knows about vomiting at other locations). "There's not a whole lot of research that separates dry heaves from true vomiting," he warned us.

What is known is that there is a place in the brain that controls this explosive event. It is called, straightforwardly enough, the vomiting center. (This would be a great name for a shopping mall.)

Certain cells in the stomach and intestines can detect the presence of toxins. In addition, a section of the brain called the chemoreceptor trigger zone samples your blood supply constantly to see if any toxins have already infiltrated. In either case, a signal travels to the vomiting center, which then sends out the barfing orders.

The key thing to understand here is that your guts don't decide to retch; your brain decides. If your gut is all emptied out but your brain is still shouting HEAVE-HO!, then you have dry heaves.

What we do not wish to report are some of the troublesome side effects of vomiting that Feldman has told us about. Like death. See, you can rupture your esophagus, and . . . oh, never mind. What's even more disturbing—indeed, the most disturbing thing we have ever heard—is that "projectile vomiting" has been known to occur "without premonitory nausea," as Feldman put it. In other words, it just happens. You're feeling fine, then suddenly (Your Sound Effect Here) you are power-booting across the room.

Feldman noted that "projectile vomiting" is only vaguely defined. There are no official standards, and no distance requirements.

THE BATTLE OVER WHO WE ARE

(In which we ask: Where did the human species come from? And learn that the Smithsonian Institution is not the place to find out.)

Something ugly is lurking inside the National Museum of Natural History. It lives among the bones of the dead. In a word: racism.

It can be sensed, for example, in a corner of the Ice Age Mammals hall, in an antiquated exhibit called "The Emergence of Man" that might better be labeled "The Emergence of White Man." *Homo erectus*, an ancestor of modern humans, is represented by a painting of light-skinned brutes throwing spears at a mammoth in what is now northern Spain. Next in line comes Neanderthal man, that most famous of protohumans, and not coincidentally a European too. Then comes the anatomically modern human. An illustration on the wall shows what he looks like. Caucasoid, naturally. Perhaps—judging from the features—a Swede.

The irony is, this white guy on the wall was supposed to represent a liberal, progressive view of the world when painted back in 1966. The caption underneath makes the point that, over time, biological differences among humans have diminished but cultural diversity has increased. The white guy represents this cultural diversity simply because he's got long stringy hair and raggedy jeans, and is barefoot. He's a hippie! (The real tip-off is that he's playing a flute, the ultimate hippie musical instrument.)

In the 1990s, this mural looks hopelessly reactionary.

"The implication is that there's this ascending progress that ends up with white hippies," says Bob Sullivan, the museum's associate director of public programming. "Issue number one we're facing is how to get the Eurocentrism out and how to replace it with a balanced view."

That's an official talking. Others have a more visceral reaction.

"The first time I saw it, my stomach turned over," says Helen Maddox, queen mother (that's her official title) of the Tu-Wa-Moja African Study Group, which has pushed for a more Afrocentric reading of the paleontological record.

What is happening in this little corner of the Natural History Museum is a collision of two irresistible forces: science and politics. Or, if you prefer, scientific correctness and political correctness. They are not mutually exclusive; both require that the existing exhibits be junked. But beyond that, the harmony shatters.

The problem is that anthropology is in a state of scientific turbulence that is only exacerbated by the divisive politics of our society. Scientists aren't sure what a "balanced" view of human evolution would show. Should the museum show Neanderthals as white, black, or something in between? Should modern humans be portrayed as a closely related brotherhood that emerged fairly recently from Africa? Or as a species that evolved over a much longer period in many places at once? Does the scientific record show that our ancestors replaced Neanderthal man and *Homo erectus* through a benign competition for resources? Through interbreeding? Or through homicide?

It's no wonder that the museum is putting up a warning at the entrance to "The Emergence of Man." The warning says that the exhibit is defective. The museum calls this a "dilemma label."

The entire Smithsonian Institution is going through a revolutionary phase. Various curators have embraced multiculturalism to the point that Christopher Columbus and his European ilk are barely footnotes to the quincentenary commemoration of 1492. The Smithsonian might be described as a nineteenth-century place trying to prepare itself for the twenty-first century; as a place that once glorified the white man's culture, and now finds itself in an era in which that culture is often seen as overemphasized or even villainous.

At the same time, museums are inherently stodgy and stale. They can't be quickly revised the way textbooks can. There's too much *stuff* lying around: fossils, skulls, skeletons, tribal costumes, spears, knives, and the occasional life-size fiberglass whale and stuffed woolly mammoth. It costs millions of dollars to put together a new exhibit, and so the existing ones stay for decades.

The gloomy, cavernous Natural History Museum is particularly stricken with this kind of museumness. A visit is like browsing through your grandparents' collection of *National Geographics*. Sullivan estimates that it would take $100 million to bring all the existing exhibits up to date, yet Congress authorizes only $2.5 million a year for that purpose.

The cheaper alternative is to start shutting doors. That's what happened. In September 1990, the museum simply closed up Hall 25, the Human Origins and Variation exhibit.

This was shortly after Sullivan arrived at the museum. His first act that summer was producing a paper entitled "The Unity of All Creation: A New Paradigm for the National Museum of Natural History." The old paradigm, as he saw it, was the nineteenth-century belief in progress— the conceit that Western civilization, through logic, science, and technology, was leading humankind out of its former condition of barbarism. Sullivan declared that era over; Western civilization can no longer presume itself the master of nature or of other societies. In an environmentally degraded world, he wrote, science museums "must be engaged institutions committed to the necessity for global survival."

Meanwhile, the community was insisting on changes. Local residents, academics, and minority interns within the museum were all complaining about the biases, sexism, and racism within the exhibits. Museum scientists also wanted a "complete overhaul" of the evolution exhibits, says anthropologist Rick Potts, but had been frustrated by four changes in the museum's directorship since 1985. And so one day everyone—scientists, critics, administrators—met inside Hall 25 to look at the exhibit more carefully.

In one room there was a large painting showing a white, middle-class, modern family, with an older man measuring the height of a boy. On the other side of the room was an identically sized painting showing two pre-Columbian Peruvian Indians pinning a boy to the ground while an Indian doctor drilled a surgical hole in his blood-spurting head.

Another exhibit implied, by its design, that a male Greco-Roman figure was the perfect human body type. A mural depicting the diversity of modern people showed a white man in modern dress and every person of color in some kind of tribal costume. A sign asked a question: What causes black skin? Implicit was the assumption that white skin is normal. Another case said that Indians and Eskimos, like "all people with simple cultures," used "inadequate procedures" to treat broken bones, resulting in "deformities and lameness." Five display cases about the races included such statements as "Excessive development of fat on the buttocks (Steatopygia) is common among Bushman and Hottentot women."

Hall 25, in short, was a disaster. Could it be fixed? No, said the critics. Sullivan agreed. The Human Origins and Variation hall was roped off.

"Outside groups, like Tu-Wa-Moja, convinced us of the urgency of this," Sullivan said.

Now comes the tougher question: What should be put up next? One person who will participate in that decision, on an advisory basis, is Michael Blakey, an anthropologist at Howard University who has written extensively on museum bias. Blakey doesn't mince words: "Exhibits of the Natural History Museum not only depict people of African, Asian, and Native American descent as inferior, they show little interest in the participation of minority scholars."

He says the Smithsonian is called "The Plantation" by some minority scholars because the scientific corps is almost exclusively white, while the custodial and security staffers are mostly people of color. "The problem from the beginning with these exhibits is that they have always been created by white, mostly but not entirely male, scholars," Blakey says.

Donald Ortner, chairman of the museum's Department of Anthropology, said the curators who put the exhibits together in the 1950s and 1960s intended no malice or racism. He points out that the European fossil record is much more detailed than that from anywhere else. "There may not be any sort of malice involved in that at all. It may be just a matter of history," he says.

Both Ortner and Sullivan declare that the museum wants and needs more minority scholars, but that the museum often can't compete with higher-paying institutions. It will take years, and about $9 million, to put a new human origins exhibit in Hall 25. In the meantime, museum visitors will see nothing about the evolution of human beings—one of the most important, dynamic areas of natural history—except for the flute-playing hippie, a few piles of bones, and some life-size plaster Neanderthals.

The members of the Tu-Wa-Moja (Swahili for "We Are One") African Study Group are not scientists, but they have immersed themselves in the academic literature on human evolution. They argue that facts, not merely fairness, require a far greater emphasis on African history in textbooks and museums. The pharaohs were black, they say. Cleopatra was black. They argue that even Neanderthal man, traditionally shown as white, was black.

"We believe they were black from the beginning to the

end," Helen Maddox says of the Neanderthals. "The scientists have no way of saying that the Neanderthal was white."

One figure who is particularly important to Afrocentrists is Grimaldi Man, the name given to the remains of two bodies unearthed in Italy at the start of this century. The bones were initially thought to be Negroid. Afrocentrists say Grimaldi Man slightly predates the remains of Cro-Magnon man, the anatomically modern human who appeared in Europe about 35,000 years ago. Conclusion: The first modern people in Europe were black.

The problem is, most scientists claim Grimaldi Man was a scientific blunder. They say the initial reconstruction of the bones was inept, and a later reconstruction showed a less distinctly Negroid appearance. Blakey, for one, says this is a sign of white scholars' resistance to the idea of an African origin of modern humans. One of Blakey's colleagues at Howard, anthropologist Shomarka Keita, says of the museum officials, "They are sensitive to a white public and they are concerned about the confusion they might cause to the white public."

Sullivan says the inconclusive nature of Grimaldi Man prevents his inclusion in any exhibit.

"That's not because we're racists; that's because we're scientists," Sullivan says. "What we won't do and can't do is replace Eurocentrism with another centrism. The point is not to use science in the service of cultural therapy or issues of self-esteem."

Ironically, while racial consciousness has become more important in the larger community, scientists are moving away from any discussion of race. Many scientists have adopted the position that human variation doesn't correspond to a classic racial breakdown, because there is far more variation within racial groups than between them. Races, they say, don't really exist at the genetic level.

"The concept of race is a political and economic one," Sullivan says. "It's not a scientific concept."

This might initially look like a case of emotional, politically minded citizens versus detached, accurate scientists.

In truth, scientists have their own political history that to this day influences their research and theories. Modern anthropology is still haunted by the bogus racial theories used by scientists early in this century to justify Jim Crow laws, and then by Nazi scientists to justify the killing of the supposedly inferior "Jewish race."

A political undercurrent flows through the hottest debate in anthropology today: the origin of modern humans. The lay person might be surprised that this is still an issue. Everyone knows that humans evolved first in Africa. But what remains a matter of contention is when and where *modern-looking* people, members of the subspecies *Homo sapiens sapiens*, first appeared, and what they did when they met up with those jut-browed, large-headed Neanderthals and other early humans. The Neanderthals mysteriously disappeared in Europe at about the same time that modern humans appeared there.

There are two major, utterly contradictory schools of thought. The first school argues that we evolved in many places simultaneously, with populations interbreeding, the genes flowing from continent to continent. This is called multiregional evolution.

That perspective has been challenged, however, by recent genetic evidence for a strictly African origin of modern humans. The so-called out-of-Africa model, or "Eve hypothesis," studies the genetic code within a cell structure called mitochondria. Geneticists say their research shows that everyone on the planet has a common ancestor who lived in Africa about 200,000 years ago, far more recently than other theories had predicted. These researchers say the descendants of that African gradually spread around the world and "replaced" other human species. (More recently, several scientists have argued that the mitochondrial studies were mathematically flawed, and the Eve hypothesis has lost some of its popularity.)

It's a complicated scientific question made still more contentious by political sensitivities. For example, what does "replaced" mean, exactly? Is that a peaceful process of competition for resources? Or does that include murder? Critics of the out-of-Africa model have used the phrase "killer Africans" to describe the theory. Christopher Stringer, a paleontologist at the Natural History Museum in London, says "killer Africans" is a term used with the intent of making the theory sound racist—which it can't be, by definition, since all human beings on the planet then would be descendants of those Africans. What might be more easily "construed" as racist, Stringer says, is the multiregional evolution view, because "that's more likely to be seen as demonstrating greater differences between the races."

Stephen Jay Gould, the Harvard paleobiologist, told *Newsweek* in 1988 that the new mitochondrial DNA research has an inspiring message: "It makes us realize that all human beings, despite differences in external appearance, are really members of a single entity that's had a very recent origin in one place. There is a kind of biological brotherhood that's much more profound than we ever realized."

In contrast, Milford Wolpoff, a University of Michigan anthropologist who is the most vocal of the multiregionalists, says he has been called a racist for suggesting, among other things, that modern Australian aborigines have some physical features similar to those of an archaic hominid called Java Man.

"People have made me uncomfortable because my ideas are not politically correct," he says. "I find the whole thing very disturbing. I hope people grow up and get over it. The politicizing of paleoanthropology might well do it in."

This debate is fundamentally absurd, because no one disputes the fact that humans had an African ancestor at some point. The issue is whether that ancestor lived about a million years ago or 200,000 years ago. And the debate is also absurd because the essential biological brotherhood of human beings is an established fact; we already know that we are genetically quite homogeneous, and this conclusion does not depend on the outcome of this latest scientific debate. The brotherhood/sisterhood of human beings will remain a reality regardless of which human evolution theory proves most persuasive over time.

Ultimately, the evolution issue will be decided on scientific merit, not political whim. It's hard to see how both schools of thought could be right. The researchers who have studied mitochondrial DNA say there's no sign of Neanderthal genes in any modern human. But the multiregionalists say they have the bones that prove their point. David Frayer, a University of Kansas anthropologist, says, for example, that both Neanderthals and the early modern humans in Europe had a specialized trait called the horizontal oval mandibular foremen, a hole that receives the mandibular nerve. The out-of-Africa view would require such things to evolve twice, first in Neanderthals and then, independently, in the modern humans that replaced the Neanderthals.

The Natural History Museum has already decided where it stands on this, says Sullivan: It will promote the out-of-Africa view. What about multiregional evolution? That, says Sullivan, will be included too—in a separate "dilemma label."

The Natural History Museum has one problem that won't easily be fixed. It is filled with the cultural treasures of nonwhite, non-European societies. These things make great exhibits. But they also convey an old, colonial-era message: Other societies are so primitive, so locked into a timeless past, that they belong alongside the skeletons of dinosaurs and the fossils of trilobites. Other societies are a part of nature, while American society has its own museum.

"One of the serious problems with the cultural exhibits in the Natural History Museum is that they're in a *natural history* museum," says Ivan Karp, curator of African ethnology.

One might say these things are silly inferences, irrelevant subtleties. But inference and subtlety matter. An anecdote:

Last spring, the members of Tu-Wa-Moja went on a tour of the museum. As they were leaving the "Emergence of Man" exhibit, they entered the Africa hall. One of the first glass cases there is titled "The Bushmen," the European name for the San people of Southern Africa. It shows black men and women squatting in the dirt outside a grass hut. They are making bows and arrows. They wear loin-cloths.

A mother and her children were looking at the exhibit. The family looked Asian, say the members of Tu-Wa-Moja. One of the kids asked the mother why the Bushmen lived that way.

The mother replied, "That's the way they eat. That's what they do. That's the way they are."

The woman then saw the approaching group of well-dressed African Americans.

"And here they are!" she said.

LANGUAGE

Why can't apes talk worth a hoot?

For years we've been trying to teach these allegedly brilliant creatures to speak, or at least learn sign language, and so far just about the only thing they've been able to tell us is that they like fruit.

Here's the longest (if not the most complex) statement ever recorded from an ape, delivered in sign language by Nim Chimpsky, one of the many chimpanzees who supposedly have learned English: "Give orange me give eat orange me eat orange give me eat orange give me you." (Translation: "The oranges here are *fabulous*.")

Derek Bickerton's book *Language and Species* argues that it is the representational nature of human language—the fact that we know that "orange" is a word *representing* a piece of fruit, but is not the *same* thing as the fruit or the wanting of the fruit—that allows us to process information and survive as a species. Chimps apparently only use words as a technique for getting something; they don't gab simply for the delight of intellectual stimulation. They can be taught many words, in sign language, but these don't seem to spawn what you would call thoughts. Human cerebration appears to be different from that of every other creature on the planet. We are thinkers; it defines us as a species.

Trying to teach apes to speak probably reveals as much about human presumptuousness as it does about simian linguistics. We are so wrapped up in the significance of language that we insist that our pets and primate cousins have languages too. It's a prejudice. We want dogs and dolphins and chimpanzees to be *just like us*.

Gradually it has dawned on much of the scientific community that apes will never be able to create a sentence. No amount of teaching, training, cajoling, and banana bribery will change this. Nonetheless, some gung-ho, true-believing researchers press on, periodically announcing in a breathless voice that there's a new critter that any moment now may start talking like John Chancellor.

Complex language is what makes humans human. Were it not for language we would not be so very different from chimpanzees. We share the same genes—not just similar genes, but the identical ones. Only about two percent of our genetic code is different from that of chimps. Chimpanzees have eyes and ears and hearts and lungs essentially identical to ours. (Okay, their hair is a little different.) They have complex emotions. They engage in protracted warfare within their species. They use tools. They will methodically crush walnuts with rocks. When primatologist Jane Goodall told the paleontologist Louis Leakey that she had seen a chimp use a blade of grass and twigs to root out termites, he responded with a telegram saying, "Now we must redefine *tool*, redefine *man*, or accept chimpanzees as humans."

(Fair enough. Man: A creature who not only uses "tools" but can also identify a dessert fork.)

In any case, why don't apes speak?

The main reason is that they don't need to. They're perfectly adapted to their environment as it is. (See "Why don't apes evolve into humans anymore?" in the first *Why* book.)

Still, what everyone wants to know is what the physiological impediment is that prevents apes, or dogs, or, for that matter, fish, from talking. What's wrong with them? The answer is that they all have two problems: the throat and the brain.

The general region of anatomy that controls speech is called the supralaryngeal vocal tract. In humans, this area is elongated. One key piece of anatomy that is different in humans and apes is the larynx, a valvelike device that lets air from the windpipe into the throat. In apes, the larynx is up high and can form an airtight lock with the nasal cavity, allowing the creature to breathe even as it is eating or drinking. In humans, the larynx is much lower, and if we eat and breathe at the same time we're likely to choke. Indeed, choking is a direct side effect of the anatomy that allows human speech. Charles Darwin himself noted what a boneheaded thing it was for humans to have food pass right by a hole leading into the lungs. One major advantage of the low larynx, unbeknownst to Darwin, is that it allows us to make nonnasal sounds, which can be far more distinct than nasal noises (Bob Dylan has yet to perfect this).

But even if apes had throats like humans, they *still* couldn't speak the way we do. Their brains are different. At some point in their evolution human beings developed the ability not only to speak easily but also to create a sophisticated language, to manipulate words in meaningful patterns. A mynah bird can "speak," after all, but it is just making sounds, without a clue in its knobby little head as to what it is saying. As Philip Lieberman states in his book *Uniquely Human*, chimpanzees can acquire a limited vocabulary but cannot grasp the rules of syntax that a three-year-old child can master.

"Nor do chimpanzees or other animals ever create works of art or complex devices, or convey 'creative' thoughts," he writes. "Nor do they, in their natural state, adhere to the most basic aspects of higher human moral sense."

They're a bunch of animals!

The miracle of language, wrote Lord Zuckerman (great byline!) in the May 30, 1991, *New York Review of Books*, "was, and remains, the critical evolutionary development that made man a unique primate, and one that released him from the immediate present within which apes and monkeys are tied, and by so doing opened for us human beings a world of our own creation, with a past, a present, and a future, one limitless in time and space."

Footnote: The Gorilla Foundation in Woodside, California, was not pleased with this answer. Foundation president Francine Patterson informed us that one of her research partners is the famous Koko, a lowland gorilla with a vocabulary of more than six hundred words in sign language. Patterson said that Koko does, in fact, use grammar and syntax.

"Tool use, toolmaking, and recognizing words as symbols, were formerly assumed to be uniquely human. We have discovered once again that we are not alone in our abilities," Patterson writes. She says gorillas also make art. One of her "partners," an eighteen-year-old gorilla named Michael, "enjoys painting and his works are quite impressive in color and composition." Patterson says she was disturbed by our line, "They're a bunch of animals!" and says, "Try inserting 'journalists' or 'women' or 'Jews' or any other human classification term into that sentence in place of 'animals' and see how it sounds."

We must protest: If Koko is so smart, then why didn't *Koko* write that letter? Huh? Answer that one!

We wrote, "Complex language is what makes humans human," and we see no reason to abandon that statement just because Koko knows six hundred words. Can she write a one-column, three-deck headline?

Our intent was not to insult gorillas. We pointed out that apes have no need to evolve into humans, because *they do just fine as apes*. The real mystery is the prosperity of humans: Why did this one species overrun the planet and push it toward environmental catastrophe? It's not the strongest, nor the largest, nor the most fecund species on the planet. But it is the only species in the history of the planet with the mental and anatomical ability to create and manipulate a sophisticated language. The end result is that today there are too many humans and too few apes.

Why are there so many languages in our world?

The real question is, why do people still speak, for example, Manx? Yes, there's a language called Manx. It has, according to the journal *Linguistic Geography*, "half a dozen" fluent speakers in the United Kingdom. That would be six, yes? And what do you bet half of them aren't even good conversationalists.

The strange fact is, in the British Isles, where you'd think people had a perfect excuse to speak English, they speak all sorts of tongues. Cornish, for example, is an entirely separate language, no doubt named after the hen. It has a couple hundred speakers. About half a million inhabitants of Wales still speak Welsh; a like number of French-men speak Breton. In Scotland there are 80,000 speakers of Gaelic, and in Ireland there are 340,000 who speak a completely different version of Gaelic that is sometimes called simply "Irish." Even though Welsh is spoken by peo-ple living geographically right next door to people who speak English, Welsh is a Celtic language and English is Germanic in origin. English has more in common with Ice-landic or Flemish or Afrikaans than it does with Welsh.

All over the world, people are struggling to understand one another. In Spain, Basque is not even distantly related to Castilian. India has 150 languages and only 30 percent of the population speaks Hindi. On the island of New Guinea there are hundreds of languages. There are about three thousand languages around the world. *Why so many?*

1. It's hard for two people to sound alike. We are not so good at mimicking. This may seem like an obvious com-ment, but if you pause for a moment you'll realize that this is the perfect explanation of a worldwide phenomenon. It takes relatively little isolation to get a good accent going, and with a little more separation the accent becomes a dialect and then a separate language.

2. People like to have their own code, because they *want* to be different. Language is probably the most powerful tool for social organization. If you want to restrict who's in the club, or make members dependent on the club, you establish a code language and enforce it.

Both of these explanations imply that two or three or even a hundred languages can sprout out of a common source, and that languages ought to multiply over time rather than decrease in number. In fact, that's exactly what has happened. For example, English is related to San-skrit—the ancient language of India. There is a whole class of languages called Indo-European, which share common grammatical structures and similar-sounding verbs, and which span a vast distance, from Iceland to India (but which do not include some languages in between, such as Basque).

Take the word "birch." In German it is *birke*, in Lithuanian *berzas*, in Old Slavonic *breza*, and in Sanskrit *bhurja*. Close enough. Linguists and archaeologists think the Indo-European languages may have descended from an original tongue, spoken by people who came from some long-forgotten homeland, the *Urheimat*, to use the German term. No one knows where this homeland was.

Colin Renfrew, author of *Archaeology and Language: The Puzzle of Indo-European Origins*, says the languages were slowly carried from east to west along with the techniques of agriculture. The first farmers in Europe lived in Greece and Crete around 6500 B.C., and by the year 3500 B.C. there was farming as far west as Scotland. This doesn't mean that no one knew how to speak before they knew how to farm. It is presumed that for tens of thousands of years, "modern" humans have possessed language skills that set them apart from earlier humans. Before the farmers fanned across Europe there were already people living there—Mesolithic hunter-gatherers—but they would not have been as prosperous as the farmers, and as they became a numerical minority of the population their language would have been supplanted by the new Indo-European tongue.

Now we are seeing a reversal of the old process of language dispersal and differentiation. English is in an imperialistic phase, encroaching on the territory of other tongues. As of 1986, about 400 million people spoke English, second only to Mandarin Chinese. Indeed, English is the language of international business. Airline pilots around the world speak in English to the control towers. The Welsh language, by contrast, is spoken by half as many people today as it was at the beginning of the century. Moreover, languages get watered down by English words, a process called code mixing. That eventually leads to code switching, in which the speaker stumbles or struggles in the original language and then switches into English.

Language decline signals the homogenization of the world. Within a couple of decades it will be almost impossible to find a single person—even a Stone Age tribesman in Borneo—who hasn't ordered the Grand Slam Breakfast at Denny's and been forced to decide between "two bacon and two sausage or four of either meat."

Why do people say they "literally died laughing" when the word they want is "figuratively"?

People don't use the word "literally" literally.

Even famous writers do this. In *The Great Gatsby*, F. Scott Fitzgerald wrote, "He literally glowed; without a word or a gesture of exultation a new well-being radiated from him and filled the little room." But did he literally glow, or just figuratively glow? Wouldn't you be alarmed if someone were literally glowing? Wouldn't you want to put on a protective radiation suit?

In *Nicholas Nickleby*, Charles Dickens wrote, " 'Lift him out,' said Squeers, after he had literally feasted his eyes in silence upon the culprit."

Is this a mistake, or some kind of cleverness? *Webster's Dictionary of English Usage* defends the hyperbolic, nonliteral use of "literally." It points out that, as far back as the early 1700s, people began using "literally" as an intensifier of the words that follow; it was synonymous with "really" or "actually." Then it gradually came to be used in conjunction with figurative statements, as in "I literally died laughing."

The Why staff, though notoriously lax about anything resembling a rule, has to side with the language snobs on this. The hyperbolic use always raises suspicions that the writer or speaker is being lazy and careless.

Quite frankly, we're shocked that Dickens and Fitzgerald wrote "literally" in a nonliteral sense. Come to think of it, name one book Fitzgerald wrote, other than *Gatsby*, that isn't kind of lame. And Dickens? Way too many kids in his books. Mangy, obnoxious kids. And his books are too thick; *Bleak House* could've easily been shortened to something more like the length of *Bright Lights, Big City*. But that's enough highbrow lit crit for today.

Why are there so many different dictionaries named *Web-ster's*?

Because the name is not trademarked. The cheap paperback dictionaries that you can buy in a grocery store might say *Webster's*, but they have no relation to either *Webster's New World Dictionary of American English* or the rival, unrelated Merriam-Webster dictionary. We have been told by Merriam-Webster that it has proper dibs on the Webster name, but the simple reality is that Noah Webster, who published the first great American dictionary in 1828, never managed to get his name trademarked.

You might note that the name *Webster's New World Dictionary of American English* has a bothersome redundancy, but this too can be explained. The company that makes the dictionaries used to be called World. In the early 1950s, World put out a sweeping new edition, and, thinking it would be a rather clever play on words, called it the New World dictionary. You know those dictionary people: a bunch of cards!

Why do so many people think a British accent sounds sophisticated and intellectual?

Like Americans, the British are, for the most part, a vulgar, crude people. Most have impenetrably thick accents and a lexicon filled with bizarre scatological epithets. "He's a bloody sod," for example, is not something you could print in a British newspaper.

But Britain, more than America, is a nation split into classes, and the upper-class accent is the one we continually hear on "Masterpiece Theatre," on BBC broadcasts, and in the infernal British drawing-room comedies and teacup dramas. Though most of Britain speaks in a downstairs accent, what we hear is the upstairs one: A British accent, to us, is what Alistair Cooke sounds like, or Laurence Olivier, or Alec Guinness. Those people are sophisticates and intellectuals, so it is only natural that we associate the accent with learnedness and good breeding. The British do too!

Occasionally we hear a cockney or Liverpudlian accent—via Michael Caine or Ringo Starr, respectively—but we instantly register that it sounds low-class.

Another explanation comes from Norman Schur, author of the book *British English: A to Zed*: "The people who came over on the Mayflower, or say they did, congregated in New England and Boston. Aristocrats in America pretty much held on to their English accents. The rest of the country looked up to Boston as the cultural leaders of the country. And that's the English accent."

In both Boston and London the broad *a* is used: Take a bahth, go to the dahnce, enroll at Hahvahd, etc.

Of course, there must be a tertiary reason, because otherwise we'd have no chance to use the word "tertiary": Rebecca Eaton, executive producer of "Masterpiece Theatre," notes that the well-heeled British speak more clearly and more precisely and faster than we do. It sounds so intellectual when a Brit says "in-EX-plicable" without mumbling or spreading the accents among the first and third syllables, as would an American. The tea-and-crumpets Britons think we are all drawling morons.

Sod, because you were curious, is short for sodomite.

Why do we use the verb "to be," in its various conjugations, so much?

The verb "to be" is a crutch. The word "is" is horribly overused. But it is natural to use "is-speak." The only thing that is worse than is-speak is was-speak. As it were.

Ronald Reagan, speaking of the Iran-Contra hijinks, uttered the immortal line "Mistakes were made." In that instance "were" is not just a verbal crutch but a smoke screen, to mix metaphors. It's an intentionally obscurant-ist verb designed to hide the perpetrator of the mistakes.

To understand why we use "to be" so much, you have to think about what happens when we speak or write. We don't simply deliver information. Rather, we use meta-phors. A metaphor is a kind of verbal equation, and "is" or "am" or "are" is the equals sign.

To take the simplest example, you routinely greet some-one with the bland line, "How's life?" and you get the an-swer, "I'm hangin' in there." The word "hangin' " is, one hopes, metaphorical; if the person wanted to be more spe-cific (and avoid is-speak), he or she might answer, "I awoke this morning to find a grotesque carbuncle protruding from my chin."

The benefit of metaphorical thinking is that it helps us organize the world in a manner that goes beyond mere facts; we can turn "He owes me twenty bucks" into "He's a jerk," and somehow that's more satisfying. But you see the danger: In its worst manifestations, "to be" is inaccu-rate, overly general, and prejudicial. You end up with lines like, "They are all hoodlums in that neighborhood."

Wouldn't you know it, there is an entire movement, de-cades old, to eradicate "to be" from the language. The movement, recently described in *The Atlantic Monthly*, is called general semantics, and one of its tenets is that "to be" is dangerous. As general semanticist Emory Menefee put it in the journal *ETC.*, "These little verbs (or their equivalent in other languages) may have contributed to two millennia of intellectual sloth and Aristotelian darkness."

Instead, say these semanticists, people should use a lan-guage called E-Prime, which essentially is English minus the verb "to be." And they're not joking. They are deadly serious. They argue that is-speak distorts and pigeonholes reality, and inspires such ludicrous questions as "What is art?"

"What we're trying to do is do some fine tuning, making language a little more accurate, and less ambiguously rep-resent what we're trying to say," says Paul Dennithorne Johnston, executive director of the International Society for General Semantics, who writes in E-Prime and is still learning to speak it. "If you say, 'I am a reporter,' what about all the other things you do?"

(From now on, we will say, "I am a reporter and bowling fanatic.")

There are dissenters within the general semantics community. Menefee, former president of ISGS, favors a moderated form of E-Prime that he calls E-Choice.

"The verb 'to be' in its less pejorative forms is, in my opinion, a useful way of condensing a large amount of information," says Menefee. "If I say the pencil is green, most of us have no difficulty agreeing with that." But still, he says, "the hardcore E-Primer believes that if you don't do away with all of the verb forms of 'to be,' you haven't achieved the Nirvana of E-Prime."

A few of these folks are actually fluent in E-Prime. One, E. W. Kellogg III, says he thinks in E-Prime.

"I even dream in E-Prime," he told us.

In a twenty-minute interview he spoke at normal speed, with elegant articulation, and never used any form of the verb "to be." He said that anyone who uses "is" elevates his or her own subjective opinion to the godlike status of objective fact. He would never say, "That is a great restaurant," because it might be a steak house and his listener could be a vegetarian.

But what if we asked him who that fellow is, standing over there? Would he answer, "That is Dave"? No, he said, he'd just say, "Dave." Or, "I'd like you to meet Dave."

Yes, it's painful to contemplate.

It may be true that "to be" leads us into temptation, toward the conversion of fact and nuance into abstraction and generalization. But some of us *like* abstraction and generalization.

Frankly, we agree with what Hamlet said to Descartes: "To be, I think, therefore I am not to be."

Footnote: You may have noticed that the very title of this book contains the dreaded "are," and thus our endeavor is surely offensive and noxious to E-Primers. Indeed, true aficionados know that the word to be stressed in *Why Things Are* is not, as you'd guess, the Why, and certainly not the lame Things in the middle, but rather the Are. Why Things ARE. How it IS. Whut it BE. You get the picture. Kellogg suggested to us that we could change *Why Things Are* to *The Way I See It*. Unfortunately, this has a major flaw, beyond the obvious destruction of the Royal We affectation. Basically, it just sounds too humble.

WORDS

Why is there a _g_ in gnat? Why is there a _k_ in knight? Why are words spelled so stupidly?

You can't write a simple sentence without hitting one of these psychotic words. Write. Psychotic. That's two already. (And let's not even talk about "two," a word that so baffles schoolchildren it should be jailed for child abuse.)

What we have here is a quirk of language: Pronunciation changes, but not spelling. Pronunciation is the ultimate democratic enterprise; it can't be controlled by government fiat or by rich snobs who talk as though they have lockjaw. If enough people say the word "harass" with the accent on the second syllable, instead of as a homonym of Harris, then that must be acknowledged as an acceptable pronunciation, if not the standard pronunciation.

Unfortunately, spelling isn't like that; it is absurdly conservative. The reason there's a _g_ at the front of "gnat" is that the _g_ wasn't silent back in the days of King Arthur. They said it: "Guh-nat."

"It's strange. It's a little glimpse back into the past,"

says David Jost, senior lexicographer for the *American Heritage Dictionary.*

When King Arthur's knights sat 'round the Round Table, they said the word "knight" with a *k* sound at the start.

So why hasn't spelling also changed? Because of the invention of the dictionary. Words were spelled all manner of ways in Old and Middle English, but with the spread of printing technology there was a movement toward standardization. Samuel Johnson and Noah Webster, the great dictionary authors, enforced those standards in Britain and America. Dictionaries also enforce pronunciation, of course, but they are organized according to the spelling of words, not the way the words sound, and so any spelling changes would create more chaos within dictionaries than changes in pronunciation.

Moreover, who would have the authority to declare that a word is now spelled differently? Norman Mailer, maybe? Or do we want to fall under the heel of some global spelling enforcement agency?

"Language isn't something that a group or country or a government has a prerogative over, so it has to be changed by a general movement," says John Simpson, coeditor of the *Oxford English Dictionary.*

And such movements don't arise. People are insufficiently outraged over the spelling of "pneumatic" to demand a change. (And even if they insisted on something simpler, the powerful spelling bee industry would lobby against it.)

Our own idea is: Let's keep the psycho letters, and start *saying* them. Why say "write" the normal way when you can say "Wuh-rite"? Isn't that more straightforward? Let's be mad dogs and say the *p* in "pneumonia"! Let's say the *m* in "mnemonic"! We'll tie those dictionary people up in knots! (Pronounced: Kuh-NOTS.)

Why are there no words that rhyme with "purple," "orange," or "silver"?

Clement Wood's *Rhyming Dictionary* confirms that there are no rhymes for "orange" and "silver," and he offers only this for "purple": "chirp'll." To which we say: Chirp'll? We guess he means something like this:

> *Horrible birds,*
> *Black, yellow, purple,*
> *If the peck doesn't drive you mad,*
> *The chirp'll.*

One initially suspects that "purple," "orange," and "silver" have no rhymes because they're the words for colors, and someone a long time ago decided that colors were too special to be rhymeable. But "orange" comes from French, "purple" from Latin by way of Old English, and "silver" from Old English going back to the 5th century A.D., when "English" was not yet a meaningful concept and the only tourist attraction in Britain was Stonehenge. (To be precise, the *Oxford English Dictionary* lists "curple," an archaic Scottish word meaning buttocks. But we'd never allow that on our Scrabble board, you can bet your sweet curple.)

That these words have no rhymes is simply the luck of the draw. It's an anomaly. But it's hardly as anomalous as, say, waking up one morning to discover an arm growing out of your forehead, because rhymes aren't actually that common.

Check the dictionary. Victoria Neufeldt, former editor-in-chief of *Webster's New World Dictionary*, asks, "Is there a rhyme for purpose? *Murpose*?"

Which brings up a more profound why question: Why isn't "murpose" a word? Why isn't "milver" in use? Why not "gazurple"?

James Hartman, a University of Kansas professor who specializes in American pronunciation, points out that there are zillions of potential words that are never employed, including simple three-letter consonant-vowel-consonant constructions such as "daf" and "zat" and "fot" and "lep." These aren't used because there's not a great crushing need for new words. We got enough! ("Got," for example, can be used in thousands of ways, some of them quite proper.) There are something like 500,000 words available for English speakers, and many of those words do double and triple duty ("racket" can mean something you hit a tennis ball with, or a loud noise, or a criminal enterprise).

More importantly, words grow out of other, already existing words.

"Making up some absolutely new words is one of the less frequent ways we have of creating new meanings," says Hartman. "Extending old words is the more typical way, or we can borrow a word from another language." This has the great advantage of helping us understand what words mean. If we simply declared that a person who speaks out loud during a movie at a theater is a "milver," there'd be no way to trace the etymology. And eventually the professional etymologists would have to find another career.

Why is B.C. an abbreviation for an English term, while A.D. is an abbreviation for a Latin term?

Didn't you used to think that A.D. stood for "After Death"? Or does that say something about the humble backwoods origins of the Why staff?

Now we know that A.D. stands for *Anno Domini*, Latin for "the year of the Lord." It was first used around the year A.D. 540 by an abbot named Dionysius Exiguus ("Dion" to his pals). This fellow was trying to get a better handle on when Easter should be celebrated. In those days there were many ways of stating what year it was, not to mention formulas for reckoning time. For example, the Greeks made reference to Olympiads, the Egyptians and Chinese used dynasties, and the Romans dated everything to the founding of the city of Rome.

Dionysius Exiguus came up with a new calendar based on Jesus Christ's birth. Unfortunately, he miscalculated by about four years. That's why Jesus was born, according to modern calculations, about four years before Christ.

The concept of B.C. is of fairly recent vintage compared with A.D. This English term dates back only to the Renaissance era. Before that, medieval historians dealing with pre-Christ history usually referred to the reign of various kings and emperors.

Incidentally, historians do not insert a zero year between 1 B.C. and A.D. 1; astronomers do.

And by the way: We abhor and despise the oft-made assertion that, for complex calendar reasons, the next millennium will begin on January 1, 2001, and not on January 1, 2000. These numbers are not fixed in place by a divine being; they are a purely human creation, essentially arbitrary, and we are thus free to celebrate whatever date we choose. We'll be breaking out the champagne in the Why bunker the moment that odometer spins over to the big 2000. Armageddon notwithstanding.

Why are people with orange hair called redheads?

Naturally, we turned to the Color Association of the United States for help. Associate director Margaret Walch confirmed our worst suspicions: Redheads are actually orangeheads. "The hue is orange, but we call it red," Walch said.

The Standard Color Reference of America lists 198 individual colors. One is "henna," which as a hair coloring is designed to make someone a redhead, but which Walch describes as "terra cotta orange." We asked her to clarify that and she said it was "rust colored." Unfortunately, the chromatically illiterate Why staff comprehends only the colors red, blue, green, yellow, orange, brown, and purple, and therefore we insisted on a yet simpler description, finally getting what we wanted: "It's a brown-orange."

So why do we call it red?

"I think there is a psychological connotation here. Red has positive connotations, as opposed to orange, which has a banal, pedestrian quality," she said. "Red implies more energy, more drama."

No need to tell Clairol. They don't sell "orange" hair coloring. And they take "red" to an entirely new level. One Clairol hair color is called "Flame." Another is "Sparkling Sherry." But the one that we like most is "Miss Clairol Audacious Red." Clairol spokeswoman Lisa Carvalho says red coloring is selling like mad. She sees a bigger picture in this.

"For a long time women didn't feel secure enough to venture into those color ranges. Now it's very common," she told us. "As women have become more aggressive and bold, redheads have become more popular."

Incidentally, if you've ever wondered why fashionable people use such absurd terms for various colors—you know, "cardinal" instead of "red"—it's because those are the official colors listed in the extremely official *Standard Color Reference of America*. There is no red in there. But there is "scarlet" and "geranium."

There's also "flax," "toast brown," "grotto blue," "amber light," "moss tone" (which is green with a touch of gray), and the bizarre "leghorn." It's a sort of phlegm yellow. To use an unofficial term.

Why isn't "amn't" a commonly used contraction?

Let's say that you walk into a job interview about ninety minutes late. You need a good excuse. Do you say you were in a bar and lost track of time? Do you say you were engrossed in game shows at home? Do you say you were detained by authorities for questioning in a drive-by gang shooting? It's a tough call. So you just go with the obvious: You say, "I'm a little late, aren't I?"

Aren't I? As in, "Are not I?" As in, "I are?" The sound of this makes an intelligent person wince. Obviously, what you really ought to say, if the world made any sense at all, is, "I'm a little late, amn't I?"

But "amn't," unfortunately, isn't a word used in American English. It is, however, a word used by Scots and the Irish. In American English, "aren't I" is standard usage. Some people say "ain't," which is delicious to the ear of the Why staff but is eschewed by language snobs. Another contraction that might work, according to *Webster's Dictionary of English Usage*, is "a'n't," but that's a case of preposterous apostrophes.

Perhaps the reason we don't say "amn't" is that the *m* and the *n* don't flow well together. You have to insert a vowel sound and make it "ammint," which lacks the punch of the "arnt" pronunciation.

For now, says Frederick Mish, editorial director of

Merriam-Webster, there's no sign of an emerging "amn't" in American English.

"We've already filled in that need by using the 'aren't' expression. Everybody does it naturally," he said. "It's only if you get too concerned about logic that you start worrying about it. But language isn't primarily a matter of logic."

Which explains "won't."

Why is anything written by George Bernard Shaw called "Shavian"? Why is the philosophy of Rene Descartes called "Cartesian"?

Who, exactly, makes the rules on turning proper names into adjectives? Why is it "Rubenesque" and not "Rubensesque"? Why is "Kafkaesque" a common term, but there's no word to describe things that remind you of Twain? Why is it "Dickensian" and not "Dickensesque"?

The answer is: Whatever pleases the ear is what survives.

"You do it when it sounds good," says Victoria Neufeldt, dictionary editor.

Shaw becomes Shavian because if you were to say "Shawian" people might wonder if all your teeth had been extracted. There's another reason: The latinized version of Shaw was "Shavius," and in classical Latin the v is pronounced as a w. From Shavius we get the adjective Shavian. The real question is: Why did anyone want to latinize the name of George Bernard Shaw? Was this Shaw's idea? Was it just an incredible affectation, like an ascot or a monocle?

Descartes, for his part, became "Cartesius" in Latin, thus inspiring "Cartesian."

The moral: Latin isn't as dead a language as you think.

Why are detectives sometimes called "dicks"?

This has always bothered us.

The literature says "dicks" is a shortening, an alteration, of "detectives."

It still bothers us.

Why do we pronounce Wednesday as though it were spelled Wenzday?

The problem with the English language is that it was invented by people who didn't actually speak English. Foreigners, in fact.

Norwegians are to blame for the word "Wednesday," which comes from Woden, which is another name for the Norse god Odin, whom we all know from reading the comic book "Thor" was a rather dour, overly powerful guy with a big white beard and a serious need to get on a jogging program.

The word "Wednesday" is not pronounced "Wed-nez-day," but rather "Wenzday," or even "Wenzdee," though we vow never to associate with the kind of people who use the -dee ending. In British dictionaries, just to be wacky, the pronunciation "Wednzday" is also permitted, but we dare anyone to say "Wednzday." That first d should disappear unless you make a major production of it and talk like a fool.

The reason that we naturally elide the d is that it is a "stopped" sound, meaning that it cannot be prolonged, and it is followed immediately by a continuable sound, the n, which is formed in the same part of the mouth, by touching the tongue to the alveolar ridge on the roof of the mouth just behind the front teeth. The d sound is made by popping the tongue off the alveolar ridge, while the n sound is formed by holding the tongue on the bridge and exhaling. To do the first and the second consecutively requires too much up-and-down business with the tongue.

(The sounds that can't be prolonged, in addition to *d*, are *p, b, t, k,* and *g.*)

To make things even more confusing, we'll note that there is a hint of the *d* sound between the *n* and the subsequent *z.* This is because the *d* sound rides the coattails of the *n* sound as the tongue lifts off the ridge. So, if you want to be really picky, you could argue that we pronounce the word "Wendzday." It's like the word "prince." The dictionary says that we pronounce it "prins," but you can actually hear a *t* in there, as though you were saying "prints."

Now, you may have noticed that in the word "Wednesday" there are not one but two elisions. The second elision is the *e* between the *n* and the *s.* ("Elision," by the way, is not to be confused with Elysian. That's some kind of a field.) Many words in English lose a lightly spoken vowel between two consonants—"every" is pronounced "evry." The unwritten but spoken vowel between the *d* and the *l* in "fiddle" suddenly disappears when we say the word "fiddler."

There is economy in such changes: "Wednesday," like "every," looks like it must be a three-syllable word, but in fact we get them out in a mere two. This saves labor.

Of course, we don't know this stuff off the top of our knobby little heads. Our indubitable source is Arthur Bronstein, a phonetician at the University of California at Berkeley and the author of the pronunciation essay in the *Unabridged Random House Dictionary.* The real question is whether there were ever any Phoenician phoneticians. Hold that thought.

Why did the name Bambi, made famous by a male deer, come to be the prototypical name of an unintelligent woman?

In the case of Disney's cartoon Bambi, we don't think of him as particularly male or female, but rather as childishly androgynous. Bambi echoes *bambino*, Italian for "baby." The gradual coming-of-age of Bambi and his discovery of a masculine sexual identity are part of the drama of the movie. By the end, he's a big buck, unrecognizable and kind of a disappointment, really (just what we need, another guy with his chest stuck out).

As a name for a person, Bambi not only suggests the babyish, sweet qualities of the famed deer but also echoes the word "bimbo." That said, Bambi is not perceived as a common name; it's too much of a joke. (By the way, Lance Alworth, the fleet, baby-faced football player, was called Bambi.)

Now for the bigger picture: In English, the way a name becomes a diminutive—a term of endearment—is usually by adding an *i* or *ie* or *y* at the end. This is routine among children, but when they become adults they often switch back to the more formal construction—Billy becomes William, Suzie becomes Suzanne, and so on. This switch is more common among men.

"There's a tendency for feminine names to be diminutive more often than adult masculine names," says Linda Coleman, a University of Maryland linguist.

There's not necessarily anything wrong with retaining the diminutive form—Jimmy Carter did, to try to seem unpretentious—but the risk is that it will suggest naivete or a childish cutesiness. The weird thing is, some men find those qualities appealing, which explains why the centerfolds in *Playboy* so often have diminutive names, such as Nancie Li Brandi and Brandi Brandt. (Nancy, which spawned Nancie, was originally a diminution of Ann.)

"What we've all discovered here is that for a majority of the Playmates, it seems like their names have the *i* sound in it, like Carrie, Teri, Tawnnee, Debbie," says Lorna Hart, di-

CALL NOW
1-900-HI-BAMBI
or just send money

rector of Playmate promotions at Playboy Enterprises. Three Playmates in the last three years have been named Carrie, Kari, and Kerri, she said, including the almost identically named Kari Kennell and Kerri Kendall. "We say, 'How are we going to tell all these Kerris apart?' We say, 'Is it Kari with the long blond hair or Kerri with the short blond hair?'"

Over the years there have been five Kimberlys (or Kymberly or Kimberley, not to mention two Kims and a Kym), but not a single plain Jane. And certainly there are no Berthas or Sadies. For the first five months of 1991, the Playmates were named Stacy, Cristy, Julie, Christina, and Carrie.

This raises the obvious question: Are these women Playmates because they have names like Kimberly and Kari, or do they have names like Kimberly and Kari because they are Playmates?

Hart says most of the women use their real names. She speculates that these kinds of names are just popular.

We asked our friend and colleague Laura Misch, a Colorado journalist, about her experiences as Miss February 1975. She says she was pointedly asked if she wanted to change her name for the centerfold. She declined.

"I think a lot of them change their name," she says. She joked, "They're not all named Kimberly. There's also some Brittanys and Tiffanys."

Even if the names are real, the ethnic bias of *Playboy*, favoring blonde women, contributes to a glut of white-bread names, which then are made diminutive in order to be perceived as sexier—that is, more childlike, more kittenish, and less intellectually threatening to the male "reader."

Why is a dollar sometimes called a "simoleon"?

This is crusty, old-guy slang, along the lines of "sawbuck" and "dame." A young, hip person nowadays refers to dollars as "bones," as in "I'm jonesing for those killer spikes, but they cost 125 bones." (Translation: The nice shoes I very much desire are too expensive.)

"Simoleon" is pretty mysterious. The earliest known usage was in a George Ade story in 1896: "He said I could have it for 400 samoleons." The spelling "simoleon" soon became standard. The *Oxford English Dictionary* says, lamely, that it might be derived from "Napoleon." That's it. End of explanation.

Fortunately, we got emergency word service from David Jost, at the *American Heritage Dictionary*, and he filled in some more of the background. A "simon" was, prior to about 1700, a slang term in England for a sixpence, though it's not clear who the Simon was who inspired the slang. The term emigrated to the United States and by the mid-1800s was slang for a dollar.

At the same time, the French were using a twenty-franc gold coin called a Napoleon. Someone (by the time of

George Ade) managed to combine "simon" with "Napoleon" to get "simoleon." That's the best we can do at the moment.

Frankly, we prefer the contemporary slang of today's younger generation. We're perusing *Slang U: The Official Dictionary of College Slang*, by Pamela Munro, and note such charming terms as "eye booger" (so much for "sleepy sand"); "buttly," an adjective for someone who's unattractive; "squid," a new name for a jerk or a nerd; and "zuke," one of thirty-one listed terms for throwing up (it has, you must confess, an economy that does not grace the synonymous "talking to Ralph on the big white phone").

Why doesn't "Arkansas" rhyme with "Kansas"?

This discrepancy wouldn't have happened if the French had ever learned to spell.

John L. Ferguson, state historian for Arkansas, tells us that there used to be some Native Americans living at the juncture of the Mississippi River and what we now call the Arkansas River. We now refer to these as the Quapaws, but in the 1700s the French explorers called them the "Arkansas" Indians, which was the name used by Algonquin-speaking Indian guides who lived up on the Ohio River. "Arkansas" meant "people of the south wind." The Indians didn't have a written language, so the French were merely approximating the spoken sound "Arkansaw," using their own peculiar spelling habits that have also given us "lingerie," "bouquet," "denouement," and "contretemps," words that, as far as we're concerned, are horribly misspelled.

Actually, the French didn't say "Arkansaw," exactly. They had a Frenchier way of emitting that last vowel. The "Arkansaw" pronunciation is an American approximation of the French. Some maps and some people have actually preferred that spelling. Other folks, seeing it spelled "Arkansas," have insisted on pronouncing it to rhyme with

Kansas (which, by the way, is named after the Kanza Indian tribe; there is probably an etymological connection to the Algonquin word "Arkansas").

This matter became so heated that in 1880 a group called the Eclectic Society teamed up with the Arkansas Historical Society and delved into the origin of the name.

The report concluded, as we have noted, that Arkansas is a gallicized Indian name and should be pronounced with the "saw" at the end. This was duly decreed in a special legislative resolution by the Arkansas general assembly in 1881. This leaves the problem of how people from Arkansas should identify themselves. "ARK-an-san" is too weird.

So they say Ar-KAN-san.

Why did Yankee Doodle stick a feather in his cap and call it Macaroni?

Was he soused? Stoned? *Tripping?* No. Just foolish. The "Yankee Doodle" song dates to pre-Revolutionary America. It became popular among British soldiers, in derision of colonial Americans, or "Yankees." In those days it was the rage, particularly in London, for young men to dress in elaborate, ludicrous finery. They were called "Macaronis," in derisive reference to flamboyant Italians.

Yankee Doodle, by contrast, was just some hayseed from the sticks, riding into town on his silly little pony, and he's so excited to be where the action is that he tries to affect the look of a dandy by sticking a feather in his cap. He thought that made him a Macaroni! What a goober.

After the battle of Bunker Hill, the Americans started singing the "Yankee Doodle" song themselves, to mock the British—a way of saying, "See here, you snobs, we Yankee Doodle Dandies just kicked your butt."

Why do we say someone is "late" rather than "dead"?

There ought to be a better way to denote that someone is no longer in possession of the characterisics that denote what we call "life." Late? What kind of stupid label is that? Just imagine what "Star Trek" would have been like if on every episode Bones felt the pulse of a hapless crewman and said to Captain Kirk, "He's late, Jim."

The term goes back to Middle English. The first known use was in the early 1400s with a reference to "Richard, late King of England."

Apparently the idea is that someone has existed lately, as opposed to having existed in ancient times. "Late" is actually an ambiguous term, because it can mean either someone who has recently died or someone who has recently left a position. *A Dictionary of Modern English Usage* by H. W. Fowler discourages the use of "late" because "of the doubt whether it means that the person's life, or his tenure of office, is over." You could say "erstwhile" instead, but that sounds so fussy and British.

There seems to be no standard for how "late" or "not-so-late" a person has to be before we say he or she is "late." We would never write "the late Julius Caesar" because he's just too dead. According to *Webster's Dictionary of English Usage*, you can say someone is late if the person was alive at any point in your living memory. But even that seems a bit lenient. Some people actually remember Teddy Roosevelt!

You also shouldn't say someone is "late" if they just died in the past couple of days—"late" is too quiet a term for such a situation, which calls for something more dramatic, like that line from Joseph Conrad, "Mistah Kurtz—he dead."

PHYSICS

(For poets, naturally)

Why is it that when you have something floating in your beverage and you turn the glass, the floating thing doesn't budge?

This is a matter of fluid dynamics, and the first thing you need to know is that a fluid is not the same thing as a liquid. A liquid is a fluid. But a gas is also a fluid. A fluid is simply something that's not a solid. A solid is something in which the molecules are locked into a lattice. (Someday, we'll figure out what the heck "plasma" is.)

So there you are, at a cocktail party, talking to the host, and you suddenly realize that in your glass of chablis is a floater of unidentifiable composition. Naturally it is poised to enter your mouth the moment you take a sip, and so you pivot the glass, hoping the floater will travel 180 degrees to the other side. It refuses. You have no choice but to fish it out with your finger, and seconds later are forced to shake hands with someone very important who immediately grimaces at the sensation of your wet hand, and so you say, "Sorry, I was just retrieving a floater from my chablis."

It's a total nightmare.

Your mistake was a lack of patience. If you had waited long enough, the floater would have moved. When you spin the glass, you create shear in the liquid. "Shear means that there is a differential motion of the fluid," says Timothy Dowling, an MIT professor who studies fluids.

Imagine that the wine is in layers, like the rings of a tree; the outer layer is held by friction against the glass and moves as the glass does. The next layer in, however, "slips" a little and can't keep up with the rotation. Inside that layer is yet another layer that slips even more, until finally you reach the layer with the floater, which might not budge at all initially.

Eventually it moves, though, because the laws of physics dictate that the shear must be eliminated. Wine abhors a shear! The speed with which everything gets straightened out is a function of viscosity; a thick liquid will experience less shear than a thin one. "The whole concept that you're trying to describe here is what viscosity is," says Dowling.

So that's solved. Now, because we can't get enough of this fluid dynamics business, let's look at something the scientists call the Teacup Problem. If you stir a cup of tea, you will notice some little flakes of tea leaves collecting in the center of the bottom of the cup. If you're a tea person, you've seen this a zillion times, and it probably never occurred to you that something is wrong with this picture. Think: Shouldn't the tea leaves do precisely the opposite, and cling to the outer edge of the cup? After all, if you've ever ridden any whirling, vomitous ride at a county fair, you know about centrifugal force. Why do the tea leaves defy common sense?

The reason, scientists have concluded, is that there's an unseen secondary current. This current flows straight down along the edge of the cup, then banks at the bottom, converging from all sides into the center. That's why the leaves collect there. The current then flows upward in a column, but not with enough strength to carry the flakes against gravity to the top of the cup. So the flakes don't become floaters. We are guessing that shear is also a factor in there, somewhere.

Why is marble always so cold?

Do an experiment. Touch different objects around you. Metal is cold. Glass is cool. Plastic is warmer than glass. Styrofoam is room temperature. It makes no sense! Shouldn't everything feel the same? Isn't every surface 72 degrees, whatever the ambient temperature is?

While you're thinking about this, lie down naked on a marble floor. Notice how the marble sucks the heat right out of your body, and keeps on sucking. Kind of like a vampire. But this doesn't happen on a wood floor. What's going on?

This: You've discovered conductivity. (How exciting! Get the beers!) What you are feeling is the rate at which heat is being transferred from your finger (the surface of which is about 85 degrees Fahrenheit, probably) to these various objects, which are, indeed, at room temperature. Marble conducts heat better than, say, sandstone. Marble is very dense and makes more contact with your skin than sandstone, which is a loose collection of sandy bits with lots of tiny air pockets in between (air is a good insulator, which means it impedes conductivity of heat). Styrofoam, which is mostly air, is therefore a great thing to put coffee in.

There's a second factor to consider: specific heat. Very important term. Keep those two words twined: "specific heat." This is the extent to which it is difficult to heat something up or cool it down. When you lie down on marble, it not only feels cold, it stays cold, rather than warming up. Wood is fairly quick to warm up. So we'd say that marble has a higher specific heat than wood.

The second law of thermodynamics dictates that heat

will continue to flow from the warm body (you) to the cold one (the floor). Water has the highest specific heat of any common substance, which is why it takes so ridiculously long for a small pot of water to boil, and even longer if you watch it (due to the first law of kitchen proverbs).

Why wasn't Ben Franklin electrocuted when he flew that kite in the thunderstorm?

Because lightning didn't strike the kite. Had it done so, "then it's bye-bye," says Martin Uman, professor of electrical engineering at the University of Florida and author of *All About Lightning*. (Someday we will do away with these prolonged identifications and simply stick with "expert.")

"He was lucky he didn't get killed," Uman says. "He didn't know quite what he was doing."

Thank you, thank you, Dr. Uman. For years, since we were wee babes, we had been bothered by the Franklin experiment, because it seemed about as wise as sticking a knife in a wall socket, or pulling on a mule's tail, or dangling your younger brother over the edge of a balcony.

Franklin himself never described the kite experiment. The secondhand account of Joseph Priestley states that Franklin flew a kite with string that could conduct electricity. At the bottom of the string was a key. Franklin did not touch either the string or the key, but was instead linked by a short piece of silk thread that could *not* conduct electricity.

The payoff came when a sizable spark jumped from the key to Franklin's knuckle. But lightning did not cause the spark. What did? Energy. Just plain old energy, zooming down from the sky. There is always a flow of electrons between the sky and the ground, and it's magnified during a thunderstorm. This doesn't always result in the massive

surge we call lightning; usually, we can't see it. Franklin's kite string, however, provided a channel for that energy flow, a relatively modest current.

The year after Franklin's experiment, a Swedish physicist tried something similar with a metal rod. Lightning struck. Alas, he became a fritter.

Why do falling cats always land on their feet?

This might seem like a simple matter of twisting, but that undervalues the subtle genius of a plummeting feline. You must understand that there are certain rules in nature that cannot be violated, and one of them is the Newtonian law that says an object cannot change its angular momentum unless acted upon by an outside force.

For a cat falling backward toward the ground, there is no outside force handy, nothing to push against. Believe it or not, the same thing is true of an Olympic diver: He or she cannot drop straight off the board and suddenly, in midair, do a complete flip. All those double gainers are the result of an initial spin that occurs prior to pushing off the board.

Obviously, the falling cat can twist and squirm. But the great achievement of the descending cat is that, after a sudden spasm of twisting, it has somehow achieved a perfect 180-degree rotation, so that it lands squarely on its feet.

We have a book here called *The Essential Cat*, which says that cats have "specialized structures within the inner ear," and that as a cat falls "crystals and liquid inside the inner ear are affected," and then the brain "sends ultrafast nerve commands" that make the head and body turn square to the ground. Awright already! We readily acknowledge that cats are totally spiffy creatures—but what the heck allows them to circumvent Newton? *Please* don't say "crystals."

(And also, while we're at it, why the heck is our balance determined by, of all things, the ear? Doesn't that seem kind of weird and arbitrary? Why not the nose? Why not the lymph nodes? Why not some specialized organ in the buttocks? The buttocks need a more complex function if they're ever going to get any respect.)

Scientists were so rattled by the ability of cats to spin in midair that for a long time it was thought that cats could tap into some hidden force that humans couldn't perceive. But it turns out there is nothing supernatural about it. The answer lies in geometry.

First, our falling cat pulls its legs close to the body, turns its head toward the ground in one direction, and twists its tail in the other. The head and tail offset one another and result in no net change in angular momentum—totally within Newton's rules. At this point, though, the cat is utterly twisted. Now what? The answer is peculiar: The cat reverses the previous move, but this time the legs are extended rather than pulled in. Although the cat returns to its initial, untwisted posture, it has wound up facing the opposite direction, with legs extended forward. A physicist would say that the cat took a round trip in something called parameter space resulting in a "geometric phase change," but all we need to understand is that the cat exploited a simple rule of geometry that allows this dramatic but limited acrobatic move.

Rather than straining too hard to picture this, consider the analogy. Physicist Hans Christian von Bayer, writing in *The Sciences*, describes two figure skaters spinning side by side, in sync, with arms outstretched. If one pulls her arms inward, her rotational speed will increase, even though there's no outside force giving her an extra spin. We've all seen this on TV. Then, if she extends her arms, she will slow down again to precisely the speed of her partner—*but no longer will their bodies be in sync.* The skater who changed speeds may have gained an extra quarter or half rotation, without ever altering her overall angular momentum.

See, it's all geometry. No doubt we've done a brilliant job of explaining this and cleared up all your concerns. To summarize: Cats land on their feet because figure skaters spin fast. (Hey, if *we* can't understand this stuff, how can the *cat*?)

Why is time travel impossible?

The other day we were watching *Terminator 2*, which is about an evil robot who is beamed from the future into the present to try to kill a little boy who is destined to grow up to lead the human resistance against the robots when they control the planet in the twenty-first century, only the evil robot first has to get around a good robot who also is beamed from the future and has the

advantage of being Arnold Schwarzenegger, and about an hour into the film we began to say to ourselves, "Hey, wait a minute, *is this realistic?*"

We later did some checking and discovered something disturbing. It turns out that time travel to the past might be possible after all. And we were so ready to pooh-pooh it!

You probably already know that time travel into the future is theoretically simple, if impractical. You just have to travel in a rocket ship really fast, like 99 percent of the speed of light, and you won't age as rapidly as people stuck down here. So, if you return to Earth, you will be in "the future" (sort of; we never really leave the present, but let's not make it any more confusing). This all is due to one of those great Einstein discoveries, that things moving at different speeds experience time at different rates.

What isn't widely known is that time travel to the past doesn't necessarily violate any of the laws of physics.

The main objection that scientists have to the idea of traveling to the past is really a philosophical one: They say it would create "causality" problems. What happens if you build a time machine, go back to the past, find your mother as a young girl, and kill her? Then you wouldn't come into existence. Or, more simply, what if you go back in time and kill yourself as a child? Then you couldn't grow up and get into the time machine that lets you go into the past to kill yourself.

"Most of us believe there must be something that prevents us from building such a machine," Alan Guth, the renowned MIT theoretical physicist, told us. "We'd be very hard-pressed to make sense out of the world in any way if time travel were to happen."

But he is quick to admit that modern physics "does not in any obvious way prevent time travel from happening."

In fact, Rich Gott, a Princeton physicist, has figured out how you might theoretically travel to the past. First, you need two adjacent "cosmic strings." These cannot be purchased in Kmart. In fact, no one is sure they really exist, though theories about the origin of the universe say they ought to be here and there. They are like piano wire on a grand scale: exceedingly thin and dense and stretching far across the cosmos. If two such strings are accelerating at great speed in opposite directions, the gravitational turbulence could twist "spacetime" like one of those sticks of licorice. The geometry is so weird that you could take off in a rocket ship, zoom really fast in a big loop, and come back to where you started from, only you'll have rejoined your strand of spacetime at a point in time prior to when you started—that is, the past.

Sure, the Gott time machine is hypothetical—it resembles an old Superman plot—but it's not mere nonsense. The physics are not in question. The idea that spacetime can be warped is accepted in modern physics. The main problem is still this dadgum causality issue. Gott, too, seems to be disturbed by the implication of his work.

"You could arrive back at the [starting] place and shake hands with yourself, yes. It's embarrassing," Gott says.

Some theorists try to solve the causality problem by arguing that there might be multiple realities, constantly branching into ever more strands, and thus no single reality is the right one. Thus you could go back and change time and causality be damned.

But maybe the best solution to the causality problem has been proposed by Kip Thorne, a Caltech physicist who, like Gott, has designed theoretical time machines. He says that time travel to the past simply requires a "self-consistent solution" that prevents any causality problems. You can go into the past, find your mother when she's still a girl, but you can't kill her.

Or, to be accurate, you can kill her, but you won't. Why won't you? Because you didn't.

This, in our opinion, is one of the most brilliant philosophical solutions that we've ever encountered. You won't because you didn't! That's beautiful.

Here's an example: You jump in your time machine and go back to November 22, 1963. You catch the morning plane to Dallas. Soon you're on the sixth floor of the Texas School Book Depository. You peek in a room. There's Lee Harvey Oswald. He's pointing a rifle out the window. You tell yourself that you're going to charge in there and wrestle him to the floor before he fires. But you don't. You slink away silently. Why? You're not sure. Or maybe what happens is, you slip on a banana peel and conk out. Whatever. There's nothing obvious that in and of itself prevents you from saving John F. Kennedy's life. You just . . . won't do it. Because that's not how the story goes. Kennedy dies in this script.

Okay, one last variation: You rush in, grab Oswald, pin him to the floor. You feel like a hero. Then you hear three, maybe four shots. You slap your forehead. Dammit, it *was* someone on the grassy knoll.

Why haven't scientists invented artificial photosynthesis, to turn sunlight into food?

Admit it, you were just wondering this. Once again we've snatched a question right off your quivering little tongue.

Photosynthesis is underappreciated. The very term brings back unpleasant memories of fourth-grade science tests. The simple fact is that photosynthesis is one of the few truly decent things about this planet. It's the mechanism by which we all survive. (The only exceptions are those bizarre creatures that live around volcanic vents deep in the ocean.) Everything we humans eat originally obtained its energy from little photosynthetic plants and bacteria.

But photosynthesis, contrary to common perception, doesn't turn sunlight into food. Why does everyone think that in the first place? Because schools teach lies. What photosynthesis does do is turn sunlight into *energy*. Plants become Eveready batteries in the sun. This energy then allows plants to manufacture sugars and other types of "food" from various elements in the environment.

The miraculous trick takes place at the molecular level. We all know that plants contain a pigment called chlorophyll, which in turn is full of tiny bacteria-like bodies that can absorb energy from light. What happens is, an electron gets whapped upside the head by a photon (a unit of light) and wanders to one end of an extremely funky molecule. Since electrons are negatively charged, the molecule is suddenly like a battery, with a negative charge at one end and a positive charge at the other. Thus the plant is able to use a simple form of electricity to start separating carbon from carbon dioxide in the air, and neat stuff like that. If you want a more detailed explanation, go to graduate school.

Why can't we imitate this in the lab? We can. "There's no reason why you can't do that artificially," says Devens Gust, professor of chemistry at Arizona State University. He and his colleagues have mimicked photosynthesis. Their goal is to learn how to doctor plants so that they can grow in hostile environments. Plants might also teach us some new tricks for exploiting solar energy; there is a new technology known as molecular electronics, which takes silicon-chip microprocessors to an even smaller level.

But these scientists are not trying to grow food to feed the world.

"It's a lot easier to grow a plant," Gust says.

Why doesn't some enterprising company follow Superman's example and compress lumps of graphite into diamonds?

You sneer? Fools, you'll never get anywhere in life without a little imagination and/or a subscription to comic books. Superman used his superstrength to make diamonds, but General Electric can do it through a machine. Yes! In fact, the technology is decades old; the factories are built, and diamonds are coming off the assembly line right now.

Unfortunately, the diamonds from GE look like the brown "natural sugar" crystals served in finer restaurants nationwide.

GE and a few competitors—very few, being as how GE is accused of monopolist ploys in this area—make synthetic diamonds just like the Man of Steel, by putting pure graphite, mixed with a liquid metal like iron, under high pressure and temperature. The pressure might reach 50,000 atmospheres (imagine a freight train resting on the tip of a pencil) and the temperature 2,000 degrees Celsius. Gradually, the diamond "grows," to use the insider terminology. There is nothing too remarkable about this trick, because a diamond is exactly the same thing as graphite—carbon. The difference is that in graphite, the molecules are in sheets, lying softly on top of one another, which gives a pencil marking that smudgy quality, while a diamond is a three-dimensional rigid matrix, so firm that nothing yet discovered on Earth is harder.

Hence diamonds, in addition to aesthetic charms, have great industrial handiness. They're great for cutting, abrading, grinding. Those linear grooves on treacherous highway curves are cut by diamonds.

Now, the appearance problem. Though synthetic diamonds on the market are sort of ugly—the Japanese make big yellow ones—there is no technological impediment to making diamonds that look like the rocks that adorn necks and fingers. The Russians once sent some fancy synthetics to Western European diamond merchants, and no one figured out they weren't for "real."

So why can't you buy synthetic diamonds in the store? Because, for now, the cost of crunching and baking the graphite into gemstone-quality diamonds is way too high. A synthetic quality diamond, manufactured to be identical in every way to a "real" diamond, would actually cost *more*!

Compounding the problem is that customers have a snobby attitude toward synthetic gems already on the market, like sapphires and emeralds. They think "synthetic" means "fake," and won't pay as much as they would for gems that come out of the ground. Since there are plenty of fakes that are actual "fakes" around—that is, imitation diamonds made of glass or whatnot—it's hard for anyone to grasp the idea that synthetic diamonds are not just another tricky form of costume jewelry.

"People somehow think that something that's dug out of the ground, that God made, is better than something synthetic that man made," says John Angus, a diamond-growing professor of chemical engineering at Case Western Reserve University in Cleveland. Nonetheless, he guesses that synthetic diamonds will be marketed within a few years as production techniques are perfected. (They should call them "Superman Brand" diamonds.)

Why is it impossible to see an atom, even with a really powerful microscope?

The problem with seeing with light is that light is kind of big. Repeat: *Light is big.* It comes in waves with several hundred nanometers in between the crests, while the average atom is only about a fifth of a nanometer across. Trying to measure an atom with a wave of light would be like trying to pick your nose with a bulldozer.

That's where electron microscopes come in handy. Electrons can bounce off an object and leave an image on a piece of film. This image can show objects only a few dozen atoms across. So why can't electron microscopes make images of *individual* atoms? Because these electrons pack quite a wallop, and when they hit a mere lonely atom they can easily obliterate it. The mere act of observation alters the thing that is observed.

James Trefil, coauthor of *Science Matters: Achieving Scientific Literacy*, told us, "It's like you have a long dark tunnel, and you want to see if there's a car down at the end of it, and the only way you can find out is by sending another car down the tunnel and listening for a crash."

In the past decade, a new type of device, called the scanning-probe or scanning-tunneling microscope, has made it possible to make images of atoms themselves. Not exactly pictures, but images. The tip of a teensy wire floats over the atom and picks up the electrical charge at its surface. When the probe is directly above an atom, the current is stronger, and when it is to the side or between two atoms, the current is weaker. From this it is possible to make an image showing the contour of the object.

Of course, atoms aren't the smallest objects known to man. Smaller still are quarks and a half dozen particles collectively known as leptons, including muons, neutrinos, and electrons. But these are "point particles" that—this is the official word—have no physical dimensions. They're just points. No width, no breadth, no depth. Let's meditate on that for a while. Also let's all consider naming our firstborn child "Muon."

Why do things get darker when they get wet?

The expert on this is Craig Bohren of Penn State University. He says that when something gets wet, it gets more transparent. A T-shirt has a lower "refractive index" when the medium surrounding it changes from air to water; that means that light rays don't bounce back into our eyes as easily, but instead sink into the T-shirt and shine on the skin underneath.

You could do an experiment. Hold a pane of glass horizontally, in the sun, and spread sand on it. The sand will be fairly bright. If you crouch underneath the glass and look up, you see a darkened pane. Then, wet the sand. It will instantly look darker from above—but it'll be brighter when viewed from below. (Better yet, skip the experiment and take our word for it.)

You may notice that only objects that are porous—clothes, certain stones, the bark on a tree—get darker when they get wet. Mirrors—or "specular reflectors," as experts call them—don't get darker when they get wet, because they're not porous.

Why are huge ships able to float, even when they're made out of steel or concrete?

You could build a ship out of lead if you wanted to. Or plutonium, even. (They'll have to do something with that stuff now that the Cold War is over.) A ship may look amazingly heavy, but so is the water displaced by its hull.

Water, you may not realize, is heavy stuff. Imagine yourself picking up a cubic foot of fresh water. Now imagine yourself getting a hernia. The water cube would weigh 62.4 pounds. The same sized cube of steel would weigh more, of course—about 490 pounds, estimates naval architect Charlie O'Brien of M. Rosenblatt & Sons in Washington—but ships aren't *solid* steel. They're hollow. Even a loaded

uSS Cumbersome.
contains; steel, lead,
cement, pig iron, rocks,
old National Geographics,
franks & beans, the
works of James Michener
& a bunch of sailors
with weight problems

oil tanker can float, because it has empty parts below the water, and because oil is also lighter than water.

When you see a freighter loaded down with what appears to be billions of pounds of material, remember that there's a lot of hull under the water line, displacing a lot of heavy water. If you could weigh the amount of water displaced by the hull, it would equal the weight of everything in and on the ship above the water line.

By the way, we always wonder how those huge ships are built. What bothers us is that, obviously, you can't build them in the water, but if you build them on dry land they'll be too heavy to move. The answer is: They don't have to be moved. The ships are built in a dry pit next to a body of water. When finished, the pit is flooded. The ship floats and sails away. (We would *never* have thought of that.)

The Helium Balloon Problem

Let's drop the Q&A format for a moment and discuss an intriguing little puzzle.

You're driving down the highway. There's a helium balloon inside your car. Where did it come from? Who knows. Maybe you stole it from a child. Who was having a birthday party. It doesn't matter. The point is, there's a helium balloon hovering about the ceiling of your car. Suddenly a small, furry quadruped crosses the highway in front of you. It's a kitty cat! You slam on the brakes. What happens? Your body lurches forward. Your groceries fly off the seat and smash into the dashboard. But the balloon flies straight back to the rear of the car.

So how come? (That should be the name of this book: *How Come That Is?*)

We are told by physicist Frank Kelly of Washington, D.C., that the deceleration of the car creates an artificial gravity throughout the interior. "Artificial gravity" is not really a scientific term, but it will do here. What has happened is that the contents of the car are accelerating forward relative to the rigid frame of the car. This is exactly what gravity is, a kind of acceleration through space. This artificial gravity pulls everything toward the dashboard.

But since helium is lighter than air, it "rises" in relation to the rest of the air in the car. And since the air is moving forward, the helium balloon rises by flying toward the *back* of the car.

Naturally, when we first wrote this our readers had to send in the usual argumentative letters.

A particularly cogent letter came from Edward S. of Bedford, Virginia, who sweetly suggested that we go back to Physics 101 (as though we took it to begin with!). What happens, he says, is that when you hit the brakes, the windshield and dashboard compress the air inside the car, with higher pressure at the front than the back. There is a "pressure gradient across the balloon which forces it to the rear of the car." There is "no gravity, artificial or otherwise," he wrote.

Dear Eddie: Experimental verification is the cornerstone of science. Never forget that!

We got two balloons. One was inflated with helium, the other inflated with our breath. And we got a car. Honda Accord, if you must know (not that we have anything against Detroit). We drove around town, slamming on the brakes, accelerating, decelerating, studying the motion of the balloons intently, getting traffic tickets, sending bikers veering off bridges, etc.

Results: The helium balloon flies backward when we slam on the brakes. The breath-filled balloon flies forward. Precisely the results we expected.

But this doesn't mean Eddie is wrong. In fact, he's right—except to the extent that he doesn't admit that we're right too. There is, indeed, a pressure gradient that forces the helium balloon backward. But our experiment shows that this pressure differential isn't strong enough to overcome the inertia of the heavier breath-filled balloon and keep it from falling forward.

When we spoke of artificial gravity, we were using shorthand for the equivalency of gravity and acceleration. The balloons in the car behave, in the horizontal plane, exactly as they would in a vertical gravitational field. A helium balloon rises through the sky because of the pressure gradient in the air; that gradient exists because gravity pulls the atmosphere toward Earth. So we are *both* right, in a sense.

Real gravity, artificial gravity—it's all pretty much the same. Our eyes feel heavy just thinking about it.

SERIAL KILLERS

*I*n the spring of 1991 I went back to my hometown of Gainesville, Florida, to write a story for the Washington Post *on the unsolved and ghastly murders of five students the previous year. By chance, my trip coincided with the ascendancy of* The Silence of the Lambs *as the most popular movie in the country, as well as with the publication of a number of best-selling novels featuring serial killers. Although I had read about serial killers for many years and, like everyone else in North Florida, had followed closely the case of Ted Bundy, I was astonished to discover how misinformed I had been about the true nature of these crimes. Here, then, is a search for what really happened in Gainesville, and why.*

GAINESVILLE, Fla.

The killer used a knife enthusiastically, to create a picture, to manipulate the human form, to alter for his own delight the appearance of the female nude. He proudly placed mirrors next to one body, at disparate angles, to intensify the visual impact of the deed.

But there was no artistry in his work. He was just a butcher. He mutilated the first girl. At his second stop, he entered a frenzy so profound he left his victim's head on a shelf. By the time of his third and final break-in his work had grown still sloppier, his fantasy punctured by the presence of his victim's athletic 200-pound boyfriend. The boyfriend, too, died under the knife.

The Gainesville murders shocked the country in August 1990. When we visited in March 1991 they were still unsolved. The police were faced with five bodies at three separate murder scenes. Once they had dealt with the initial horror, and contained their overpowering nausea, they had to figure out what it all meant.

Gainesville Police Lieutenant Sadie Darnell saw the first two bodies.

"It was a much different murder scene than I had ever experienced before," she says. "I was only in there maybe ten or fifteen minutes but it seemed much longer. It was as if I was absorbing things in slow motion, because there was so much on a sensory level to absorb. It was an eerie feeling and very much a feeling of the presence of evil."

She pronounces the last word cautiously, aware of its power.

"That all sounds so trite, I know, but it was a feeling I had never had before," she says. "The only thing that could have caused that was something that was evil."

He's a genius, he quotes poetry, he kills and eats his fellow human beings. His name is Hannibal "the Cannibal" Lecter, and he's the star of the novel and the movie *The Silence of the Lambs*, a sensational success in both media. In the book, Lecter has a series of tense discussions with Clarice Starling, a pretty young FBI trainee who has come to prison to interview him. She says she wants to find out what "happened" to him.

"Nothing happened to me, Officer Starling," Lecter lectures. "*I* happened. You can't reduce me to a set of influences. You've given up good and evil for behaviorism, Officer Starling. You've got everybody in moral dignity pants—nothing is ever anybody's fault. Look at me, Officer Starling. Can you stand to say I'm evil? Am I evil?"

• • •

The serial killer has become an American Original. He's almost a romantic icon, like the cowboy, the astronaut. He is enjoying a Golden Age both in reality and in fiction.

In real life, the past twenty years have seen a boom in serial homicide, the bogeyman type of murder, the kind where a sadistic stranger of unknown and incomprehensible motives steps out of the shadows and savages an innocent. Before the 1970s, serial killers were fairly rare. In most countries, they still are. In America, they have become so commonplace that criminologists estimate there are as many as twenty serial killers roaming the country at any given time.

And then there are the ones who inhabit the pages of books and the screens of movie theaters. Authors and filmmakers know that the public loves a good serial killer.

Between the fact and fiction of serial killers lies a gulf of ridiculous romanticization.

The imaginary serial killer is a powerful creature, brilliant at his craft, an implacable death machine. He's like a shark, driven not by mindless hunger but by an elaborate malevolence—evil, if you will.

Real life is not so gothic. When police bag a serial killer, he is usually a weak man, cowardly, not terribly savvy, and a failure at most everything he's ever done in life. He's a loser. He manages to get away with multiple murders not because he's smart, but because he kills strangers and keeps moving; in real life, unlike on "Murder, She Wrote" or any other TV drama, such crimes are always hard to solve.

"The bottom line is that most of these serial killers are not that clever," says Vernon Geberth, a former New York City cop and author of an authoritative text on homicide investigations.

This confusion between the real and the fake may explain the peculiar reaction of the people in Gainesville in recent months to the announcement that police have a prime suspect in the murders—Danny Rolling. [Author's note: he was eventually indicted.] You would think Gainesville might collectively untense, would gratefully accept an end to its terror. It hasn't happened. When you listen to the talk at off-campus hangouts like the Purple Porpoise and P.J. O'Riley's sports bar and the Market Street Pub, you find hardly a soul who thinks the police have cracked the case.

"Whoever did it is probably in another state by now," says Marti Sullivan, a University of Florida senior standing warily in the dark parking lot of the Gatorwood Apartments, where the last two bodies were found.

The problem is Rolling himself. He is a two-bit grocery-store robber, a nondescript thirty-six-year-old drifter from Shreveport, Louisiana, where he is wanted for allegedly shooting his father in the face in May 1990. Police say that on August 30, two days after the last bodies were found in Gainesville, Rolling stole a car from a university student, drove south to Tampa, held up a grocery store, crashed the car when chased by the cops, escaped on foot, and four days later got nabbed in a similarly bungled robbery at a supermarket in Ocala. He's inept. He's uneducated. He's a zero.

"We don't want it to be someone who is, say, less intelligent than we are," theorizes police officer Darnell. "We don't want it to be someone who is *ordinary*."

People aren't satisfied. They want Hannibal the Cannibal. There is something reassuring in imagining our killers to be driven by an almost supernatural monstrousness. Perhaps our attempt to make them larger than life is a way of distancing ourselves from them, of making sure that we have nothing in common with these creatures. It is almost too terrifying to think that they are merely a diseased product of human nature, that they are driven by the same forces that are in every human being and particularly characterize men: predatory aggression and lust. This is the dirty secret of serial killers: They are horribly twisted, but they are us.

The Gainesville killer was fastidious. The bodies were scrubbed with a cleanser. There were signs he had used masking tape to bind the victims, then removed it later.

One investigator told reporters that it was as though the killer created a "play" for the cops, that he was leaving messages. This remark helped foster the image of the killer as a demonic fiend who was toying with the police.

Police did find some important physical evidence. It has been mentioned in some of the news accounts of the killings, but often in passing, a minor detail.

Not fingerprints. Semen.

The typical serial killer, criminologists say, is a sexually dysfunctional man who lives alone or with a parent. He is not capable of a healthy sexual relationship with another person. He is likely to treasure pornography and those detective magazines with the staged pictures of women being menaced by knives, with impotency relief ads in the back. He gets drunk before he kills.

His immediate motive is hardly grand: He wants sexual gratification. The simple fact is that *serial killers are rapists*. Killing is one of the characteristics of the way they perpetrate rape. What's amazing is that the public doesn't realize the universal link between serial killing and rape, largely because the police and the press tend to withhold such nasty information.

Consider the Jeffrey Dahmer case. All the early reports focused on the number of bodies and the way the body parts were stored. There was hardly a word about any sexual motivation. Only later, during Dahmer's trial, did the public learn that Dahmer was a necrophiliac. All his deeds, from imprisoning his victims to saving their body parts, were committed in the hope of satisfying his unusual sexual cravings.

Except for a subgenre of "nurse killers" who like to play God and decide which of their patients will live or die, serial killers have always been sexual sadists.

Ed Kemper, a California killer in the early seventies, had sex with the headless corpses of his victims.

A few years later and not far away, Leonard Lake videotaped himself raping and torturing his captives.

Floridian Christopher Wilder asked pretty women if he could take their pictures, then kidnapped, raped, and killed them.

Absurdly, some writers have suggested that serial kill-ing has arisen in response to the growing economic and political power of women. The quickest of glances at the record shows, however, that the victims are often male. John Gacy of Illinois raped and tortured to death thirty-three boys and buried them in his basement. Randy Steven Kraft drove around the freeways of Los Angeles picking up young men, whom he then drugged, sodomized, tortured, killed, and mutilated. Juan Corona raped and murdered twenty-five migrant farm workers in California in 1970. The grisly list goes on.

The common attribute of serial killing cases is not the type of victim but the type of perpetrator—a rapist for whom violence is the key to sexual gratification. All classic serial killers have been men except for Aileen Wurnos of Florida.

"I have yet to see a serial killing that didn't have some sexual motivation," says Bob Ressler, a former FBI agent who was a leading figure in developing profiles of serial killers at the FBI academy at Quantico, Virginia. "I have never seen a serial killer who is a happily married family man, or who had a long-term successful relationship with a woman."

In recent years it has been popular among psychologists and some law enforcement authorities to say that these crimes are not acts of sex but of violence and power and domination. This is the same politically correct line used by sensitive people when discussing rape in general. It's not sex! Sex is good, this is bad! It's a ridiculous message. There are very few cases in which violence, power, and dominance are wielded without an accompanying sexual climax. Maybe the Son of Sam case falls into that category, because David Berkowitz didn't rape his victims, but his choice of young lovers in parked cars indicates a sexual element.

"It became vogue to say this was just an act of violence," says Ressler, but "it's an act of violence that's based on sexual maladjustment."

When people think about America's most famous serial

killer, Ted Bundy, they think of how diabolically clever he supposedly was, how he went to law school, how he easily blended into normal society for so long. In a movie he was played by Mark Harmon, once labeled the "Sexiest Man Alive" by *People* magazine. What people don't think about is the fact that Bundy was a necrophiliac. He craved sex with the dead. [Author's note: When this story was first printed, several other journalists questioned the accuracy of this detail. It was news to them! But it's true.]

Bundy was a failure in his normal life and a cowardly brand of killer. He would wear a cast or a sling on one arm and lure young college students into helping him carry his books to his car. Then, when the woman turned her back, he'd pick up a tire iron from the ground and kill her with a blow to the back of the head. Upon reaching a safe location he would have sex with the corpse. This would sometimes occur even days after the murder—one account says that he would wash the victim's hair and apply makeup to her face.

Yet these details are often deleted from Ted Bundy's public image. He was romanticized relentlessly. His cell on Death Row in Florida filled up with love letters. He received literally thousands of them. During one of his murder trials an admirer married him in the courtroom. She now claims that she bore him a child after a Death Row visit.

"I've been contacted by all these Bundy aficionados, all women. They're either in love with him, they want to talk to the person who was last with him, they have some feeling of attachment to him, many of them wrote to him in prison," says Bob Keppel, a Seattle prosecutor who tracked Bundy and spoke to him near the end. He is dismayed by the glorification of serial killers. "They are not romantic at all. They are just the lowest-level slimeball you would ever want to run across. They're the lowest dregs of society."

In a sense, the serial killing phenomenon is an extension of this country's rape problem, which is growing faster even than the homicide rate. Per capita, the United States has fifteen times as many reported rapes as England, twenty-three times as many as Italy, and twenty-six times as many as Japan.

But people don't like to think about rape. It is too low, too vulgar, too crass.

"We are fascinated by murder. We are not fascinated by rape," says James Alan Fox, coauthor of the book *Mass Murder: America's Growing Menace.* "Crime stories focus on murder, not rape. Rape has never been fashionable, it's always been seen as disgusting and demented. We can be fascinated by murder, it's so extreme, it's so bizarre, but we're only sickened by rape."

Steven Egger, author of *Serial Murder: An Elusive Phenomenon*, mentions in his book that in all of the academic literature on the subject, there is almost no mention that nearly all serial killers are men. It is as though people want to steer away from any explanation for these crimes that addresses a hormonal factor—people don't want to think of it as a testosterone explosion. But the behavior of serial killers is an exaggeration of the kinds of behavior found throughout the male population—predatory sexuality, treating women as objects, aggressiveness, desiring immediate gratification, narcissism, and so on.

There is something out there that we might call Male Pattern Badness. And it's so obvious we just ignore it. We take it for granted that women don't go around murdering people for pleasure, that women aren't rapists, that women don't videotape themselves beating up someone and laughing all the while.

When the story broke in Milwaukee that parts of fifteen human bodies were found in Jeffrey Dahmer's home, people did not take in a startled breath and say, "Was it a *man* who did this?" Because we knew already that only men are cannibals.

•   •   •

Fictional serial killers don't tend to rape anyone. Orgasm via sadism is never a motive. That would not be sufficiently entertaining.

Instead, they're just plain evil.

One absurd creature is Patrick Bateman, the murderous yuppie of *American Psycho* by Bret Easton Ellis. Bateman is handsome, Harvard-educated, works on Wall Street, buys expensive clothes, and goes to all the trendy night clubs. He also tortures and kills people in the most ghastly ways. The reader is led to believe that Bateman is the product of the excessively commercial, shallow, greed-infested era of the 1980s. He cares about things but not people. In one breath he says, "I'm wearing a wool suit by Armani, shoes by Allen-Edmonds, pocket square by Brooks Brothers," and the next he says, "Today I was obsessed with the idea of faxing Sarah's blood ... over to her office in the mergers division at Chase Manhattan."

Bateman is not merely fictional, he's totally improbable. Serial killers are invariably professional failures—even the ones like Ted Bundy and Christopher Wilder, whose few minor achievements were exaggerated by the news media. No known serial killer in America has ever been remotely as well educated, affluent, and successful as Ellis's murderer.

"I have never seen a person like that," says Ressler, the former FBI agent.

Thomas Harris, author of *The Silence of the Lambs*, did a lot of research for his book, and gained the cooperation of the FBI. Ressler, among others, gave Harris advice. Nonetheless, the two psychos of the novel and movie are not terribly realistic. Hannibal Lecter is just a vampire. The second-string psycho is James "Buffalo Bill" Gumb, who captures women and flays them so he can make clothing out of their skin. The character is based on three real serial killers: Ted Bundy, Ed Gein, and Gary Heidnik.

From Bundy, Buffalo Bill gets his cleverness, including the technique of using an arm cast to attract sympathy from women.

From Gein he gets his interest in skin. Gein dug up graves and took the corpses back to his lonely Wisconsin farmhouse, where he did "experiments" with the body parts; one favorite activity was making masks out of human faces and skulls. One day in 1957 he went into a nearby town and murdered a middle-aged woman, then killed another. Both resembled his deceased mother. He died in a mental institution in 1984, his actions immortalized by Alfred Hitchcock's 1960 film *Psycho.*

From Heidnik, Buffalo Bill gets his basement dungeon. In March 1987 police raided Heidnik's house in Philadelphia and found three women in chains in the basement, emaciated but alive. Two others were already dead, the body parts of one found in pots on a stove and in the freezer.

The FBI looks at these three killers and puts them in two separate categories: organized and unorganized. Gein was unorganized; Bundy and, to a lesser extent, Heidnik were organized.

What the FBI does not find, however, is someone like "Buffalo Bill": extremely clever, but also interested in something incredibly bizarre, in this case making dresses out of human skin.

"The reality of a person like Gumb is just not possible, because he has very psychotic tendencies and at the same time he's very organized and premeditating," says Ressler. "The movie is a joke. It's a joke on society and it's a joke on the FBI."

•   •   •

There are no good explanations for why someone becomes a sexual sadist. There are only mushy theories from experts who squabble with one another and manipulate a tiny and scientifically almost meaningless database culled from a few dozen bad guys. We are expected to hang the entirety of these bizarre pathologies on the flimsiest of nails—child torture as the product of a Bad Mommy, cannibalism as a desire to "dominate." The problem with the psychological theories is that a lot of people have bad childhoods and awful environments and do not grow up into anything resembling Ted Bundy or the Gainesville killer.

There is also a biological explanation. Ray Jeffery, professor of criminology at Florida State University, claims that virtually all serial killers have brain damage. "They can't control the violent areas of the brain," he says. "Everybody has a 'violent brain,' if you want to use that phrase. It's part of the evolution of survival. If you're not going to protect yourself in a predator/prey situation, you're not going to survive."

Finally, there are the sociological theories. These state that serial killers are consciously assaulting a society that they are alienated from. Elliott Leyton, an anthropologist, has written that the multiple murderer is "a profoundly conservative figure who comes to feel excluded from the class he so devoutly wishes to join. In an extended campaign of vengeance, he murders people unknown to him, but who represent to him in their behavior, their appearance, or their location the class that has rejected him."

The underlying cause of these crimes is something the experts can bat around and argue about forever in their analyses. It's not even clear what these people should be called. Killers who lack conscience and remorse are informally called "sociopathic" or "psychopathic."

The Diagnostic and Statistical Manual of Mental Disorders rejects those terms. Its preference: "Antisocial personality disorder."

"You know what's funny?" says Annie Hunter. She's a senior at the University of Florida. "Nobody talks about it anymore. People call it 'the incident.' "

It's over. People go on. They absorb the horror into their daily risk calculus.

"It's not even a topic of discussion anymore," says Spencer Mann, spokesman for the sheriff's office.

"I haven't thought about it recently because I prefer not to think about it," says Amy Barnard, a twenty-seven-year-old bartender in downtown Gainesville. "I'm tired of it."

The psyche heals, the fear subsides, and life goes back to normal.

Only now, normal has a new definition. Normal incorporates an astonishing glut of violence throughout American society. More violence in the media, more violence in real life: They seem to feed on one another.

The crime statistics are ominous. Despite great leaps in forensic technology to solve murders, the clearance rate has fallen from 86 percent in 1970 to 68 percent by 1989. The reason, in part, is that more and more murders are "stranger homicides," says Jim Wright, an FBI agent who analyzes violent crime. Another disturbing trend is that serial killers are racking up larger and larger body counts; there are more cases like that of Randy Kraft, who may have slain as many as sixty-five people in Los Angeles. "They learn from their mistakes. Every time they commit a crime, they learn. And they get better," says Wright.

Celebrated, probed, fussed over, the rapist-killer is now a familiar figure on the American landscape. He is probably here to stay. He is beyond the bounds of governance, beyond social engineering, beyond control. Perhaps he is the price we pay for slavish devotion to individualism, mobility, the right to ignore one's neighbors even when they seem weird. He can come through town and no one will ask him any questions. This is the way it is going to be, as long as this remains a nation of strangers.

Author Norman Mailer once made a prediction:

"The psychopath may indeed be the perverted and dangerous front-runner of a new kind of personality which could become the central expression of human nature before the twentieth century is over."

He wrote that in 1959. At the time it seemed preposterous. Now it's just an exaggeration.

THE KITCHEN

Why is it so much better to slice a sandwich diagonally than straight across?

This is a matter of almost infinite complexity, subtlety, and nuance. And yet our enemies say this is a trivia book!

There are three (3) reasons why triangular sandwich halves are better than rectangular halves:

1. The hypotenuse. You want geometry that reveals *maximum meat*. If you cut a five-inch-square piece of bread straight up and down (a "drugstore cut," in the dismissive phrase of Stuart Gurewitz of Parkway Deli Restaurant in Silver Spring, Maryland), the exposed middle of the sandwich is five inches long. But a diagonal cut gives you slightly more than seven inches of exposure (you need merely solve for C in the equation, A squared plus B squared equals C squared, with C being the hypotenuse of the half-sandwich). Gurewitz lays the halves back to back: "That way, no matter which way you look, the meat's facing outside. It's better presentation."

2. Flatness. Rectangular sandwiches don't lie as flat. "If you cut a piece of white bread right straight in half, it has a tendency to open, just unfold," says Walter Loeb, owner of Loeb's Perfect New York Deli in Washington, D.C. "Corner to corner it will stay down better. It's better divided weightwise, I guess." Note: Loeb, unlike Gurewitz, slices oval-shaped pumpernickel and rye breads down the middle, because "there aren't four corners."

3. Mouth action. It's easier to bite into the acutely angled corner of a diagonally sliced sandwich than into the regular right-angled corner of a rectangular sandwich.

Both Gurewitz and Loeb mentioned this, but the best description of the phenomenon can be found in Nicholson Baker's nutty novel *The Mezzanine*. "In the case of rectangular toast," he notes, "you had to angle the shape into your mouth, as you angle a big dresser through a hall doorway: you had to catch one corner of your mouth with one corner of the toast and then carefully *turn* the toast, drawing the mouth open with it so that its other edge could clear; only then did you chomp down."

You have the full picture. Cut your sandwich accordingly.

Why do NutraSweet and saccharin taste so much like sugar, yet have no calories?

True fact: Saccharin has been used industrially to make car bumpers shinier. No wonder there's an aftertaste.

Saccharin is a form of benzene, which means it comes from petroleum distillates. Both saccharin and aspartame (NutraSweet) are shaped similarly to the sugar molecule and thereby fit into the taste receptors on the end of the tongue. Taste buds aren't smart. They're just holes, basically. Your tongue thinks saccharin is sugar, but your gut doesn't recognize it as food, or anything else worth keeping around, and so it zips right through your system.

Aspartame, moreover, is a compound of amino acids that is metabolized, and it contains plenty of calories in its pure form. But the secret of aspartame is that it's two hundred times as sweet as sugar, so you don't have to use much to achieve the same sweetness as a teaspoon of sugar. And saccharin is *five hundred times* as sweet as sugar. This means that when you pick up a packet of these artificial sweeteners you're really holding only the slightest trace of the sweet stuff; the rest is filler that's put there to give it bulk.

"It's simply there so that the product can be packaged, because the aspartame itself is so sweet you couldn't handle it," says NutraSweet spokesman Rich Nelson.

Saccharin was invented way back in 1879. Aspartame was synthesized several decades ago, but no one knew it was sweet until a fellow named James Schlatter, a chemist with G.D. Searle & Co., serendipitously licked his finger after handling some of the stuff.

Why don't we ever eat turkey eggs?

Turkeys are poultry, right? They lay eggs, right? So why don't we ever scramble up a batch? Why don't we ever "egg" a house with turkey eggs? Why don't we paint turkey eggs at Easter?

We rejoiced at the chance to call our friends at the National Turkey Federation. They told us that turkey eggs are a mite expensive—about seventy-five cents per. Then again, you do get a bigger egg, nearly twice the size of what comes out of a hen.

The true reason that turkey eggs are used only for breeding, not for eating, is palatability: They don't taste good. More precisely, they don't have as much water in them as chicken eggs. The next time you eat a couple of chicken eggs, think about how wet they are. But a turkey egg, if exposed to high heat, turns rubbery. And who wants to eat a rubbery turkey egg for breakfast ... although it might make a nifty bathtub toy for a child.

Why doesn't yeast, which is a living organism, die when it gets dried out and packaged and put on grocery store shelves?

We find that it's easiest to think of yeast as a form of baking soda, and not even contend with the perplexing concept that it's actually alive. But let's proceed. After nine million phone calls in search of a yeast expert, we reached Bill McKeown, quality assurance manager for Fleischmann's Yeast in San Ramon, California, and he said by way of explanation, in that way that quality assurance managers have of talking, "The packages are nitrogen-flushed."

Of course! Nitrogen-flushed packages. Everyone knows that. One minor question, though: What in tarnation is a yeast, anyway? Is it a bug? A germ? A virus?

No, it's a form of mold, part of the fungus kingdom, which means it's a living organism that doesn't fit into the category of "animal" or "vegetable" or "bacteria." It replicates when fed a nice mixture of sugar and molasses, and McKeown can take a single yeast spore on Monday and grow sixty thousand pounds by Saturday.

The yeast is dried to a precise moisture level, then tightly sealed in nitrogen-filled (and oxygen-free) packages. Without oxygen and with little water, the yeast can't metabolize much. The spores will last at least a year in this sloweddown but not entirely suspended animation. They're like seeds, alive but amazingly mellow.

Why do humans eat cooked food, even though all other animals eat it raw and bloody?

The vegetarian lobby has promoted the notion that the consumption of meat is an unnatural act, not merely unhealthy but actually a distortion of the human palate, a kind of self-induced madness. They claim charred flesh doesn't actually taste good. Our intestines don't even recognize it. Send a greasy burger down there and it gets mistaken for a shoe. The only reason that we think we like this stuff is that we're brainwashed by corporate greedheads who run the beef lobby. We want to eat real food so we'll be "real people."

Frankly, we think only a dolt would argue that a bowl of granola tastes as good as a burger. (What would happen if you ate granola with a side of fries? Would your taste buds go into shock?)

The traditional (nonpolitical) explanation for why we eat cooked meat is that it's more tender that way, and is easier to eat, saving time and energy and allowing us to have smaller jaws than our forebears, who tended to have those big Carly Simon features. Moreover, the cooking of food kills unsavory smells and unhealthy bacteria.

But this doesn't explain why people *like* the taste of cooked food. This is a matter of chemistry: When food is heated, the complex sugars and amino acids break down into new and exciting molecular combinations, each of which has a distinct aroma and flavor. If you heat sugar to 320 degrees Fahrenheit, it melts, and at 335 degrees it starts to turn brown and give off a rich aroma. These heat-induced changes are called the browning reaction. The carbon, hydrogen, and oxygen atoms in the sugar molecules are reacting with oxygen in the air to make hundreds of molecular compounds, many of which are registered by our olfactory organ and contribute to what we think of as "taste."

We have a book here, *The Curious Cook*, by Harold McGee, that says cooked beef has at least six hundred "flavor compounds," compared with only a few flavor com-

pounds for your basic staffs of life, like wheat and barley. Raw meat is also extremely bland. Those wild creatures who gnaw on bloody flesh would probably savor a medium-rare steak, but they lack stoves.

The only foods that naturally have lots of flavor compounds are fruits. A strawberry has about three hundred flavors, a raspberry about two hundred. McGee argues that all well-prepared food aspires to the condition of fruit.

"Fruits probably provided our evolutionary ancestors with refreshing sensory interludes in an otherwise bland and dull diet. Perhaps cooking with fire was valued in part because it transformed blandness into fruitlike richness."

McGee notes that a similar browning reaction also takes place when organic material decomposes in the soil, which is why rich soil is darker than infertile sand. So if you're going to eat dirt, make it compost. Medium rare.

Why do we love coffee so much, even though it is bitter and odd-tasting?

Every morning you cherish that cup of coffee, maybe even a second cup, maybe even so many cups that your entire body develops an internal hum and your coworkers suddenly can't get you in sharp focus. But you probably have no idea why you like the stuff—even though the economies of no fewer than sixty nations depend on how much you like it.

The only word that people can usually summon to describe the "appealing" flavor of coffee (other than "coffee-flavored") is "richness." But true coffee experts disdain this term. Richness! Hah! That's not a flavor, that's just a vague description of *mouth feel*, they say.

Real experts use words like "grassy," "earthy," "winey," "woody," "acidy," "brackish," "briny," "caramelly," and "sharp." They also will say that a "sharp" coffee has a secondary taste that is either "rough" or "astringent." An "acidy" coffee can be either "nippy" or "piquant." Our favorite coffee term is "Rioy," which means "tastes like it came from Rio." Apparently some Brazilian beans have an unpleasant iodine or medicinal taste.

The experts have a special way of drinking coffee too, called "cupping." According to *The Coffee Cupper's Handbook* by Ted R. Lingle, a spoonful of coffee should be quickly slurped from a silver-plated spoon and sloshed around the tongue. He instructs, "First swallow a small portion of the brew after holding it in the mouth for a few seconds, and then rapidly pump the larnyx to force up into the nasal cavity the vapors in the back of the palate."

(We presume you should then wipe your mouth with the back of your hand and say, "Yessiree bob, that's a great cuppa joe!")

So why do we like this hot, sometimes nippy, occasionally piquant beverage? There's no simple answer—and the lack of simplicity is, in fact, the key to the mystery. Coffee, like cooked meat, provides an unusually complex taste, a result of the roasting process. Lingle writes that there are at least four hundred chemical compounds mixed together in a single cup, each one contributing somehow to the taste and smell of coffee.

"Roasted coffee has some things in it that are similar to what you find in cooked meat," says Tim Castle, author of *The Perfect Cup*. It also has a slight barbecue taste. "A lot of people have used it in barbecue sauce," Castle told us.

So, in essence, we like coffee because it reminds us of ribs.

Of course, we can't totally dismiss the caffeine angle. True, some people drink only decaffeinated coffee, but it is the addiction to caffeine that makes coffee drinking a national compulsion rather than a mere pleasure. Moreover, kids who grow up with the familiar smell of coffee (and, in the old days, the sound of a percolator) find coffee a reassuring, comforting beverage when they become adults.

That raises a final question: Why don't kids like coffee? The answer is that they don't like bitter, sour things. They won't drink beer either. (Imagine!) Put a daub of beer or coffee on a baby's tongue and it will cringe and draw back. Yet later in life the palate mysteriously changes. This is probably an adaptive trait of the species: Poisons in the environment often are bitter or sour-tasting, and therefore only when we become older, and savvier, does our palate encourage us to experiment with some of the weirder substances found in nature.

A final note: Coffee, miracle beverage though it may be, provides almost no nutrition whatsoever. And no calories. It's mostly just hot water.

Why isn't salt colored, so you can see how much you are putting on your food?

Everyone has shakers of salt and pepper on the dinner table: salt because food tastes bland without it, and pepper because it satisfies the primitive urge of diners to use a condiment that's visible. Applying salt is like

writing your signature: it's a muscular contraction preprogrammed into your hand and wrist, a brief and frenzied flurry impossible to shake. So to speak.

So why can't they make salt that's not virtually invisible? This question has been asked so frequently of the people at Morton Salt that they have been compelled to perform exotic experiments and marketing studies with colored salt. Conclusion: bad idea.

For one thing, people like their salt to be white. It looks cleaner. Happily, that's how it occurs in nature too. "We are very proud of the pure white salt that we sell," says Nancy Hobor, spokeswoman for Morton International.

There's a better reason, though, to keep salt white: Salt, colored or not, disappears the moment it touches hot, moist food. Salt is extremely soluble.

Even colored salt would disappear in this melting process, unless massive amounts of dye were used, says Arie Hoogendoorn, director of scientific research at Morton.

Also, if you colored your salt, you would require several different colors to contrast with food of different colors.

"You could color salt green. That would be good on potatoes, but on spinach or a salad, that would be a waste," says Hoogendoorn.

Our advice: Be satisfied with regular salt but be sure to shake it on your palm first.

Why is concentrated orange juice cheaper than nonconcentrated orange juice, even though it is presumably costly to concentrate the stuff?

Because it costs money to store and ship water. For example, Tropicana's "Pure Premium," which is pasteurized orange juice that's never been concentrated, takes up more storage space per drinkable ounce than thick concentrated sludge. Moreover, it has to be made from Florida oranges, unlike the concentrated stuff, which can be made from cheaper Brazilian oranges. (It costs too much to ship unconcentrated Brazilian juice to the United States, which is why OJ in this form isn't available.)

There's an interesting frozen OJ anecdote in John McPhee's neat little book *Oranges*. Frozen concentrate is of relatively recent invention—the mid-1940s. Before then, growers knew it was simple enough to concentrate the juice, but when it was later reconstituted it tasted "like a glass of water with two teaspoons of sugar and one aspirin dissolved in it," writes McPhee. Enter Dr. Louis Gardner MacDowell, of the Florida Citrus Commission. "Just as simple as that, it occurred to me to overconcentrate the juice and then add fresh juice to it. And that was that," MacDowell told McPhee.

In other words, the juice companies evaporate so much water that nothing is left but some gunk about seven times as thick as normal juice. Then they add fresh juice (and maybe some orange peel oil and other "essences") to make it only about three times the normal viscosity. That's your frozen concentrate currently available.

Nowadays, more and more people buy cartons of reconstituted concentrate, or never-concentrated "premium" juice, rather than the thick frozen stuff. Ed Moore, who along with MacDowell and C. D. Atkins won the patent for concentrated orange juice, told us that the days have passed when people thought it nifty to add three containers of water to frozen concentrate and stir up a batch of OJ.

"Today, that's a little bit too much work," Moore said. "It's easier to just pay someone else to add water."

Why do people think vodka is made out of potatoes, when it's not?

Vodka is the most social-climbing of all the spirits. This unsophisticated beverage has gradually become respectable, not to mention commercially triumphant. In 1955 only 3.5 percent of the hooch purchased in America was vodka, but by 1982 the amount had risen to 22 percent, and it has continued to rise. Why is vodka so hot? Because it's so boring, and we live in a boring era. Vodka is essentially nothing but alcohol, watered down.

Vodka can be made from almost any grain or vegetable. It used to be made primarily from potatoes, but only because they were available to Russians centuries ago. Today, all domestic vodkas and every quality imported vodka are made from grain. Vodka is produced by distilling almost pure alcohol—virtually 200 proof—from grain, then adding water and perhaps a tiny bit of sugar syrup or glycerin to provide a sleek mouth feel.

The difference between bad vodka and good vodka is mainly one of purity—the good stuff comes from the "heart of the run," the middle portion of the distilling process. The rotgut comes from the beginning and end. According to Harriet Lembeck, author of the newest edition of *Grossman's Guide to Wine, Beers and Spirits*, vodka is defined as "a neutral spirit that is distilled without any color, aroma or flavor."

Mr. Vodka Head

If you add the flavor of juniper berries and a few other things, you've made gin. If you start with sugar cane, distill it at something like 130 proof, and age it in a wooden cask, you have rum. If you take perfectly good grapes and treat them like dirt, you have a wine cooler.

SHOPPING TIPS

(All great literature should double as a consumer guide.)

Why aren't cans of soup alphabetically arranged on grocery store shelves?

The average person spends seven months and fourteen days, over the course of his or her lifetime, staring at the Campbell's Soup display, wondering where the heck they put the chicken noodle.

Even though we concocted that statistic mere seconds ago, the fact remains that the soup display is weirdly disorganized and subtly manipulative, which makes you feel that you're being toyed with by the all-powerful Soup Cartel. Unless, that is, you are a certified Smart Shopper, in which case you know that chicken noodle is always, as surely as the sun rises in the east, on the bottom shelf.

But does the Smart Shopper know the other two soups in the triad that the Campbell Soup Co. refers to as "the Big Three," and that accompany chicken noodle on the bottom shelf? Tomato, obviously. The stumper is the third one. Cream of mushroom. (This is the kind of compelling

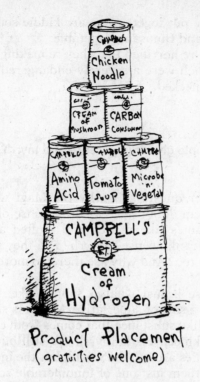

Product Placement
(gratuities welcome)

information that you simply don't get in a hardcover book.)

Kevin Lowery, spokesman for Campbell's Soup, says the Big Three are on the bottom shelf because that shelf is bigger and stronger, and can therefore hold a couple cases of soup cans. It's also easier to restock.

"Many people aren't aware that our Big Three are the fastest-moving dry grocery items in supermarkets nationally," he said. (We were tempted to reply, "Yeah, people are really stupid.")

The shelving system is not as random and incomprehensible as it looks, even though it is unforgivably anticonsumer. The company has "planograms" that show grocery stores how the soups ought to be arranged. New soups that need exposure (like the "vignette label" cream of broccoli) are put at eye level. Your cooking soups, like chicken and beef broth, are put together, as are kiddie soups, like Superstar Soup and Dinosaur Vegetable.

Frankly, we're horrified that they're making soup out of dinosaurs, which were a severely endangered species the last time we checked.

Why don't people give frankincense and myrrh as gifts anymore?

The bigger question is why the Magi who went to Bethlehem didn't have a better sense of baby presents. Babies like rattles and stuffed animals and mobiles. But frankincense? Myrrh? Did they give the Kid some matches too? And why are there no more Magi these days?

Frankincense is just what it sounds like: incense, the "frank" being a sort of superlative. Myrrh is similar. It's a gummy, resinlike substance that comes from certain types of trees. Frankincense and myrrh are still burned in religious ceremonies around the world, but the incense industry has made them just one of innumerable scent options. We called several health food and botanical shops and they said they actually do a fair business with frankincense and myrrh. (These scents certainly *sound* as though they smell good.)

According to *Spiritual Cleansing*, by Draja Mickaharic, frankincense "is really wonderful for attracting a beneficial influence to a place." The book adds, "Myrrh fumes bring the astral realms closer to the earth, opening up the spiritual doorway so the influences attracted by the frankincense may manifest."

No thanks, we'll just take what's in the third chest over there—ah, yes, the gold.

Why do coupons often say in tiny print, "Cash value 1/20th of one cent"?

Whenever we're feeling poor and poverty-stricken, and so forth, we look at our collection of coupons, scrutinize the tiny statement about cash value at the bottom, and think: "If we cash these in, maybe we can get that Cadillac after all."

Why would anything be worth 1/20th of a cent? Or 1/100th, as some coupons are? We found the answer to this mystery, but it's pretty daffy. Apparently some states, with Kansas being the prime example, have strict "trading stamp laws" that can also be applied to coupons. Trading stamps are nearly extinct—you remember, you used to get them at the grocery store and fill up booklets with them so that, after three years of diligent collection, you could trade them all in for a gooseneck lamp—but the restrictive laws are still on the books.

The regulatory goal was to prevent unscrupulous characters from trying to persuade gullible people that a coupon worth "forty cents off regular price" is actually worth forty cents. So by law, coupon issuers have to put a real cash price at the bottom. And yes, you really can cash them in to the issuing company—but otherwise they're not worth the paper they're printed on.

Why is perfume so expensive?

Calculators came down in price. So did digital watches. Why didn't Chanel No. 5? Is perfume really that hard to make? Don't they just boil up a bunch of flowers or something?

We asked. Chanel scoffed.

"Do you have two hundred acres of roses? Then you couldn't make an ounce of perfume. You're talking about tons of flowers that would go into making pounds of essence from which you could extract the oils," said Jack Mausner, a senior executive at Chanel, Inc.

The flowers have to be picked by hand, he said, to make sure that there's no mold or disease that might spread into the entire batch and ruin it. And they're grown in France! These are *sophisticated* flowers. "Only very good flowers can go into the mix," he said.

Makes you almost want to mail them a check, just to help out.

Speaking of the mix, two natural ingredients that Chanel and some other companies don't use anymore are musk and civet. They stopped because of the animal rights movement and subsequent legislation. Musk comes from a gland inside a deer. That requires the deer be placed in a deceased condition. This is nothing compared with the fate of the civet cat. These cats, like skunks, spray their adversaries with a horrible excretion. "The odor is disgustingly obnoxious, but like many odors of animal origin it becomes very pleasant and attractive on extreme dilution," says a reference book called *Perfumes, Cosmetics and Soaps*.

The fox-sized civets have been the target of industrial exploitation for years, and no doubt still are, despite the new laws. Because they produce their scent when traumatized, civet traders obligingly torment them. Our book says calmly, "Since heat increases the yield, several cages [of civets] are kept in specially heated huts. . . . Teasing increases the yield."

Torture: Both fun *and* practical. (No thanks, we'll take a splash of skunk instead.)

Why aren't postage stamps flavored?

Sickness. Death. Unhappiness.

"Any flavoring you put into a stamp could result in allergic reaction by customers," says Dick Rustin, manager of stamp product development at the U.S. Postal Service.

Citizens have suggested such flavors as "pretzels and

beer," he says, but he adds, "There's no flavor that you could come up with that would satisfy everyone." (What? *Beer* wouldn't?!)

So stamps just taste like glue, or, more specifically, like corn-based dextrin and/or polyvinyl alcohol (which satisfies no one).

Why does your hair lather so much better the second time you shampoo it?

Because your hair is already clean. The lather is compelling evidence that your hair got clean the first time.

"You get most of the dirt and oil off with just one treatment—assuming that you have a normal amount of oil on your head," says Julie Leet, a chemical engineer for Procter & Gamble. (She didn't realize that most Why staffers like the "10W-30 look.")

Soaps are really efficient; one washing removes about 99 percent of the oil. But initially that dirt and oil prevent the shampoo from forming nice firm bubbles, which together make up lather.

The only point of reapplying the shampoo is that it's psychologically pleasing (the instructions say "repeat if desired," which is a squirrelly attempt to be intellectually honest while still encouraging the consumer to use more of the product). But our advice is to refrain from the redundant scrub: You are wasting shampoo, wasting water, wasting the energy that goes into making the water hot, increasing water pollution, having deleterious effects on the entire biosphere, and probably leaving excessive soap scum in the shower.

Why do packages of Q-Tips say you aren't supposed to insert them in your ear?

Some people fear death. Others fear, more specifically, a painful death. What *we* fear is a silly death, like maybe a banana-peel accident or a plucked-nose-hair infection or, worst of all, a death by Q-Tip. It doesn't get any worse than that. One minute you're using a Q-Tip while riding a pogo stick, the next . . .

The Q-Tip package specifically instructs you to "stroke swab gently around the outer surfaces of the ear without entering the ear canal." Right. Soon we'll probably see cigarettes with the instructions, "Let dangle from lips in Gary Cooperish fashion. Do not ignite."

We called Chesebrough-Pond's, Inc., the maker of the product, and asked if the company seriously thinks that Q-Tips are not designed specifically to stick into the ear to clean out ear wax. A spokesman said, "Our feeling is that nothing should be entering the ear canal. Clearly this is a misuse of the swab."

The swabs were called Baby Gays when introduced by inventor Leo Gerstenzang in 1923. He supposedly saw his wife use a toothpick with a cotton ball on the end to apply stuff to their baby. A couple of years later he changed the name to Q-Tips Baby Gays, and then they became just Q-Tips, though no one is sure what the Q stands for. "Quality," the company suggested.

Chesebrough-Pond's bought Q-Tips, Inc. in 1962 and, sometime in the 1970s, added the warning about not sticking the thing in your ear. The company has no details on why it did this. Readers have anecdotally told us of various Q-Tip accidents, like the time the sailor answered the phone while swabbing out his ear and . . . well, you don't want to know.

Responsible journalism forces us to note that it is, indeed, dangerous to stick things in your ear. In fact, there probably ought to be a Surgeon General's warning on a Q-Tips box, as well as "No Q-Tips" sections in restaurants and airplanes. (Ear canal swabbing would, of course, be allowed on flights longer than six hours.)

Why do car horns sound so wimpy?

Cars used to go *Bah-WOOG-ah*. Then for a while they all went *WHAWWNK*. Now they go *NEEP, NEEP*. Some jerk pulls out in front of you on the interstate, you hit the horn, *NEEP NEEP*, and he just laughs. It's humiliating.

Why the change? Naturally, you would presume this has something to do with the fact that cars, in general, are getting wimpier, and as they do their voices rise a few octaves through some quasi-biological process. When cars were covered with steel, chrome, and chest hair, they had deep horns; nowadays we drive fuel-efficient econoboxes and they sound prepubescent. It's just nature, you figure. It would be weird if a Toyota Tercel went *WHAWWNK*. This is a car so wimpy that if you run out of gas you can simply plug the engine into the cigarette lighter.

So naturally the horn sounds like a baby's squeeze toy. Little cars, squeaky horns, right?

Erroneous presumption. In fact, horns have gradually gotten wimpier since the late 1960s because automakers have discovered that a whiny, tinny sound gets the attention of other drivers better. It's more obviously a man-made sound. The *WHAWWNK* was deemed too much like a normal traffic noise.

"This began changing back in the late sixties or early seventies. The big old blasting horns have really kind of been gone for a long time now," says Don Postma, a General Motors spokesman.

"It's nothing more than customer preference," says Dave Sloan, another GM mouth. He explains, in case anyone cares, that a car horn uses a combination of four notes (someone told us they are A, F, C, and D, but someone else said that isn't so, so we'll chalk it down as another mystery for the ages), but the cheaper cars may use only two notes— say, A and F. Yet another factor to contemplate the next time you car shop. Tell 'em you want a car with all the notes.

Why do car speedometers go up to 120 miles per hour even though such speeds are incredibly unsafe and illegal?

When we buy a car, we always look for one with a speedometer that stops right at 55. With a frightening red zone going all the way up to 65. Just in case we might want to open 'er up and clean 'er out on a rural interstate.

The real question is: Why does the Ford Taurus SHO speedometer go up to 140? Isn't that irresponsible?

"We are only indicating the top performance level of a vehicle," says Nick Sharkey, a Ford spokesman. "Although we don't want people to drive the Taurus SHO at 140, it does show them that when they get in difficult driving conditions, the car does have quicker pickup than cars with a slower driving range."

In other words, let's say you're in a school zone and you need to pass a stopped school bus before ... oh, never mind. The truth, of course, is that the 140 on the speedometer is a "selling point." Some people feel better about themselves when they own high-speed machines.

Maybe they should just put a flashing red light on the dashboard saying, "You Are a Major Hunk-0-Burning-Love."

MONEY

Why are dimes so wimpy, even though they are more valuable than pennies or nickels, which are larger?

It's pathetic. Dimes are worth twice as much as nickels, yet they're only about half as big. That's life: a travesty, all the way down to the coinage.

This horrifying situation is left over from the days when the value of coins was a function not of size but of metallic composition. See, money didn't use to be simply symbolic; it used to have real value. You weren't asked to simply believe that a green piece of paper was worth one dollar, you were assured it could be redeemed in actual gold. And coins, in similar no-nonsense fashion, contained valuable metals. Long ago, dimes were about 90 percent silver and 10 percent copper. Before the Civil War, there were no "nickels," only "half-dimes," worth five cents and, appropriately, half the weight of a dime. (Talk about a pathetic little coin.)

In 1866, the brawny "nickel" debuted, so called because it was 25 percent nickel and 75 percent copper. No silver in it. It was big, but the ingredients were cheap.

In 1965, the U.S. Mint stopped putting silver in dimes

and started making them with a copper core and a copper-nickel exterior. Dimes are now about 92 percent copper, all told. In other words, a dime is a penny, with a little bit of gloss.

So here's the latest twist: Dimes are now worth less than nickels, if you're judging strictly by metal. In fact, even two dimes are worth less than a single nickel.

"Logically the larger coin of these two should be worth ten cents and the smaller should be five cents," says Arlyn Sieber, editor of *Numismatic News.* "But the fact that the dime is smaller than the nickel is something we've lived with all our lives. It would be a pretty radical change in our coinage system."

One final bonus fact: According to the U.S. Mint, it costs 1.42 cents to make a ten-cent coin, and 2.59 cents to make a five-cent coin. So obviously, the easiest way to balance the federal budget and eliminate the deficit is to stop making those expensive nickels, and to use the metal instead to make dimes, which are clearly far more profitable.

It's amazing that no one has campaigned for president on this platform.

Why are airline companies dropping like flies? Why don't they make money?

One of these days we will start an airline specially designed for thrill-seekers. It will be famous for spins, nose dives, and mock emergencies. Sometimes the jet would not lift off the runway but instead drive down the interstate at 150 miles an hour, occasionally hopping over annoying slower traffic.

And it would probably go bankrupt. But we probably couldn't even enter Chapter 11 because there's no space left in there for any more airlines.

Why are airlines dropping like flies? Because flying requires too much fancy hardware. It costs a fortune to build a plane and a fortune to keep it running. And such terrible gas mileage! What it all adds up to, says Ray Neidl, an airline analyst with the securities firm Dillon Read, is a fundamental problem: "Costs are higher than revenues."

Neidl says, "Airlines have the worst of all worlds. They're a cyclical business; they're highly unionized, which takes away cost flexibility; they're highly dependent on fuel, which lately has been volatile; they're a service industry, which means that you have to have a lot of employees who are motivated; and on top of that, they're highly capital-intensive."

Oh yes, and terrorism. Bad people like to do things to planes.

This is not to say that airlines are blameless. In the 1980s, corporations everywhere decided that the secret to success was to go wildly into debt. Eastern cranked up debts to the tune of several billion dollars. Ultimately, the airline had to shut down and its planes sold to satisfy the debtors. The underlying problem all dates back to deregulation of the industry in 1978: New carriers like People

Express started offering cheapie fares, and suddenly there were bitter fare wars that sapped everyone's profits.

It's like that old joke about selling books:

He: "It costs me $20 to make a book, and I sell it for only $15."

She: "How can you make money?"

He: "Volume."

Why don't the Japanese make airplanes, since they seem to make everything else in the entire universe?

They do. They just aren't famous for it. Yet.

The victors in World War II (Ford and General Motors, for example) prohibited the Japanese from making any aircraft for seven years. Those seven years were critical in aviation history, because that's when jet engines started replacing propellers. The Japanese company that made the infamous Zero fighter plane—Mitsubishi—went on to make cars and TVs.

In recent decades the revitalized Japanese aviation industry has grown into a hungry adolescence, and there are now incipient fears in the United States that someday we'll all be flying in Hondas. U.S. firms want to head off the Japanese by entering into partial partnerships. For example, Boeing has made a deal with three Japanese aerospace companies, Kawasaki, Fuji, and dear old Mitsubishi, but Boeing claims that this relationship won't allow the superior American aerospace technology to slip into foreign hands. Another possibility, unless the U.S. government intervened, is that a Japanese aerospace firm could simply buy an American one. (Then all in-flight movies presumably would be from Columbia Pictures.)

Why does the economy have recessions but not depressions anymore? Or is this just a government word game?

The thing you really have to fear is when the economy goes into an *obsession*. This is when the normal human drive to become pleasantly rich turns into a craving to be shamelessly, heroically rich—to be the lead guitarist in one's own band of rock-and-roll financiers.

This change of personality needs only a little prodding, which the U.S. government happily provided in the early 1980s. We'll try to summarize what happened in bland, nonpartisan terms (and keep in mind that we're talking about the subject of Economics, which, as a science, ranks somewhere down near Comparative Literature).

First, the government canceled many of the old regulations that restricted how money could be loaned, while keeping intact the extremely favorable tax laws and federal deposit insurance programs that took the sting out of any losses due to boneheaded investments. In effect, the government said to investors, "Go for it, you mad dog."

Soon, the economy was in an obsession. The typical modest business-oriented guy who once contented himself with shooting a round of golf every Wednesday afternoon suddenly decided that, henceforth, he was going to be one of life's Big Winners. He would build hotels! With fancy marble imported from his own private Italian quarry! And so he went to his pal at the local S&L, which would give money to any creature above the evolutionary level of a marmoset. Soon there was this dazzling new hotel on the skyline—the only problem being that at night there were very few actual hotel guests, because they were scattered around town in dozens of other dazzling new hotels.

Ordinary citizens would stare at all the darkened hotel windows at night and wonder, "How does that place make money? Who is paying for that thing?" And these ordinary citizens would presume that they just didn't understand high finance.

But naturally, the answer to the question is that the *or-*

dinary citizens ended up paying for it, through the obscenely expensive government bailout of the S&Ls.

Even if these ambitious new structures weren't foolish enough to begin with, the government compounded the problem in 1986 by eliminating many of the tax breaks for the speculators. It might have been a "good" or a "fair" thing to do, but it essentially changed the rules in the middle of the game. Speculation was initially encouraged and then punished. The government suckered the greedheads.

The direct result was a total collapse of the real estate market, which in turn led to the S&L debacle and the even more frightening crisis that has appeared at this writing in the banking and insurance business. And all that contributed to the 1990–92 recession.

Still, recessions are not quirks. They are part of the "business cycle."

"If it weren't for the '86 tax act, something else would have popped the balloon," argues Robert Reich, Secretary of Labor. He says there's an inevitable tendency for an expanding economy to get out of hand, for debt to become excessive, for speculators to build too many shopping malls in suburbs where no one lives.

"Supply outruns demand," he says. "On the upward swing of an expansionary cycle, everybody anticipates more of the same, and there's some speculation."

So, if a little kid asks you why there are recessions, just say "excessiveness."

Now then: Why no more depressions? One reason is that when consumer demand for stuff is too low, the government can spend more money or cut taxes, which gives everyone a bit more pocket change. Also, various government programs, like unemployment insurance, Social Security, and welfare, function as a kind of ongoing Prozac medication for the economy, preventing capitalism from ever getting too depressed.

On the other hand, as we've seen, government can screw things up too. Indeed, "To some extent, every recession since World War II can be traced to federal budgetary policies," write Robert L. Heilbroner and Lester C. Thurow in their helpful little book, *Economics Explained*.

Actually, some recessions are even desirable. The recession of 1982 was a government invention designed to lower the runaway inflation rate. The Federal Reserve squeezed the money supply so tight that interest rates hit 20 percent. That threw the economy into a recession, which caused prices to level out. In the meantime, unfortunately, lots of folks lost their jobs.

The scary thing is that economics doesn't seem to be getting less mysterious over time. It's an ever more dismal science.

"There are so many things going on in the world economy that are beyond our capability to fully understand," says Jeff Garten, managing director of The Blackstone Group, an investment bank. "There's an enormous amount of money that is sloshing around. There's tremendous liabilities of financial institutions that are not on their balance sheets, exotic financial transactions where risk is swapped, and all kinds of fancy hedges that very few people understand, even the ones that are doing the trades."

Could we ever have another depression, Mr. Smart Businessperson?

"To say there is not going to be another depression is to be a fool," Garten says.

Oh well. Karl Marx said capitalism wouldn't even last this long, so let's count our blessings. (And then get more blessings. And then get huge numbers of blessings, and then borrow some more blessings against our anticipated future blessings, and then . . .)

Why are credit card interest rates so hideously high?

Your passbook savings account gives you a wimpy 3 percent return, yet a bank that issues a credit card wants 19 percent interest. They used to call this "usury" and "loan sharking" when hoodlums did it, but we're more civil now. (Also, federal usury laws were repealed in the early 1980s.)

We have read, here and there, that the reason these rates

are so obscene is that people just don't pay attention. That's probably a piece of the answer: People seem to care more about annual fees than about interest rates. They delude themselves, when they first sign up for the card, into thinking that they will always pay their balance in full and won't pay *any* interest.

But we'll offer two better reasons why the credit card companies charge so much:

1. To make up for the people who don't pay.
2. To make up for all the other bad loans the credit card–issuing banks have made.

About six of every hundred credit card accounts in America end in default, according to Al Lerner, chief executive officer of MBNA, a credit card company. The cost of those defaults is essentially passed on to the rest of us honest folk. A credit card account is just a signature loan; there's no collateral to back up the borrowing. Plus, it's expensive to make itty-bitty loans to millions of people. American Express was charging 16.5 percent on its Optima credit card in 1991, but, according to *The Wall Street Journal*, the operation still lost millions of dollars.

Lerner says the credit card business is very competitive. And it's true that some banks offer cards at 14 percent interest or even less. But most banks are so hard up for money after making horrible loans on real estate during the 1980s that they need to turn a good profit on credit cards. So you, a regular bill-paying customer, are paying 19 percent on your credit card account as a way of subsidizing the grotesque spending habits of millions of over-extended consumers *and* the stupid loans that helped build all those stores in the first place.

The next time you are at a department store, wondering how anyone can afford a $450 dress or an $800 sweater or a $2,000 overcoat, remember that all it takes is a plastic card and a willingness to declare personal bankruptcy or move to an undisclosed location.

Why don't rich people, on their deathbeds, hand over their money to their heirs, rather than waiting and letting the government claim estate taxes?

It's illegal. They say this is a free country and yet your extremely rich and extremely dying Uncle Carbuncle can't hand you a wad of cash moments before he expires. If he does, the Internal Revenue Service will demand its inch of green.

Of course, the IRS has to draw a line somewhere. Each year, Dad and Mom each can give $10,000 tax-free to each deserving child. Every additional dollar over the limit gets hit with a gift tax (33 percent last we checked, but it has probably gone up).

How is this law enforced? By the honor system. Okay, all kidding aside, the government makes you fill out a form if you deposit more than $10,000 in a bank account. You have to say where you got the bread.

There's an easy way to get around the government regulations: put your money in an offshore bank account. In the Cayman Islands, a dozen "banks" may occupy a single small storefront office. In 1984 the Caymans had eighteen thousand residents and eighteen thousand registered corporations. The bank accounts have numbers, no names. Only the banker knows the identity of the depositors. (Cayman Islands law ensures total secrecy.) American newspapers are in heavy demand at the Cayman airport—for the obituaries. If the banker is the only one who knows that the deceased had a secret offshore account, the banker has a *moral obligation* to call the survivors and inform them of the hidden wealth.

This, also, is enforced by the honor system.

GADGETS

Why do we have time-saving gadgets like fax machines and personal computers, and yet feel just as rushed and harried as ever?

There is chaos and lamentation throughout the Why Things Are empire. We're always feeling so rushed, despite all the modern technology that's supposed to save us time and effort—the fax machines, the express overnight mail, the word-processing programs on the personal computer, the LaserJet printers, the electronic databases, our six-seater corporate jet with the built-in Jacuzzi, and so on.

Where, we ask, does the "time saved" go? It seems to disappear. And so we find ourselves strangely nostalgic for inkwells and feather pens, for battered typewriters and carbon paper, for calculators the size of laundry hampers.

This annoying situation is easily explained. These new systems are not designed to save you time. They are designed to *increase your output*.

If the distinction confuses you, ask your boss. She didn't buy these gadgets so you could leave work early.

This is a simple phenomenon of industrial engineering.

ED LAOCOÖN

If it becomes possible to do three days' worth of work in a single day, you won't suddenly get two days off; instead, the labor market changes the definition of "one day's work" (and it reads, "What used to take three days").

Michael Smith, a professor of industrial engineering at the University of Wisconsin, Madison, and an expert in the "human factors" in engineering, points out that this phenomenon has annoyed and frustrated blue-collar workers throughout the twentieth century. Only in recent years, however, has it had a major impact on office workers, and the white-collar crowd is squawking.

"I feel a hell of a lot more time-stressed now," says Smith, "because I can do so much more."

Gavriel Salvendy, editor of the *Handbook of Industrial Engineering*, points out another reason why we're still rushed: That's the American Way. New technology makes us more productive, but as a society we choose to take the financial rewards without changing our basic working life.

In Germany, by contrast, the work week now averages

only thirty-four hours, and six weeks of vacation a year is normal. But Germans don't have our standard of living, Salvendy says. "In America the main thing is to excel and climb up the hierarchy," he says. "In some countries, take France for example, the key issue is to have a good time, to be able to go to nice restaurants."

We should note, by the way, that some of the "efficient" technology of today isn't so efficient after all. Like replacing human switchboard operators with computers. Humans did that job better. Computers are just cheaper.

Is call waiting so great? Not if you like coherent, uninterrupted conversations. What about answering machines? They become surrogates for ourselves, inanimate liaisons that do as much to separate people as bring them together.

Our advice is to put your instruments aside and . . . well, reach out and touch someone. And not just metaphorically.

Why are automatic teller machines uncannily accurate at counting money, even though fresh, crisp bills tend to stick together?

The opacity test. That's the secret.

When you ask for money from an ATM, several factors ensure that you won't get ripped off or get too much. First, you're dealing with a gadget that costs upwards of $25,000. The most important part of the machine, obviously, is the dispensing mechanism. It first counts out your money, then tests the length of each bill, in case one bill is stuck to another and the two are imperfectly overlapping.

Then comes the opacity test. The machine simply shines a light through the bill, onto a photoelectric plate. If the light comes through too dimly, there are probably two bills stuck together. The machine dumps the money into what's called the purge bin and starts the transaction anew.

"A lot of time and effort has gone into that dispenser,"

brags Dave Sacco, a spokesman for NCR, one of the leading makers of ATMs.

But the system still isn't foolproof. A bank employee could accidentally put $20 bills in a canister meant for $10 bills. The machine has no way of telling a Jackson from a Hamilton, Sacco says, but he adds that the government may someday put magnetic markers in the bills that will allow ATMs to distinguish one denomination from another. The Japanese already do that with their yen, wouldn't you know.

Why is there a hesitation before a soda machine coughs up the goods?

We live in an electronic world and have every right to expect machines to behave in chop-chop fashion, like maybe the speed of light wouldn't be too shabby. Yet if you pop seventy-five cents into a soda machine and hit the Diet Cherry 7-Up button, there is always a long pause as though the machine is trying to decide whether it has any Diet Cherry 7-Up left, or, even if it did, whether this is truly a well-conceived beverage.

The thing is, if you intensely crave a Diet Cherry 7-Up, this interval seems to last approximately as long as the entire Falklands War. It may even trigger a memory of the time in high school that you asked a dreamy person to go on a date with you and the answer came back after a delay sufficiently long to allow you to plan your entire suicide, including the dosage-to-body-weight ratios.

Who makes these machines? Intrepidly, we journeyed to the vending alcove of the Why Things Are International Command Bunker, and on the side of the Coke machine we found a small metal plate that read: Dixie-Narco. That's a company in Ranson, West Virginia. (Kids, yet another possible name for your new garage band: Dixie Narco and the Soda Jerks.)

Dick Bline, manager of engineering for the company,

gave us the answers. There are two styles of machines. "Serpentine" is the kind in which the instant you hit the button the can makes a noise inside the machine and appears a second later at the bottom. This is because a hinged panel has dropped out from under the can, allowing the can to roll down a winding rail.

But serpentine machines are not quite as popular anymore, giving way to what Bline calls "dual-adaptable" machines that can handle either cans or bottles. And these are slower—painfully slower for some of us. That's because these machines must be gentler, so as not to break any bottles. The can or bottle rests on its side in a trough. When you put your money in and hit the button, a motor turns a shaft that slowly tilts the trough to one side, until the can or bottle spills out and rolls down a slanted panel. But in the meantime there's that horrible delay while the trough tilts.

We timed it, by the way. It ranges from about 1.75 to 3.5 seconds. Either way, an eternity.

Why does everyone know who invented the light bulb and the telephone and the airplane, but no one knows who invented the television and the computer?

The computer, the computer . . . wasn't it IBM? And the television, that was, uh, let's see . . . Milton Berle?

See, we're just guessing, because the schoolbooks have for some reason refused to distill the historical gibberish down to a single memorable mental nugget, along the lines of "Alexander Graham Bell invented the telephone."

In the haste to simplify history, textbooks tend to promote the myth of the lone genius inventor, and, more broadly, of the "technological breakthrough." A close look at inventions, though, reveals that they are the result of painfully small advances achieved through the toil of countless obscure and forgotten thinkers. Even the Kitty Hawk flight of the Wright brothers, a grand and exhilarating moment, is merely a mechanical triumph, prefigured by the work of countless aeronautic theorists and Icaruses of the past.

"Technological breakthrough is a myth," proclaims Jon Eklund, who ought to know, being curator of the Computers, Information and Society division of the National Museum of American History in Washington, D.C. "On really complex inventions, there really are no inventors."

Inventions are like baby talk: There is a prolonged period of babbling, nonsense, and incoherence, and endless experimentation with simple consonants—*dah*—before finally there emerges a sound that might conceivably and inconclusively be described as a word.

The uncertainty with which we regard the origin of the TV and the computer ought to be applied retroactively to earlier inventions. For example, Alexander Bell and Elisha Gray independently produced telephone prototypes in 1876. Gray arrived at the New York patent office two hours after Bell on February 14, 1876, a delay that may have swayed the judges in a subsequent lawsuit to grant Bell the patent. Bell thereby made a lot of money and bequeathed his name to Ma Bell, but this speaks as much to his travel skills, legal advice, and entrepreneurial instincts as to his inventiveness.

Thomas Edison has clearer title to the light bulb, though he had many helpers in his large lab in Menlo Park, New Jersey. The invention itself didn't come in a flash but rather after studious trial and error with all sorts of filaments and structures and pressure levels and such. His greater breakthrough was to think of illumination *systems*, conceiving of whole cities powered by central generating stations. He didn't just light a bulb, he lit up New York.

The person who probably ought to get credit for the TV is Vladimir K. Zworykin. Zworykin demonstrated the first practical electronic TV system in 1929. But he built on the work of others and has a challenger in Philo T. Farnsworth, who arguably has the better name and who, as early as 1922, developed the electronic scanning system used in TV.

The computer is more troublesome, because it's hard to

say exactly what a computer is. If it's just a calculator, then you have to go back to the seventeenth-century mathematicians Blaise Pascal and Gottfried Leibniz, who made mechanical devices that could count, multiply, divide, and calculate square roots. If you want a more narrow function for your Original Computer, then you have to look at a host of people. Vannevar Bush built a mechanical device in 1930, called a differential analyzer, that is sometimes considered the first computer. We're not sure exactly what it did, but we think it analyzed differentials. Not until 1939, though, did someone apply electricity to such a device, he being John V. Atanasoff. Alan Turing is another candidate for Inventor of Computer stature; he created Colossus, an electronic monstrosity with two thousand tubes that kept track of Nazi coded messages in World War II.

Then there's J. Presper Eckert . . . John W. Mauchly . . . John Von Neumann . . . they all are major players.

Frankly, we think it would be easier if we simply agreed that, henceforth, all textbooks say, "Alexander Graham Bell invented the computer."

Why are the controls on VCRs so complicated that most people can't even set the clock, much less record a program?

This is just the leading edge of a broader crisis: hypergadgetry. What is hypergadgetry? It's a word we made up about five seconds ago, and it will have to do until we can find a more elegant way to label a truly horrible development, namely, that there are too many buttons in our lives.

We have heard estimates that 75 percent of VCR owners have never learned how to record a TV show. For most people, VCRs are just holes into which they can pop a rented movie.

Hypergadgetry began with push-button watches and car dashboards, then extended to photocopiers and fax machines. Now, our beloved telephones, which worked just fine when they only had numbers on them, suddenly look like they could order up an entire nuclear war. The fancy new AT&T phones in the Why Things Are bunker have fifty-three buttons each, and we have this horrible suspicion that all of them have multiple functions, and the total number of uses could be something like fifty-three *cubed*. There is also a helpful digital screen that flashes such messages as "Clock needs to be reset." Some of the buttons have inscrutable labels: One says "Drop," with a smaller word underneath, "Test." No way are we going to press that button. (We are guessing that if you hit the "Test" button the digital display screen says something like, "What is the central theme of *Finnegans Wake*?")

There is a simple technical explanation for what has happened here: The microchip has made it possible to cram lots of functions into a small device. But still, why has the home electronics industry gotten the idea that we want our household gadgets to become more, rather than less, complicated? Who are these fiends?

"On the design team there were engineers, marketing people, manufacturing people, component procurement people, business planners . . . and nobody who knows how to design the human interface of complex microprocessor products," explains Arnold Wasserman, dean of the school of art and design at the Pratt Institute in New York.

More simply put (ahem), nearsighted geeks who carry around very sharp pencils have designed our gadgets and written the instruction manuals without pausing to realize that actual humans must use them. For example, the Xerox Corp.'s 8200 office copier bombed when it first hit the market in the early 1980s because using it required virtually a Ph.D. in button pushing.

Many other companies are coming to the conclusion that simpler is better, *Business Week* reported in 1991. Wasserman says, "The trend [toward fancier gadgets] has not peaked. There is only a salutary counter-trend toward making things easier and simpler."

But now here's a promising new development: In the

future, you won't have to mess with lots of buttons when you want to record a program or set the clock on your VCR. Instead, you can just shout at it. That's right. You will be able to order your gadgets around. You could say, "I wanna see 'The Simpsons,' and I wanna see 'em *right now.*"

"You could just speak to the VCR. There would be speech recognition capabilities," says Daniel T. Ling, an IBM executive whose official title, Manager of Veridical User Environments, needs a bit of simplifying itself.

IBM is also designing computers that can read your handwriting. That way you can write in the old-fashioned way, scripting your thoughts, and the computer will understand. Meanwhile, all the devices in your house, ranging from the TV to the computer to the alarm clock to the burglar alarm to the coffee maker, will be interconnected electronically, and thus able, Ling said, "to speak to one another."

There's got to be a horror film in this.

Why does the alphabet on the telephone start on the 2 button rather than on the 1? And why aren't the letters *Q* and *Z* used?

Long ago, the phone system was really primitive. How primitive was it? So primitive that, instead of buttons, they had "dials." This was some kind of circular configuration with holes for your fingers corresponding to the numbers. Hard to believe, but true.

Anyway, when you dialed the 1, it sent out a pulse, a single clicking sound (a 2 sent two clicks, a 3 sent three clicks, and so on). According to Chuck Starnes of Bell Laboratories in Indianapolis, the fussy old switching equipment at the phone company got confused sometimes. A random clicking sound might cause the equipment to think someone was starting to dial a number beginning with 1, when they actually weren't. Thus a rule was made: No phone number can start with 1. This rule is still observed, though solely for the sake of tradition—you now dial 1 to get access to the long-distance network, and this doesn't cause any confusion for the modernized equipment.

As for the alphabet, it's there to help you remember numbers. This was particularly necessary in the old days, when phone books weren't as common as they are now. The telephone companies used letters instead of numbers to identify exchanges. Instead of 555-5000, the number would be labeled KL-5-5000, which would be relayed orally as "Klondike five, five thousand." (Note that we are using the standard TV phone number prefix that gives you directory assistance.) In California and New York some diehards still use letters routinely.

Since phone numbers couldn't start with 1, Ma Bell didn't want to put the ABC there. So the alphabet started with 2. Unfortunately, the 0 was reserved for "Oper," so there was space for only twenty-four letters, not twenty-six. They bumped the seldom-used Q and Z.

The real question is, what should we say now instead of "dialing the number"?

Beeping the number?

Stabbing the number?

The perfect word, unfortunately, is already taken: "Prestidigitation."

Why do some clock faces with Roman numerals use IIII instead of IV?

For symmetry. The IIII balances the VIII on the other side of the face. If they used the less substantial IV, the clock face would look slightly lopsided, throwing the entire space–time continuum out of whack.

Why can't you dry clothes in a microwave?

Fire. Death. That sort of thing.

This is not a whimsical matter: Even as we speak, smart scientist-type people are trying to develop a microwave clothes dryer.

Obviously, one problem with putting a shirt in a microwave is that you will get a hot, albeit still wet shirt. There's nothing to ventilate the moisture. But that could be easily fixed.

"The biggest problem is that you've got to have an adequate sensor system to determine that it's dry before it gets *too* dry. We don't want to have to install fire extinguishers," says Robert LaGasse, executive director of the International Microwave Power Institute.

You see, microwaves are more powerful than just plain hot air. A hot-air dryer can parch your clothing, but the temperature will never rise above about 140 degrees. A standard microwave device, however, doesn't operate on low power. It goes full blast. The only way to control this is by shutting the machine off. If you leave a cup of coffee in a microwave too long, it will simply boil off. But your drawers, as we like to call them, might get so hot they'd catch fire.

Fortunately, there is a new technology that will allow microwave devices to operate on low heat. But there's still the metal problem. We all know that if you put metal in a microwave something terrible like Three Mile Island will happen. Clothes have metal in them. Zippers. Buttons. Rivets. What the microwave people are hoping is that clothing manufacturers will help them out by making clothes that are—you got it—"microwave safe."

Why does the pipe under the kitchen sink make that funny U-turn?

You know, the one from Liquid Plumr and Drāno commercials. The one with the hair and grease and crud and scuzz slowly accreting in a thick blob of putrescence. What's it for? Isn't there a more sensible design?

Also repels Goblins
& Drain Bogeys

We started our research by simply asking folks around the office. Here's what they said:

"It's there to catch hair and stuff."

"It has something to do with more time travel for hot water."

"It collects dropped forks, knucklebones, whatever."

"It has to do with getting the hairballs to move out faster."

Wrong-o-rama! Obviously, you should never ask a journalist to fix your toilet. We got the real answer from an actual plumber, Mike Vito, of Washington, D.C.: "It's a trap to keep sewer gas from coming back up into the atmosphere."

The U-shaped portion of the pipe is literally called a "trap," and that term may have caused much of the confusion. People assume a trap is designed to trap things that fall into the drain. In fact, it's there to trap water. The sewer gas, which isn't under pressure, can't penetrate that water barrier.

Toilets have built-in traps, and showers and tubs often have them in the wall. The down side of the traps is that, yes, they trap crud and get clogged up. This makes you wonder: Are these traps actually a conspiracy of the Drano lobby and the Plumbing Industrial Complex?

"If you did away with the trap and put up with the smell for a while, I think you'd rather have the stoppages," Vito assured us.

One other thought: Do the water traps keep rats from crawling up out of the sewer? No. Rats can swim. But you shouldn't worry. Because rats don't live in sewers.

We got this information from Richard Kramer, spokesman for the National Pest Control Association in Dunn Loring, Virginia. He said it's highly unlikely that a sewer rat will turn into a toilet rat. Sewers are sealed tight, as a rule. Rats might live in storm sewers, but those aren't linked to your plumbing.

Footnote: Our column really brought the rats out of the woodwork—er, the plumbing, that is.

Laura Brown, of Washington, D.C., informs us that she found a rat in her toilet not once but twice last year. "It was a big rat. A huge rat. It was wet and it was trying to get out," she said.

Reader Laura Miller says that when she lived in Georgetown a few years ago her son found "a very large, very wet rat emerging from the toilet." It ran out the front door. "The last we saw of him, he was running down Thirty-fifth Street, his wet coat glistening in the sun."

And finally, Phillip Alcorn, of Richmond, Virginia, told us his wife found a rat in the toilet recently, abruptly ending what was to have been a potty training session for their two-year-old daughter.

We will spare you further details of this situation—suffice it to say that the Alcorns dealt with the matter with massive amounts of bug spray and a barbecue fork—but we will point out that in each case there is no firm evidence that the rat came up from the sewer. More likely the rat was in the house and was looking for a drink. The Alcorns note that they keep their lid closed, but, according to

Kramer, "a rat can lift the lid and get inside the toilet."

In an old part of a city, such as downtown Richmond, where the Alcorns live, there may be a slightly higher chance that a home's plumbing is tied into an old, beaten-up sewer system, and that might allow a sewer rat to set up camp, but in general there are no rats in sewers because the sewers are sealed tight. "I won't say it's impossible for them to come up through the sewer, but it's not a likely thing to happen," says our expert.

So calm down. Take a deep breath. Rats probably are not going to come out of the toilet.

Because they already live in the house.

Why can you recognize someone's voice over the telephone even though it has been turned into an electrical signal?

You would think that somewhere along the suboceanic cable, or in the empty space between microwave transmission towers, your voice would become that of a robot, or a total stranger—someone from Boston, for example.

The secret is inside the phone. It's a metal plate called a diaphragm. This thing is a direct steal from nature's design of the human eardrum. The process goes like this: You hold the phone to your mouth and say something like "The Czech's in the mail." The sound of your voice ripples through the air in distinctive waves, molecules knocking each other along in a chain reaction, transmitting sound in a process you are quick to call "conduction." Your own particular ripple pattern is distinctive; that's what makes a voice print ID an accurate tool. The sound hits the diaphragm inside the phone, like sheets of rain. The metal plate vibrates.

Then comes a wonderful trick. The metal plate is attached to a pack of carbon granules, as in certain cigarette filters. These granules have an electric current running through them. When the metal plate shakes, the granules jitter about, causing surges in the juice. The better the engineering of the phone, the more accurately your voice is translated into an electrical language. (Okay, so we're wobbling a bit here at the crucial moment.) Like Morse code, this electrical message races along the phone lines at close to the speed of light, directed by switches and circuits that are far beyond the Why staff's capacity to understand, much less explain, and then arrives at your friend's phone. As the electrical current hems and haws, a magnet in your friend's phone tugs at the metal diaphragm, causing the plate to vibrate. Sound ripples from the phone.

Sounds like . . . you.

Why doesn't a "busy" signal on the phone cease and desist the moment the person you are calling gets off the line?

There's both a technical reason and a business reason that you can't just stick on the line and wait for the busy signal to stop. The technical reason is that the sound isn't coming from your friend over there on the other side of town, it's coming from the central switching office of the phone company. (The tone is generated by a gadget sensibly called a tone generator.)

That said, the main reason you can't stick on the line is that the phone company doesn't want you to. You're tying up a line. So get off the phone.

Why are the numbers on calculators upside down from those on push-button telephones?

C an't we get some consistency around here? C'mon! This is driving us nuts. Look at your phone. The top three numbers, left to right, are 1, 2, and 3. That makes so much sense, doesn't it? But now look at your calculator or at any adding machine. The whole thing is inverted. The top three numbers are 7, 8, and 9.

We called Hewlett-Packard. Neither Mr. Hewlett nor Mr. Packard was available, so we talked instead to a public relations person who told us that basically the phone company was at fault.

Adding machines go way back to virtually the pre-Cambrian era, and they have always used that same configuration. But—this is the legend among the Calculator People—when the phone company created push-button phones, it intentionally inverted the numbers, to slow down the fingers of all those accountants and other people trained on adding machines. (It's not clear whether this was merely an attempt to be mean, or to ensure that people were careful and accurate when punching in the number.)

The phone company says this legend is hogwash. We spoke to Blake Wattenbarger, who is the human factors psychologist at AT&T Bell Laboratories in New Jersey ("Daddy, why can't you just be a *regular* doctor, like the other daddies?"). Wattenbarger says that when the phone company first started playing around with push buttons, it simply didn't think about the way calculators are arranged.

And you know what? That's obviously the truth. We've argued all along that life is a lot more random than you think.

Besides, he says, the phone setup is better. It's been proved. There was a study done of thirty "housewives" (what a grotesque word) reported in the journal *Ergonomics* in 1968. By a narrow margin, they could work the phone arrangement faster and more accurately than the calculator arrangement.

This whole topic, we are told, is now under review by something called—it sounds rather foreboding—the International Standards Organization.

When they finish with telephones, maybe they can do something about all the awful neckties.

Why is aluminum foil shiny on one side and dull on the other?

It has nothing to do with how you're supposed to use the stuff. That aluminum foil is shiny on one side is unintentional and meaningless. It just comes out that way at the factory. What they do is put two sheets of raw, unfinished aluminum foil on top of one another, like two bedsheets, and then they feed them through bright, high-chrome steel rolling pins. The shine comes from the contact with the metal rollers.

Thus the outer sides of the twinned aluminum sheets become shiny but not the inner sides.

The reason they double the sheets up is simply for efficiency and ease of operation. So you can wrap up the baked potato either way, but shiny side out is prettier.

Why does the passenger-side mirror on a car say, "Objects in mirror are closer than they appear"?

Truly, that is one of the great lines in the English language. It's so shamelessly blunt. It might as well say, "Mirror designed by a total ding-dong."

Surely the reason for this is obvious. As you move away from a mirror, the field of view grows smaller. Thus, that tiny mirror four or five feet away from the driver would hardly have anything in it if it weren't convex. But the convex shape has the unfortunate side effect of making things appear farther away. The safety benefit of the larger field of view is believed to outweigh the danger from the distortion. These mirror designs are covered by government regulations, which probably is why the mirrors seem to have been designed by committee.

Of course, the car could simply have a big, flat mirror over there, but that would be unsightly. And it would be a drag, literally.

Why don't they make things as well as they used to make them? Why are antiques so much better than stuff made today?

Go to the Smithsonian's National Museum of American History and you will come away wishing desperately that you could have been alive back in the days when ordinary people had furniture made of real wood, and dishes made of pewter, and cars made with gobs of chrome. Of course you died young of polio, but no matter, you had lovely possessions. What happened?

Six things:

1. Junk disintegrated. All the really lousy antiques have fallen apart by now.

"The stuff that survives is the stuff that's well made. The high-quality stuff is giving us the mistaken impression that everything was of high quality," says Peter Liebhold of the museum's Division of Engineering and Industry.

2. The stuff that survived isn't as good as you think.

"We just recently took apart an 1850s milling machine," Liebhold says, "and it really had some absolutely abysmal work done on it, but it was all tucked away where no one could see it."

He says that if you examine nineteenth-century metal artifacts you will be surprised by how poor the metal is, how the iron is full of slag, and how steel is almost nonexistent. Things had to be built sturdily—massively—to allow for a huge margin of error, in case some of the materials were weak. Today, that bulkiness strikes us as pleasantly generous.

Notwithstanding answers 1 and 2, the perceived erosion of quality isn't entirely a misimpression. A lot of things made in recent decades really have been inferior to what came before. So let's continue:

3. Cheap products are the hallmark of a relatively modern invention, the "middle class."

Prior to the Industrial Revolution, much of what was manufactured was for snotty rich people. Alexis de Tocqueville wrote, "When only the wealthy had watches they were very good ones." In her essay "The Decline of Quality," historian Barbara Tuchman wrote, "The decline that has since set in has a good historical reason: The age of privilege is over and civilization has passed into the age of the masses."

4. The middle class gradually became inept at shopping.

Roger Kennedy, director of the aforesaid museum, says that in the Olden Days, before the division of labor got out of hand, people not only knew how to make their own axes and their own butter and their own clothes, they also knew the difference between a good product and a bad product. Progressivists in the 1800s assumed that the Industrial Revolution would lead to better consumer goods because of the benefits of specialization. Instead what happened, says Kennedy, was that the "taste-making middle class" degenerated into a "readily manipulated component of the mass market."

5. Ornament became unfashionable.

Much of what we admire about older things is mere flamboyance. The rise of design theory in the early 1900s led to a backlash against ornamentation. Art nouveau gave way to modernism. The new aesthetic emphasized Function. For example, the huge machine-tool maker Brown and Sharpe redesigned its sewing machine in 1911 to get rid of all curvilinear shapes. In his 1988 article "The Theory of

Machine Design in the Second Industrial Age," in the *Journal of Design History*, Tim Putnam noted the case of a lathe with legs that looked like those of horses. Sure, they looked neat, but "they impeded working movements, were mechanically incorrect, and suggested that the machine was something other than a machine."

Yes, before there was "politically correct" there was "mechanically correct."

6. Labor and materials now cost more.

You just can't get those nimble little nine-year-old factory workers anymore.

PROGRESS OR REGRESS?

(In which we try to figure out whether
the world is getting better or worse.
Or is just consistently awful.)

I was bitterly disappointed when I walked into the World Future Society headquarters and saw that no one was wearing a space suit or wraparound goggles or even those lame pajamalike shirts that Kirk and Spock wore on "Star Trek." In fact, the World Future Society is an unassuming collection of offices in a forgettable building on a side street in Bethesda, Maryland, itself a rather pedestrian suburb of Washington. A lean Ivy League–looking gentleman named Tim Willard explained, without hint of apology, "If you went to the National Asphalt Association, you wouldn't expect people to be wearing work belts and dressed like a road crew."

I had come here with some big questions, the kind of questions that go beyond a simple "why" and "how" and get deeply into the "whither." Such as: Whither Earth? More specifically, is human civilization careening toward destruction, and taking much of the natural world with it? Or is that just an illusion, however well-supported by statistics, surveys, and anecdotes?

Long ago people believed in something called "Progress." Life got better. This was simply understood. Somewhere along the line, though, "Progress" became a reactionary notion, a cockamamie idea if not an outright hoax. We began to use the word ironically—it described a parking lot that paved over a lovely forest glen. In our new maturity we began to believe in a new paradigm. Call it Regress.

What makes the situation all the more complicated is that the very artifacts of the Progress paradigm (my car, for example) lead directly to the artifacts of Regress (air pollution).

How should we interpret this? Which is it, Progress or Regress?

Ed Cornish came into the room. He's the head of the institute, a famous futurist, a man of small stature and big ideas.

He said, "I believe it is totally impossible to scientifically prove that we have had Progress. . . . Now, if you say, have we improved humans' technological capability, the answer is yes. Yet you could say this is not really important, that what matters is humans' spiritual progress. A lot of people will say we have made no progress there, and others would argue we've deteriorated in terms of human happiness."

Hmmm . . . a good point. Are we talking about objective, measurable changes, like interstate highways and antiseptic hospitals? Or subjective, immeasurable changes, like whether the human spirit is any closer to a state of grace?

Cornish weighed in with his own verdict. "I see Progress, as of now, outweighing Regress, and I hope it will continue. My belief is that it's not possible to know if it will continue or not. That's why we're here, to see to it that it *will* continue."

My own gut feeling is that we are much better at seeing what is wrong with the world than at seeing what is right, a characteristic that probably has served the species well over the years. Gloom may be part of our nature, a survival strategy, a *skill*. For the past three decades, people have talked about the myth of Progress, but perhaps it's now time to talk about the myth of the "the myth of Progress." The world has this quirky knack of subtly improving itself even as it appears, to the skeptical investigator, to be worsening dramatically. Sure, modern life is a nightmare—but anyone who wishes he had been born 150 years ago is either crazy or a member of the English nobility.

My generation of Americans was fully indoctrinated in the politics of fear and dread. I remember an elementary school teacher telling my class that "experts" were doubtful that the world would even exist in five years—a nice thing to tell kids barely old enough to ride a bike. The specific threat, in this case, was nuclear war, but we understood that we were victims of a more general misfortune, that of being born into the modern world, a world gone mad.

All the evils that had befallen us—drugs, divorce, smokestacks, assassinations, Charles Manson, My Lai, H-bombs, and suburban tract housing—were specifically the product of modernity; they were the very things that described what modernity *meant*. And these were only the known evils, because modernity had this bad habit of springing new unforeseen terrors on you.

What had happened is that a three-century trend had been reversed. The belief in Progress, a secularized version of the Christian concept of Providence, dates back at least to the seventeenth century. At that time, Progress was a spiritual concept, something that described the gradual perfection of the human soul. Not until the nineteenth century and the arrival of the Industrial Revolution did the notion take hold that Progress would mean economic growth and the democratization of wealth and education. By the turn of the twentieth century the palpable evidence of Progress was everywhere: illuminated cities, horseless carriages, even flying machines. How could you *not* believe in Progress? It was right there in front of, and above, everyone.

"From at least the early nineteenth century until a few decades ago, belief in the progress of mankind, with Western civilization in the vanguard, was virtually a universal religion on both sides of the Atlantic," writes Robert Nisbet in *History of the Idea of Progress*. He says this idea has "led to more creativeness in more spheres, and given more strength to human hope and to individual desire for improvement than any other single idea in Western history."

Regress emerged gradually. It may have had its origins in the aftermath of World War I, that strangely pointless war of unprecedented bloodshed. As the war climaxed in 1918, Oswald Spengler, a German philosopher, argued in *The Decline of the West* that all civilizations rise and fall, a natural and irreversible process, and that Western civilization had already peaked. The coming of the Great Depression convinced many that the Marxist and Spenglerian prophecies were correct, that capitalism had run its course (though Marx would call *this* Progress!). World War II then showed that an advanced, technological civilization might be nothing more than an elaborately organized form of barbarism, and that modernity's ultimate end could as easily be mass murder as it could be utopia.

Perhaps the true progression of civilization would be toward a crushing of the individual spirit, a fear dramatized by George Orwell's postwar novel *1984*. There is a famous passage in which the torturer O'Brien says to Winston Smith, "Progress in our world will be progress toward more pain. The old civilizations claimed that they were founded on love and justice. Ours is founded upon hatred. In our world there will be no emotions except fear, rage, triumph, and self-abasement. Everything else we shall destroy—everything. . . . If you want a picture of the future, imagine a boot stamping on a human face—forever."

The book is kind of a downer, yes.

Despite these horrible visions of the future, the general public still believed in Progress. But then came the atom bomb. The superpowers built nuclear arsenals capable of destroying the world, and suddenly, how could you not believe in Regress?

Doom and gloom suddenly became marketable. Paul Ehrlich sold three million copies of his 1968 book *The Pop-*

ulation Bomb, in which he pointed out that the world's population was doubling every 35 years, and "if growth continued at that rate for about 900 years, there would be some 60,000,000,000,000,000 people on the face of the earth. Sixty million billion people. This is about 100 persons for each square yard of the Earth's surface, land and sea."

The political science professor Richard Falk wrote in his 1971 book *This Endangered Planet* that, because of multiple warheads being attached to individual nuclear missiles, "a single submarine commander, if able to overcome command and control safeguards, is thereby empowered to destroy almost all major urban life on the planet."

Yikes! How do you sleep?

The idea of Regress may have been best illustrated by the Crying Indian. You know the commercial. Some jerky suburbanites throw their litter out the window. It lands on the bank of a stream. The Indian—representing the pre-industrial, pre-Progress world—paddles up in a canoe from out of nowhere. He sheds a monster tear. How could you not cry along?

At some point, we hit a gloom glut. The Union of International Associations in Brussels came up with a list of world problems in 1986. There were more than ten thousand.

One is reminded of a line by Woody Allen in his story "My Speech to the Graduates": "Mankind stands at a crossroads. One path leads to despair and hopelessness. The other, to total destruction. Let us pray we have the wisdom to choose correctly."

Gloomy predictions have a funny way of not coming true.

The world didn't end within five years. Not even close. The superpowers somehow had the wisdom never to launch their nuclear weapons, and eventually one of the main belligerents simply closed up operations.

The world also didn't run out of oil. Gas actually got cheaper, in constant dollars.

The global birthrate, once increasing rapidly, has fallen, from about 2.1 percent in the early 1960s to about 1.8 percent today. (Hardly satisfactory, but at least the trend has gone in the right direction.)

Some mechanism seems to be at work, altering the dismal trajectory of the planet. Could it possibly be . . . Progress? Or, less lyrically, could it be that human beings are smart enough to adapt to changing conditions? Could it be that we're not so dumb after all?

The world never seems to ride that handbasket all the way to Hell. In fact, it's a safe bet that the world will get better rather than worse—as Julian Simon found out.

Simon, an economist at the University of Maryland, is the ultimate Pollyanna. He is loathed by environmentalists. He thinks the world not only is going to get better, but already is better than ever before, and that anyone who says otherwise is a ridiculous doomsayer.

Simon and Paul Ehrlich made a wager in 1980. It was Simon's idea. Simon had challenged the common-sense notion that prices for nonrenewable resources would go up over time due to increasing scarcity. Simon claimed that the reverse would happen—that human ingenuity ("the ultimate resource," in Simon's view) would make those same resources go down in price. He challenged any and all Malthusians to bet him on the issue. Ehrlich denounced Simon's view as absurd, saying Simon was the leader of a "space-age cargo cult" that believed resources would fall to the earth from heaven. And Ehrlich took the bet. He placed $1,000 on his five picks: chrome, copper, nickel, tin, and tungsten. The way the bet worked, if the prices rose after ten years (in real terms after taking inflation into account), Simon would pay Ehrlich the amount of the increase, and if the prices fell, Ehrlich would pay that amount to Simon.

Ten years passed.

The earth's population grew by 800 million.

Chrome, copper, nickel, tin, and tungsten fell in price.

Why did these metals get cheaper? Because, according to an analysis by *The New York Times*, new lodes of the metals were discovered, technology made it possible to extract them from the earth more efficiently, an international tin cartel was broken up, and cheaper materials came onto the market and made the old-fashioned metals less valuable.

Ehrlich sent Simon a check for $576.07.

Ehrlich argues that prices will eventually rise on nonrenewable resources, that Simon is like a guy who jumps off a skyscraper and, passing the tenth floor, shouts out that he's fine so far.

I visited Simon in Chevy Chase, Maryland, and he gave me his whole spiel. He said nutrition is better throughout the world; educational opportunities have improved, and that every objective measure of human welfare has shown an improvement.

"Our air and water are cleaner than ever before," he said.

I asked, "What about the depletion of natural resources that are nonrenewable?"

Silly question.

"We have more resources every year; that's the bottom line," he said.

Oil?

"We have more oil every year. I know it boggles the mind. I'm telling you things that cannot possibly be understood because they're against common sense."

Is there nothing in this world that Simon finds less than wonderful? Simon finally conceded that, good news aside, he can't really say that people are happier or better off in any way other than the purely material ones. That's a matter of philosophy.

"I'm just an economist," he said.

Hmmm . . . so he's a gung-ho believer in Progress, but only as it can be *objectively* measured. And objective measurements are possibly the least important ones; it's what we *feel* that really matters.

There's another nagging doubt here: Is optimism even useful? Would you want someone like Julian Simon—someone who says things are just wonderful—running the country? (Maybe someone like Julian Simon has been running the country in recent years, but never mind.)

This is one of the great ironies of Progress: The people who fear for the future may be more likely to construct a better world than those who are complacent. It may be true that the press and the academic experts are overly negative and have created an illusion of a world falling apart, but the alternative is worse: feel-goodism run rampant.

If the pessimists are right, or even partly correct, then the world is at a crucial juncture, a point where it must head toward long-term sustainable development or collapse in a convergence of crises. Lester Brown, head of the Worldwatch Institute, told me, "My sense is that the die is pretty well going to be cast in this decade. We'll either get a lot of these trends turned around, or we'll find that environmental degradation will lead to economic decline in more and more of the world, and the two will be feeding on one another."

In fact, whether you embrace a positive view of the future or a negative one may depend on how much value you give to intellectual achievements—understanding the structure of the universe, the charge of the atom, the hidden genius of the double-helix DNA molecule, the evolution of the octopus's eyeball. Knowledge shouldn't have to prove itself with practical applications; even the most useless and pointless knowledge should count for something.

Then again, you might argue that knowledge is dangerous, as when the secret of the atom inspires weapons of mass murder. At the least it is a contaminant of innocence, turning Eskimos into snowmobilers and Amazon tribesmen into chainsaw-wielding capitalists. The fear of knowledge goes back a bit: The Jews told of the drastic consequences when Adam and Eve ate the fruit of the tree of knowledge, and the Greeks described all manner of evils when Pandora's curiosity drove her to open that box.

The knowledge-is-bad idea is related to a more general philosophical construction: Good News Is Actually Bad News.

For example, Communism collapses. Good news, right? Silly fool, the breakdown of the post-World War II order has led to chaos! We are witnessing the rise of the most dangerous sort of political factionalism, that of ethnic nationalism—remember Hitler? (For more on this, see "On the Road to Ruin: Winning the Cold War, Losing the Economic Peace" in *Harper's*, March 1990, and "Why We Will Soon Miss the Cold War," in *The Atlantic*, August 1990.)

Another example: Life is more comfortable now, for many people. Good news? Nope. As life gets "better," it becomes somewhat less heroic, and it is possible to reach a state of discontentment even though by every measurable index one's life is wonderful.

This is part of the message of Christopher Lasch, a leading proponent of the Good News Is Bad News concept and the author of a thick book called *The True and Only Heaven: Progress and Its Critics*. Things that most people think are *objectively* good are, for Lasch, the reprehensible markers of a degenerate society. Lasch rejects many of the allegedly wonderful artifacts of Progress—better medicine, welfare society programs, child labor laws, you name it—on the grounds that they are actually ruining the human spirit, destroying our heroic selves, replacing the true man/woman with a new creation who is basically a wimp.

For example, child labor laws "obscured the positive possibility of children working alongside their parents at jobs of recognized importance," he said in a recent interview. In another book he wrote, "new ideas of sexual liberation—the celebration of oral sex, masturbation, and homosexuality—spring from the prevailing fear of heterosexual passion, even of sexual intercourse itself." As for the rise of professional armies, this usurps the rights of citizens to participate in war (war is apparently a good thing).

"The attraction of progressive ideology . . . turns out to be its greatest weakness: Its rejection of a heroic conception of life," he writes.

Excuse us while we go strangle a grizzly bear.

So, now let's float the counterargument (assuming we have license to be ridiculous). If good news is indeed a form of bad news, the reciprocal must also be true: Bad News Is Good News.

The greenhouse effect? That's good news—it has shocked us into thinking globally and, though a relatively benign catastrophe by the standards of things like nuclear war, may lead to a new approach to both resources and the environment that will serve the planet well for millennia. Almost overnight, the planet has been reexamined as a single unit, as a biosphere, and in the year 789116, people will remember the late twentieth century the way we think of the fifth century B.C. in Athens, the era of Aristotle and Socrates.

(Maybe.)

Progress has an obvious flaw as a description of human history: It is not universal.

Jonathan Kozol, in his 1975 book *The Night Is Dark and I Am Far From Home*, criticized elementary schools for continuing to teach the myth of Progress, because he said that myth provides "the sense of self-awarded respite from concern for those who *are* in trouble on the part of those who *aren't*." Kozol wrote that in his poor neighborhood of blacks and Puerto Ricans, Progress never showed up: "Things did not get better. They grew worse. Twisted, contorted lives grew only more intricately twisted."

The quincentennial of 1492 saw much controversy over whether the voyage of Columbus should be seen as a great discovery or the beginning of a genocide. What was Progress for the Europeans was Regress to the native American cultures. Do we dare glorify the ingenuity of a Genoan sailor when it led to such grief for a less technological, less militant people?

This is the paradox of Progress: It is a fitful, uneven thing, a five steps forward and four steps back process. Humankind's great challenge is not so much to build the perfect mousetrap, but to subdue and transform its own worst instincts; unfortunately it has been a slow evolution from the law of the jungle to the law of civil society, from the rule of might to the rule of right. And one of the least successful attributes of Progress has been its ability to measure out the good life in fair shares.

Now, back to the World Future Society.

There was a strange little twist to my conversation with Ed Cornish, the futurologist. We discussed a philosophical conundrum: If Progress improves our overall condition, in terms of food and housing and spare time and intellectual freedom, but we don't notice it—if, that is, we are spoiled by our own successes—is it possible that we are "objectively" happier but just don't realize it? And if we don't realize it, isn't that the same thing as *not* being happier? What's the point of Progress if no one gets off on it?

Cornish has a thought: Someday, we'll be able to measure happiness. Not with crude questionnaires, but with neurological tests. Wires. Electrodes. Brain waves. We'll root around in the endorphins. We'll know for sure.

"A lot of people who think they're unhappy are really quite happy. And once they've been shown the results of the scientific test of their happiness, they might decide that they're happy after all."

And if they're not, we can fix that too.

"We may be able to program people to be happier, to change their genetic structure. I think that's a reasonable expectation," Cornish said.

Perhaps we could even give people happy pills. They would be blissed out. (That's actually part of the plot of a novel written back in 1932: *Brave New World*.)

If that's the future—engineering human beings for perfection—I'd rather be morose and sullen and stuck in the present.

The simpler solution is the better one. People should just learn to keep their fears in perspective. There's a lot to worry about. Be happy anyway.

HISTORY

Why did the Vikings, after going to all the trouble of discovering North America, fail to populate it?

It got cold. That was a big part of it.

But first you have to realize that the Vikings didn't have royal backing the way Columbus did. They were wildcatters, freelance plunderers, show-up-without-calling-first houseguests. As marauders go, they weren't terribly ambitious: They tended to invade sparsely populated islands and set up some Viking farms. Viking fathers would gesture dramatically at these newfound lands as they told their sons, "Just imagine, someday this will all be beets."

If you look at a map of the Northern Atlantic, you see it is possible to reach North America from Europe through a series of jumps, starting at Norway, moving on to the Faeroes, then to Iceland, then Greenland, and finally Newfoundland. That's exactly how the Vikings did it.

A Viking ship headed for Iceland was blown off course and found Greenland in the tenth century. Just before the turn of the millennium, another sailor got blown off course and hit North America. He went home and told his Viking pals, and soon Leif Ericson paid a visit to Newfoundland with a few dozen hardy colonizers.

They figured they had merely found some more islands. As Daniel Boorstin notes in *The Discoverers*, the Vikings didn't really discover North America. "Was there ever so long a voyage that made so little difference?" They missed the point, just like that record company guy who turned down the Beatles in the early sixties. (In fairness, though, even Columbus missed the point; he insisted to his death that Cuba was the Asian mainland and the planet was pear-shaped.)

Why didn't the Vikings eventually drift down to Daytona Beach and hit the bars during spring break? To this day there are goofballs who insist the Vikings went all over the place. Viking myths even persist among some of the Scandinavians who settled in large numbers in the northern Midwest (which is one reason they call their football team the Minnesota Vikings). But in truth, the Vikings explored only a little bit of the East Coast, possibly getting as far down as what is now Massachusetts. The one settlement lasted only about two decades, because the Europeans didn't get along with the locals. In fact the Skraelings, as the Vikings called the native inhabitants, attacked the Vikings with moose-bladder buzz bombs. Our sources don't explain how these things were made or what they were filled with (water? codfish oil? moose pee?), but no doubt these weapons are currently being developed by Saddam Hussein. Eventually the Norsemen packed it in and shipped home.

Greenland, meanwhile, was becoming more inhospitable as the climate grew colder, and eventually all the Scandinavians left or died. The Viking era essentially ended in the mid-eleventh century as sailors drifted back to the homeland, became integrated into Western European culture, and abandoned Thor and Odin for mainstream Christian beliefs.

Let's face it, Scandinavians have been a little dull ever since. (We were deeply saddened to learn recently that the Vikings never did wear helmets with horns.)

Why is Christopher Columbus known by so many different names, such as Cristobal Colon and Cristoforo Colombo?

Hardly anyone has ever had a name as indefinite as that guy in 1492.

What did he call himself? "The Admiral," in most of his writings. In the introduction to the log of his first voyage it says "I, Cristobal Colon," but the real log itself was lost, and all that remains is a handwritten copy by a Spanish biographer. In his own hand, he once wrote his name "Xpoual Colon," in which the X is the Latin abbreviation of Christ, which hints at a bit of an ego problem.

"Columbus" is derived from the Latin version of his name, first appearing in the writings of Petrus Martyr, an Italian who held office in the church of Spain. The English, Dutch, and northern Europeans preferred this latinization.

Surely he had a name at birth, right? Well, we think he was born in Genoa (now a part of Italy) as "Cristoforo Colombo," though another record says "Christofferus de Colombo." By the time he began hanging out in Spain he called himself Colon. The switch from Colombo to Colon is strange, since Colombo would have fit the Castilian tongue just fine. What was he up to?

One biographer, Salvador de Madariaga, claims that this name change is evidence that Columbus was a Jew. (Proving Columbus was Jewish has been a cottage industry for years, though it all sounds mighty speculative.) Madariaga wrote, "May we point out how Jewish this [the name changing] all is? The men of the wandering race are so often bound to shift the conditions of their existence that, with them, change of name has become habit, practically unknown though it is to the rest of mankind."

That strikes us as ludicrous at best. Another view: Kirkpatrick Sale writes in *The Conquest of Paradise: Christopher Columbus and the Columbian Legacy* that Columbus was "a man without a settled name, and it is hard not to believe that a confusion, or at least inconstancy, of that kind reflects some sort of true psychological instability."

You can't libel a dead man! Columbus will probably always be subject to revisionist thinking and maverick theories. Let's leave it at this: He was a mysterious and peripatetic figure even by sailor standards. He bopped from place to place, trying to get the dough to make his big cruise. He didn't care what people called him; all the better if they gave him a new name that fit their language and made them feel he wasn't a stranger seeking a handout. And then, once he made his discovery, everyone wanted to nab some of the credit—the Spanish were certainly not going to call him by an Italian name!

The ultimate truth is that Columbus was a man without a home. This rootlessness is no doubt one of the reasons it was Columbus, not some other guy, who decided to sail into the Great Unknown, across what was then called the Ocean Sea.

Why did "ancient astronauts" from outer space visit places like Easter Island in the middle of the Pacific Ocean, but not Europe?

Few literary frauds in recent history surpass that of Erich von Daniken's, author of the seminally stupid but best-selling book *Chariots of the Gods*. His basic theory is that massive stone megaliths like the ones on Easter Island, along with the tales of gods in ancient mythologies and the Bible, are irrefutable signs that our ancestors were from outer space. His "ancient astronauts" are the key to understanding The Flood, the pyramids, the Book of Ezekiel, and the alleged missing link in the evolution of apes into humans.

In the early 1970s, a time when people were particularly hungry for a secular replacement for traditional religious doctrines and were discontent with orthodox science, von Daniken's fruitcake ideas caught on, inspiring an NBC "documentary" called "In Search of Ancient Astronauts," which in turned inspired the "In Search of . . ." TV series and all manner of astonishing far-out books on the frontier of reason.

Von Daniken sold more than 45 million copies of his books, including one, *Gold of the Gods*, in which he finds a hidden, enormous labyrinth in South America containing vast treasures of gold and such irrefutable proof of alien technology as a plastic chair. He wrote that he was driven away from the site by primitive, hostile Indians, and couldn't ever find it again. Later still he admitted he made the whole thing up: "That did not happen," he said, adding, "All the facts do exist but with other interpretations."

(As a young man von Daniken was described by a court psychiatrist as a liar and criminal psychopath just before serving a year in prison for forgery, embezzlement, and fraud.)

Von Daniken's message was ultimately racist: He exploited the simpleminded idea that primitives in places like the Andes and Central America could not possibly have managed their engineering feats without some kind of outside help. You know how backward those people are! Aliens *must* have shown them how to build those pyramids.

Debunker James Randi writes in *Flim Flam!* that at no point does von Daniken cite such architectural marvels as the cathedral of Chartres, Stonehenge, or the Parthenon, "because these wonders are European, built by people he *expects* to have the intelligence and ability to do such work. He cannot conceive of our brown and black brothers having the wit to conceive or the skill to build the great structures that they did leave behind."

In 1979, in *Signs of the Gods,* von Daniken looked back on his scandalous career and said smugly, "I am very pleased. Surely it speaks highly for our society that a single inspired idea can set it rocking."

Or even a single inspired lie.

Why did Civil War soldiers stand shoulder to shoulder as they advanced on the enemy, even though this made them easy targets for rifle fire and was obviously a dumb idea?

War-fighting tactics are always outpaced by man-killing technology. Generals, trained in the history of combat, go into the field and with great calculation refight some previous war—the result being that their men are ground to pieces by some new maiming device.

The Civil War commanders ordered their men to maintain "close-order" formations, just like those you see in those paintings of the Battle of Waterloo or the Battle of Bunker Hill, the ones with the neat rows of brightly uniformed soldiers in the distance and, in the foreground, a scene of unimaginable chaos, violence, and individual gallantry. Back in the Napoleonic Wars, it made sense for troops to stay close together. Soldiers could be under the voice command of a single leader. "Command and control" was the buzz phrase.

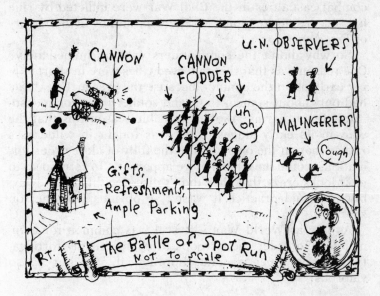

Plus, there was a psychological component: War scared the bejabbers out of you, and so you wanted someone right at your side. This way the regiment could move as a single organism, a machine of lethal impact.

The key to the success of this rugby-scrum behavior in the Napoleonic Wars was the relative feebleness of the musket as a weapon. The smooth-bore musket had limited range and poor accuracy. It took a long time to reload. A line of soldiers thus could advance to within a couple of hundred yards of the enemy and still be safe. The basic tactic was to charge the enemy, withstand a volley of musket fire, then go to work with the bayonets, slicing and dicing.

During the Civil War, however, rifles accurate at long distances made this traditional close-order formation almost suicidal. (The secret to better accuracy and distance was "rifling" the bore of the gun—using grooves to impart a spin to the bullet. While this trick had been known for many years, it was not until the mid-1800s that bullets were mass-produced with the ability to expand in the bore and go with the flow of the rifling.) About 80 percent of the combat casualties in the Civil War were inflicted by rifle fire, according to James McPherson, author of *Battle Cry of Freedom*.

So why didn't the commanders wise up immediately? One reason was that the improved rifles were in short supply early on in the conflict, because the prewar U.S. Army had only about sixteen thousand soldiers and commensurately few firearms. Another possible reason was that the war, in its early stages, often was fought in wilderness rather than in the open, where the folly of close-order formations would have been more apparent. "In retrospect to us it looks crazy that they didn't discover this right away, but in actual practice it wasn't so obvious," McPherson says.

As late as World War I, it still was common for commanders to order their troops to charge enemy fortifications across open ground. Impractical, yes, but oh so valorous!

Why didn't the American Indians invent the wheel?

They did, actually. At least the Aztecs, in what is now Mexico, did, if not the more nomadic and less technological "Indians" who roamed what is now the United States. Archaeologists have found toys with wheels among the Aztec ruins. Things like little doggies on dollies.

What no one totally understands, though, is why they didn't build *big* things with wheels, like carts and wagons. They carried stuff on their backs instead, or dragged it on sleds. You have to wonder: If they could build huge pyramids, why didn't they ever build a wheelbarrow?

The academics' answer is that it has to do with animals. The New World had an animal deficit, at least in the category of beasts of burden. In the Old World, the wheel was first used in Sumeria around 3500 B.C., in the form of wheeled vehicles. An essential ingredient was a domesticated animal to provide the propulsion. But in the New World there were no cows or horses or donkeys. The only domesticated animals in North America were dogs. Plus, "The buffalo weren't prone to that sort of thing," says Sam Wilson, an anthropologist at the University of Texas at Austin.

Yet we don't find the animal hypothesis totally satisfactory. After all, the Incas domesticated llamas and alpacas. They also had roads in the coastal plains, but the roads functioned merely as paths for men and animals. Never did they build a cart, or use a wheel for other basic functions; they had no waterwheels, no pulleys. And certainly this was not because of ignorance: The Incas and Aztecs were brilliant engineers.

The real answer may be that it is presumptuous to assume that any culture's technology should follow a fixed pattern, from stone to bronze to iron and so forth. For example, the Chinese invented gunpowder but used it only for fireworks! Technology develops according to need, and the technological cultures of pre-Columbian America did fine without the wheel. The Incas wiped out hunger in an empire of twenty million people, even though they didn't have a particularly good version of the plow.

Now for an even greater American mystery:

Why did the humongous Inca Empire fall to fewer than two hundred Spanish invaders?

In the 1530s, just under two hundred Spanish soldiers armed with swords, pikes, halberds, blunderbusses, and other scary-sounding weapons (you can just picture someone being quartered with a halberd) sailed down the western coastline of South America and invaded the Inca Empire in what is now Peru. The Spaniards were a vicious collection of mercenaries led by a former swineherd named Francisco Pizarro. The Incas were a civilization of twenty million people who worshiped their ruler (the Inca himself) as divine. At that time the Inca himself was a man named Atahualpa.

Atahualpa knew the Spanish were up to no good, but decided to pay them a personal visit, both as a formal courtesy and to get a measure of their forces. With great fanfare he was carried on a throne of gold into the Spanish camp. But he never had a chance to chat amicably with Pizarro because the Spaniards pounced on him, bound him with chains, and locked him up.

You'd figure the rest of the Inca army—thousands of armed men not far away—would rush forward and turn this little band of Spaniards into paella. But no. The army did nothing and let the invaders loot the empire of unbelievable amounts of gold.

Why were the Incas so passive?

One answer you sometimes hear is that the firearms and horses of the Europeans intimidated the Incas. That's partly true; the Incas had never seen a weapon that could kill at a distance. This small band of soldiers managed to slaughter at least two thousand natives.

A more complicated explanation is that the Inca society was essentially antlike; a single leader ruled over a vast communal enterprise with no concept of the individual. This led to disaster when the leader was killed, when "the charm that might have held the Peruvians together was dissolved," as William H. Prescott wrote long ago in *The Conquest of Peru*.

"Those Indians who let themselves be knifed or blown up into pieces that somber afternoon in Cajamarca Square lacked the ability to make their own decisions either with the sanction of authority or indeed against it, and were incapable of taking individual initiative," the Peruvian novelist Mario Vargas Llosa wrote in *Harper's*.

This has a "blame the victim" ring to it, but it's still a somewhat more logical answer than simply saying that the Incas were scared of a few guns and horses.

Oh yes, you might want to know what happened to Atahualpa. Pizarro wanted to burn him alive. But the Spanish were religious people, so they decided on a compromise.

They baptised Atahualpa, so he'd be a Christian, with the attendant afterlife perks. Then they strangled him.

Why was Henry VIII such a lousy husband?

As far as piggish, misogynistic, paranoid, blood-thirsty tyrants go, Henry really wasn't so bad. In fact, his story is more one of spectacular dissipation. He was the Orson Welles of his day, only meaner. In his younger, trimmer days, he was a dashing, brilliant, popular king, a prime mover behind the English Renaissance. For a long time he was even a decent husband, by the standards of his day. His first marriage, to Catherine of Aragon, lasted twenty-three years. Pretty good!

Then things got weird, and Hal's marital difficulties inadvertently triggered the English schism with Rome, which resulted in the Protestant Reformation, without which the Pilgrims might never have sailed to America in search of the right to be religious fanatics.

See, the king needed a male heir, but his babies by Catherine kept dying at birth or soon after, and his only surviving child was a girl. He figured that this was God's way of punishing him for violating a biblical injunction against marrying your brother's widow, which Catherine happened to be. A lame-brained idea, sure, but then again Henry lived in a relentlessly stupid era, except for the great frescoes.

After all, Henry reigned a hundred years before William Harvey realized that the blood circulates through the body, 250 years before the discovery that we need oxygen to live, and 450 years before the invention of the twenty-four-hour bank teller. Medicine was so backward in the early 1500s that the curative powers of the leech had not yet been discovered. Meanwhile, Henry started packing on the poundage. He was the classic wave-a-big-drumstick-in-the-air kind of eater. His sloppy manners should be excused, though, according to Retha Warnicke, an Arizona State University historian who has studied Henry VIII: "Those were the eating habits of everyone in sixteenth-century England. There were no forks. Forks didn't come into fashion until the seventeenth century."

So anyway, Henry asked the pope to annul his marriage. The pope refused for all sorts of political and religious reasons too complex to detail here. What could Henry do? He had always been devoted to the pope. But he had to dump Catherine! He finally decided to break with Rome altogether, and he started the independent Church of England. He got his divorce and married Anne Boleyn, his twenty-year-old mistress. She gave him another daughter, the future Queen Elizabeth, but then something happened that set him against her. There is circumstantial evidence, according to Warnicke, that Anne had a miscarriage and that the fetus was deformed. What is known is that Henry accused her of witchcraft and adultery, perhaps in an attempt to deny his own paternity of this "demon" offspring, Warnicke says.

Anne Boleyn was tried, convicted, and sent to the block. As you can see, Henry was now deeply into his Husband from Hell phase.

On to wife number three, Jane Seymour. She died in childbirth. Not his fault, okay?

Then came an arranged, politically motivated marriage to some northern European whom Henry loathed from the start and quickly dispatched with a simple divorce. Wife the Fifth was another young Anne Boleyn–type, and she really did fool around behind his back, and so he chopped her head off too.

The last wife he didn't have a chance to kill because he died first.

The final tally on Henry VIII's six wives: divorced, beheaded, died, divorced, beheaded, survived.

Why on earth was there a war in 1812?

This was the most boring war in American history. If you can name the principal combatants we will send you a free toaster. (And if the Treaty of Ghent pops to mind, you also get the Why Things Are board game, as soon as we invent it.)

The war was dull because one of the two major combatants, the United States, did not have a military. An astonishing oversight! Actually we had about ten thousand soldiers, but figure that if every soldier had a musket you would only have had the equivalent firepower of a single Miami drug dealer. Also, the U.S. Navy had only twenty ships, and several major sea battles were actually on lakes, like Lake Erie and Lake Champlain and, for all we know, the little pond in Central Park with the radio-controlled boats. So pitiful was this war that when Francis Scott Key watched the bombs bursting in air over Fort McHenry, he was appalled that the British couldn't even knock out one little flag.

The bad guys were the British, just like in the previous war. President James Madison had declared war in 1812 because the British were impinging on our foreign trade, hassling merchant ships, and yanking British-born sailors off American boats; also, they were supposedly sending arms to the Indians in the Western territories. There's also a school of thought that the war hawks in the U.S. Congress wanted the war with Great Britain so we could steal more Indian land. (In any war, there's usually an underlying real estate motive.)

Since we didn't have much of a military, and since the British were more interested in fighting the French in Europe, the War of 1812 became a scattershot affair, with conflicts popping up here and there in strange places, like semi-pro basketball franchises. At one point the Americans invaded Canada across the Detroit River, but we absent-mindedly brought only two thousand men to do the entire job, and they succeeded in running back to Detroit and getting captured, along with Detroit itself.

The low moment for the United States came when the British sauntered into Washington, D.C., and burned down the Capitol and the White House. (Where are those Redcoats *today*, when we really need them?!) Eventually we had some naval wins, thanks to freelance ship captains hired to fight the war for us. Ultimately, everyone got tired and went home. In December 1814 the Treaty of Ghent allowed both sides to claim victory and stop fighting, but there was no way to communicate in those days, except by shouting, and so on January 8, 1815, there was yet another battle, this one in New Orleans. The Americans won, but it was too late, because the fight had already been declared a draw.

Why hasn't JFK's assassination been solved once and for all?

(Note to discerning readers: This issue was briefly dealt with in the first *Why* book, but the recent outbreak of assassination mania has forced us to revisit the issue and make still more enemies.)

JFK's murder will never be solved. Sorry! In a hundred years they'll still be rehashing it, with ever more complicated and Byzantine conspiracy theories. They will still be arguing about the trajectory of the bullets, the nature of the wounds, and the significance of tiny shapes in grainy snapshots. The argument can never end because we can never know everything about a given moment in time, even one that lasted only about six seconds.

We reached this sad conclusion after seeing Oliver Stone's *JFK*, a film with roughly as much historical veracity as your average episode of "Lost in Space." It made us wonder: Why is there a seemingly permanent gap between the Official History of the assassination and the various unofficial, populist versions? Between the simple, lone-nut hypothesis and the foreboding vision of dark, unseen conspirators?

Our best guess: Official history (Lee Harvey Oswald acted

The evidence points to a CIA-FBI-CBS Triumvirate in complicity with Cuban and Mafia elements linked to rogue Illuminati working in Tandem with The PGA

Plus revelations That Oliver Stone secretly directed "BIGTOP PEEWEE" under orders of The Right wing of The Trilateral Commission raises suspicions of a murder-suicide pact between JFK and Marilyn Monroe

one   Two

alone) is based on what we do know, while unofficial history (Kennedy was killed in a conspiracy) is based on what we *don't* know—on contradictions, ambiguities, mysteries.

Bear in mind that evidence is stuff like this: the gun, the bullets, the bullet holes in the clothing, the autopsy photos and X rays, the eyewitnesses who saw Oswald, etc. This evidence indicates that Oswald shot Kennedy. This evidence, in a less sensational murder, would probably send a man to his death in the electric chair.

Evidence is *not* stuff like this: HEY, CHUMP, HOW COME THAT BULLET DID ALL THAT ZIGZAGGING? HUH? HOW COME?

Three

That is not evidence. That is a question, wrapped around a mystery, inside an enigma.

If you choose to believe in conspiracy theories, you have a wide assortment to choose from. Be judicious. A modest choice would be to believe that Oswald was in someone's hire; there is certainly evidence that people were plotting against Kennedy and there is nothing in the physical evidence of Dealey Plaza to contradict that kind of limited conspiracy.

But you are taking a bigger risk to believe, as *JFK* and most conspiracy books have it, that there was another gunman. There is no solid, irrefutable evidence of such a second (or third or fourth) gunman. What there is—and this is at the core of most conspiracy theories—is information that's inexplicable. Or suggestive. Stuff that's *fishy*.

Like, the brain disappeared after the autopsy! Doesn't that mean something? Perhaps. But while a brain itself is surely evidence, the fact that a brain is missing isn't necessarily evidence of anything.

Conspiracy theorists exploit doubt. Like, how could Oswald have fired three shots from a bolt-action rifle in merely 5.6 seconds, the interval between Kennedy's wounds? One answer: easily. The gun requires about 2.3 seconds between shots. Figure it out. Boom, reload, boom, reload, boom. You need 4.6 seconds. Where's the "evidence" of a conspiracy here?

But wasn't Oswald a terrible rifleman? Hasn't it been proved that even a top marksman couldn't replicate the feat? The simple fact is that Kennedy was eighty-eight yards from Oswald's alleged perch when the fatal bullet struck. The limousine was moving almost directly away from Oswald at eleven miles an hour. This is hardly an impossible shot!

Then there's the single-bullet theory, another doubt-inciter. The Warren Commission said there was "persuasive evidence" that a single bullet caused the nonfatal neck wound to Kennedy and the wounds to Governor John Connally. But bystander Abraham Zapruder's film seems to contradict the idea, and Connally says he was hit by a separate shot. What does this mean? Maybe it means that the Warren Commission's single-bullet theory is wrong. But the flimsiness of the official theory is not itself *evidence* of a second gunman. It is, rather, an indication that perhaps what happened that day has yet to be figured out.

Pony up an actual name, an actual gun, an actual bullet, an actual eyewitness, and then you'll have the evidentiary foundation of a conspiracy.

You might ask, what about the evidence of a gunshot from the grassy knoll? The fact is, a small minority of the people at Dealey Plaza heard a shot from that location. And, darn the luck, no one saw that gunman fire. No shell casings were found. If an invisible gunman *did* manage to fire a bullet from his invisible gun, the bullet remained invisible too; it vanished in thin air.

But what do you know, someone who looked a lot like Lee Harvey Oswald was actually seen firing a rifle out a window on the sixth floor of the Texas School Book Depository. Police immediately put out a description of the gunman, and shortly thereafter police officer J. D. Tippit was slain when he stopped a man who matched the specifics. The Tippit killer was seen by six witnesses as he fled into a theater. The police converged and arrested the man—Oswald, who, lo and behold, was an employee of the Texas School Book Depository and was being sought already for having suddenly disappeared after the shooting.

This is the pattern: sounds and shadows on one side, warm bodies and physical evidence on the other.

"Oswald's fingerprint is on the stock of the gun! I like those things! And that's what juries like too, by the way," says Ron Wright, a Fort Lauderdale medical examiner who weighs evidence for a living.

The Kennedy murder is fishy through and through: Why was the autopsy botched? Why were there two caskets? Why did that man have an umbrella on a cloudless day? Is that a man with a badge over there on the grassy knoll? Why did a cop honk twice outside Oswald's boardinghouse? Why don't the shadows look right on that photo of Oswald? And so on. Whether you think this adds up to a conspiracy depends on your tolerance for fishiness. But some of us diehard skeptics don't crave a reality that is neat, clean, and odorless.

The thing about conspiracy theories is, they can't be disproved. For one thing, the evidence that there's no conspiracy is, by definition, *a manufactured artifact of the conspiracy itself.*

For example, the movie *JFK* shows one fiend pressing a rifle against Oswald's dead hand, for a fake palmprint. The movie shows another shadowy figure planting the "magic bullet" on a stretcher. Scary stuff! Except both scenes are entirely invented.

There is one major piece of legitimate evidence for a second gunman: the acoustic analysis of a recording taken by a policeman's Dictabelt. A number of experts say it shows, with great probability, that three shots were fired from Oswald's perch and a fourth shot (which missed!) from the grassy knoll. From this one piece of evidence, the House Select Committee on Assassinations concluded in 1979 that Kennedy was probably killed as the result of a conspiracy. But a subsequent panel of experts disagreed with the acoustic analysis. Who's right? Who knows. In the meantime, that's a small nail upon which to hang a multiple-gunman (much less "triangulation of gunfire") scenario.

Okay, so what about the Zapruder film? Doesn't it show Kennedy's head violently jerking back and to the left? Yes. But that's merely a layman's idea of evidence.

"The concept that a body goes in the direction that a bullet is going is a Hollywood concept," says Michael Baden, who served as chairman of the Forensic Pathology Panel for the House Assassinations Committee.

In fact, it doesn't matter why Kennedy jerked backward: Unmentioned by Stone is that Baden and numerous colleagues examined the X rays and autopsy photos and concluded, with one dissent, that Kennedy was shot from the rear. (Ah, but we forget: David Lifton's book, *Best Evidence*, argues that this is because some mysterious person surgically altered the corpse immediately after the assassination.)

"The whole thing is silly," says Baden. "When you look at the hard evidence, the scientific evidence, everything fits with Oswald being the lone killer."

That doesn't mean he was necessarily acting on his own motives and not in the service of some other conspirators. But the lessons of *JFK* and many other conspiracy stories are probably 180 degrees wrong. The movie argues that our government (the FBI, the CIA, the Justice Department, the Secret Service, the Pentagon, the Dallas Police Department, etc.) is so diabolically brilliant, so brutally efficient, that it could perpetrate an assassination of the president, rearrange evidence and plant a plausible cover story, then cover up the crime for three decades.

The truth is that our government is inept, boneheaded, and bumbling—and conspires to delude the public into thinking otherwise.

POLITICS

Why are politicians always getting into sex scandals?

Male politicians are often sexually greedy. You might call it the JFK Syndrome—an extreme form of rakishness in which women are treated as perquisites of power, just like access to the better golf courses or free rides on military planes.

We know that, historically, sex and power have been natural partners. In pre-Columbian South America, the Inca emperor had houses of virgins spread throughout the empire—seven hundred virgins per site. He alone was permitted access. In ancient Rome, concubines were legally sanctioned, and the Emperor Commodus had three hundred. In the present-day Ache culture of Paraguay, the more skilled a man is at hunting game, the more women he is allowed to claim as mates.

"Across cultures, across space and time, power has correlated with sexual access," says Laura Betzig, an anthropologist at the University of Michigan who has studied the sex lives of leaders in premodern cultures. "It's one of the reasons people want power."

Is it possible that the powerful are abnormally horny?

(Oh, excuse us, we meant to say "sexually addicted.") Or are they, historically, men of average sexual drives who merely exploited their power? To what extent is sex drive associated with political ambition? And should we care if a guy who asks us to vote for him (or a female candidate, for that matter) is unusually randy?

This is where it gets tricky: No one wants to elect a leader who is merely out for personal gain—financial, sexual, or otherwise. Sexual behavior isn't irrelevant to the character of a leader; despots, historically, have been sexually promiscuous.

"It seems bizarre to me to hold politicians to a higher standard of sexual propriety than everybody else. On the other hand, extreme abuse of sexual privilege correlates with abuse of all sorts of other privileges," Betzig says.

It's likely that powerful men have a stronger sex drive than the average Joe, says anthropologist Helen Fisher of the American Museum of Natural History in New York. "There have been quite a few studies that show that in monkeys, and in people, levels of testosterone . . . go up when one rises in rank," Fisher told us. "Testosterone is clearly associated in both men and women with sex drive. So there's every reason to believe that these leaders should have a high sex drive."

Testosterone also is associated with aggressiveness, and the quest for power is certainly a kind of aggression. So you might conclude that the higher sex drive is a preexisting condition for politicos. But it may also be an aftereffect of leadership—a symptom of the intoxicating nature of power. Men gain power and suddenly are surrounded by women. Sex doesn't result in satiation, it results in still greater desire. Says Betzig, "Once you've tasted the perquisites, I think it's going to be difficult for a lot of men to resist."

There is something called the Coolidge effect, the gist of which is that sex drive increases in response to an increase in the number of sexual partners. The Coolidge effect is observed in both scientific experiments with animals and, in a more general way, animal husbandry. The effect is named after an anecdote, no doubt apocryphal, involving President Calvin Coolidge and his wife.

TESTOSTERONE CAL

Supposedly they were touring a farm and Mrs. Coolidge became curious about the number of times a rooster engaged in sex during a day. Astonished by the number, she told the farmer, "Please tell that to Mr. Coolidge." The president later asked the farmer if the rooster had sex with the same hen every time, or different hens. Different hens, said the farmer. "Please tell that to Mrs. Coolidge," said the president.

Why is it suddenly impossible to figure out the difference between a country, a commonwealth, a federation, and a "community," such as this new European thing?

When Mikhail Gorbachev unsuccessfully proposed that the Union of Soviet Socialist Republics reconstitute itself as something called the Union of Sovereign States, he explained that this new union would "have a federative membership on some questions, confederative on others, and associate on yet others."

Obviously, he was making this stuff up as he went along. The question was: How would Rand McNally deal with this on the maps? Would Moldavia (Moldova?) get its own color? What if Uzbekistan was confederated with Russia and Kazakhstan on questions of national defense but merely *associated* with them in matters of currency and postal delivery?

Boris Yeltsin and his associates decided that the best solution would allow almost complete independence of the former Soviet republics, within the framework of the Commonwealth of Independent States. But what is a commonwealth, anyway?

This is a new, messy era of creative governmental organization. The easily grasped, old-fashioned concept of the nation-state has been outmoded. Countries are pulled in two directions: Ethnic groups want their own turf, yet the global economy disdainfully ignores the concept of political boundaries. Serbs and Croats fight in the streets over nationhood status even as Europe coalesces into a new, countrylike thingamajig called the European Community.

"What we called a nation-state or a state for the last couple of hundred years is becoming more diverse," says Joseph Nye, a Harvard political scientist. No longer are states treated like billiard balls, "round and hard and impermeable," as he put it. "There are more things that flow across borders and there are more ways of organizing powers."

The notion of a "country" is a relatively recent invention. For example, neither Germany nor Italy as we know it was unified until the second half of the nineteenth century. Before that they were conglomerates of petty states and autonomous cities. A map of Germany in 1648, at the close of the Thirty Years' War, requires the entire Crayola box. There was the Electorate of Brandenburg, the Duchy of Saxony, the Margravate of Bayreuth, the Bishopric of Wurzburg, and the Archbishopric of Bremen, to name but a few of the hundreds of political entities.

Today, a political scientist doesn't use the word "country," but rather prefers the word "state." A state may or may not coincide with a "nation," which is defined by a language or cultural group. Quebecois make up a nation by that definition, but the province of Quebec is not a state, because it is merely a part of the state of Canada.

For thirteen years after the Declaration of Independence, the United States functioned as a loose confederation of essentially sovereign states. Then, the United States was a plural noun. The signing of the Constitution began the process of building a federation out of the confederation. A federation allows some power to be granted to the central government. Over time—through many Supreme Court decisions, the Civil War, and the expansion of the federal government during the Great Depression and World War II—the federation gradually came to be more of a unitary state, one big blot of color on the map, a thing called "America."

One might endeavor to define a "country" as a governmental entity that has a seat at the United Nations. But if so, then Byelorussia and the Ukraine have been countries since the end of World War II. They have always had their own votes, their own ambassadors, their own missions to the UN. Their status was a concession to Stalin, who argued that all of his socialist republics were sovereign states, with their own foreign policies, even though this was no more true of Byelorussia and the Ukraine than it was of, say, Idaho.

Now then: What in tarnation is Puerto Rico? Puerto Rico was a colony of Spain until the United States took it during the Spanish-American War. Since the United States didn't want to admit to having colonies, Puerto Rico became a "commonwealth." It pays no federal income tax but is eligible for some federal aid programs. It sends its own teams to the Olympics but has no seat at the United Nations. So it's not a "country."

In the fall of 1991, the Marshall Islands and the Federated States of Micronesia joined the UN. It is worth noting that the Federated States of Micronesia had not, in fact, been an official "state" for the past half-century, because it had instead been something called a "trust territory" of the United States.

But that's too complicated to get into.

Why do you always hear about the Third World but never about the Second World?

It's kind of like the *reichs* in Germany. You never hear about the first or the second because no one counted until the third came along. In other words, Hitler declared himself the leader of the Third Reich, but there was never a Second Reich. There was, however, a second reich (note the lower case), established by Bismarck when he united Germany in 1871. He called it simply *Deutsches Reich*, German Empire. The first reich was *Das Heilige Romische Reich*, the Holy Roman Empire of Charlemagne.

"Worlds" started to get numbers in 1955 when President Sukarno of Indonesia coined the term "Third World" in a speech. People quickly turned to their fingers and figured out that the capitalist "free" world was the first, and the Communist world the second.

In China, they used to think that the First World was the two superpowers, the United States and the Soviet Union, with other developed nations being the Second World and the poor countries, including China, being the Third World. Nowadays, it is gauche to say "Third World" because it implies third-rate.

For a while, people referred to the "underdeveloped" countries, but that's also insulting, hinting of underachievement. It's a bad description of those countries that, though poor economically, are rich in culture, like India.

So now we say "developing." Of course, this has accuracy problems—there are countries that are not exactly going anywhere, like Chad and Burkina Faso. (These are sometimes called the "Fourth World," in a whisper.)

In any case, the United States is part of the "developed" world, though whether this includes the district in Louisiana that elected David Duke remains a matter of argument.

Why do college professors tend to be liberal?

Some wiseacre said a while back that Marxism is dead everywhere except in North Korea, Albania, and Cambridge, Massachusetts. Since then, Albania has rejected it as well, and there is talk of Korean unification, which means that it's going to be up to Harvard to keep the torch alive.

This is hyperbole, of course, but it is true that academics tend to be, at the very least, liberal, and at elite universities in particular you would have to hunt pretty long and hard before scaring up a professor who'd confess to the sin of being a Republican.

To avoid sounding too reactionary in our question, we could turn it around: Why do people outside academia tend to be so conservative, so traditional, so insensitive to the plight of the oppressed and underprivileged? Why has the outside world not discovered that it is horribly Eurocentric, logocentric, and patriarchal?

Academia, by its nature, is going to have a relatively high share of people who are in opposition to, or somehow not suited for, the nonacademic world. If American society were left-wing, if IBM were run by someone railing about Eurocentrism, if Wall Street were a hotbed of Marxism, then perhaps Lee Iacocca would be teaching at Harvard. But America remains a generally conservative, business-oriented culture, and thus someone who develops a leftist ideology is going to want to find a safe haven.

"Often people become professional intellectuals as a way

of rejecting the values of mainstream American society," says John Searle, a professor of philosophy at Berkeley.

A harsher view comes from right-wing writer Roger Kimball, author of *Tenured Radicals: How Politics Has Corrupted Our Higher Education*. He told us that these academics essentially have never grown up: "The pose of radicalness and the rhetoric of subversion is very titillating to adolescent minds and to many academics who, though not chronologically adolescent, continue to exhibit the characteristics of adolescence in their thinking."

Our own experience contradicts that: Leftists never seem to be posturing, or playing some game. If anything, they tend to be maddeningly sincere.

We'd argue that it is the job of the professional intellectual to pick apart this creation we call society, to question it, to challenge it, perhaps even to subvert it. It is that instinct of subversion that ended feudalism and slavery and gave the world democracy. The professional intellectuals have a job—to deconstruct the world—and they're performing it with gusto.

For the rest of us, abstract ideas like "logocentrism" are not as important as finding a good parking space and keeping the boss happy. Alas, jobs in the real world don't offer tenure for life.

Why can't we use fancy ground-launched missiles to protect America from nuclear attack?

Because we promised we wouldn't.

Americans and Soviets spent much of this century united in a death pact. It was one of the crazy paradoxes of the cold war: Both sides built enormous, redundant nuclear arsenals and simultaneously agreed not to build any kind of defensive system.

The reasoning was that defensive weapons—or anything that might limit the devastation of war—were at least as dangerous as offensive weapons. Supposedly, if one side were to build a defense, it might feel invulnerable, and then might be emboldened to start a war and rain thousands of ICBMs on the enemy. Or, if one side were to start to construct a defense, the other side might say, oh-oh, we had better attack them now before it's too late.

By outlawing the use of defensive weapons, the Americans and Soviets committed themselves to a policy of Mutual Assured Destruction. As nutty as it sounds, it worked. It's logical but kind of sick: It's a pathetic species that needs to be vulnerable to total destruction in order to refrain from mass murder.

Defensive missiles were among the heroes of the Persian Gulf War, though the Patriot missile's effectiveness at blasting Iraqi Scuds out of the sky was initially exaggerated. One of the ironies of the 1972 Anti-Ballistic Missile Treaty is that it allows us to build a system that can defend against conventionally armed missiles, but we're not allowed to defend ourselves against the vastly more destructive nuclear intercontinental ballistic missiles. ("Let this one through, boys, it's a nuke.")

The perceived success of the Patriot has inspired new fervor for the Strategic Defense Initiative, which had been politically moribund—though still funded—for the last few years. Down in the Why Things Are International Command Bunker we take no position on this delicate political issue, except to suggest that SDI might be a colossal waste of taxpayers' money on behalf of greedy defense contractors.

You see, whether we base a defense in space or on the ground, it's essentially impossible to stop a concerted nuclear attack. There are two reasons:

1. A nuke isn't like a Scud.

You can't destroy an incoming nuke only a mile or two from the target; you'd still be fried. So you have to hit it farther out. What makes it all the harder is that the nuke is going to be flying much faster than a Scud, maybe ten thousand miles an hour. That bomb may also be "smart," able to juke to and fro, dodging your defensive missile. John Rhinelander, legal adviser to the SALT I negotiating team, says, "The Scud is basically a 1950s missile. It comes in big, slow, dumb, and happy. Patriot is a 1990s missile system. If the Patriot was up against a sophisticated 1990s offensive system, it couldn't do what it's doing."

2. We can build faster and better antiballistic missiles, but they still might not serve their strategic purpose, because they could be overwhelmed by huge numbers of attacking missiles and decoys, any one of which could inflict intolerable damage.

"The Soviets could hit us with tens or hundreds of RVs [reentry vehicles] at any one moment," Barry Carter, a Georgetown professor of international law who helped write the ABM treaty, told us a couple of years ago. Consider the damage wrought by a single Scud that made it through the Patriot defense and hit Tel Aviv; had that contained a nuclear warhead no one would have celebrated the overall success of the Patriot.

There was one caveat in the 1972 ABM treaty: The Americans and Soviets were allowed to have a single battery of defensive missiles, limited to one location. The Soviets decided to protect Moscow. We decided to protect a patch of North Dakota. No lie. Our antiballistic missiles are designed to protect *other missiles* (the ones we needed to bomb Moscow). The foundation of nuclear deterrence has always been that we can't let anyone hurt our bombs. That's the problem with all these antiballistic missile systems—they're good for protecting other missiles but can't protect people.

For economic reasons, by the way, we stopped operating the North Dakota facility in the mid 1970s. (A future question: Why do we need two Dakotas?)

Why is marijuana illegal?

Mary Jane has been illegal since the 1937 Marijuana Tax Act. You say you haven't *paid* your marijuana tax this year? Are you a pot head *and* a tax cheat? (All right, so the Marijuana Tax Act was replaced in 1970 by the Comprehensive Drug Abuse Act; you can get off on a technicality.)

You should be aware that some drugs are more illegal than others. Valium and other prescription medications are legally ranked as class 3 drugs, so they are the least illegal drugs out there. Cocaine and morphine, which can be prescribed only under limited circumstances, are class 2 drugs. Marijuana is a class 1 drug. So is heroin. These drugs are limited to scientific experiments. Yes, reefer is worse than crack. (Tobacco, we would guess, is the no class drug.)

The negative standing of marijuana is at least slightly due to the labor situation during the Great Depression. There was much resentment in the Southwest against Mexican immigrants taking farm jobs. Marijuana was considered a Mexican drug, although crazy jazz musicians down in New Orleans smoked it too. Middle America didn't like marijuana, but more than that it didn't like the kind of people who smoked it. Scientists were also pretty sure it made people wacko and homicidal; funny how public opinion can sway a laboratory experiment.

Marijuana remained legal even through Prohibition, because, according to Yale historian David Musto, the legal community didn't think it would be constitutional to outlaw a weed. After all, it's just a plant that grows wild all over the country. Outlawing pot would be like outlawing red ants.

Marijuana finally was outlawed when machine guns were outlawed. The Supreme Court ruled in 1937 that ultra-strict tax and license restrictions on automatic weapons were constitutional. Quickly, Congress passed the Marijuana Tax Act, which said you could not possess, barter, give, or sell pot without a license and a transfer stamp. The government then refused to print up any such licenses or stamps. The only group that was still allowed to use the hemp plant legally was the birdseed industry.

The marijuana seeds were famous for making the canaries sing terrifically.

PLANET EARTH

Why was Venice built in, like, the middle of the sea?

If you ever go to Venice, the first thing you'll notice is that someone accidentally built it underwater. It is literally in a lagoon. You can call it an architectural wonder or you can call it idiotic.

Those clever Venetians built beautiful churches and plazas, but no one even thought to install a sewer system. Human waste is dumped directly into the canals, to be carried out to sea by the tide. (What a saving on your utility bill!)

Who decided to build this crazy place? And after how many reefers?

We have to go back to the beginning of the Dark Ages. The barbarians had overrun the Roman Empire, and some northern Italians sought refuge along the thirty-two-mile-long lagoon on the northwest end of the Adriatic Sea. When the coastal marshes got too buggy and pestilential, they moved to a patch of 117 mud flats in the center of the lagoon.

This unusual location had several advantages. It was a perfect site for a port. Situated between the West and the

East, its settlers could play middlemen in trading. And it was such a bizarre place for a town, no one else wanted to live there. Venice became an independent city-state and a great trading empire.

Since then it has sunk several feet into the mud. The buildings are crumbling from water rot. The lagoon doesn't flush well anymore and gets choked by algae. One recent summer the entire city was infested with horrible flying insects, which then died and decomposed and smelled bad.

Now the Italian government wants to build billions of dollars' worth of huge floodgates to keep back the sea during storms. There's another high-tech solution we'd prefer: Pack the place up and move it to Disney World.

Why do people get swallowed up by earthquake fissures in the movies, but not in real life?

Because geologically it is absurd: The ground doesn't open up like that. Your typical earthquake fissure is usually only a few inches wide, and no deeper than about fifteen feet, so you couldn't fall in unless you had a figure like Nancy Reagan. On the rare occasions when a wide fissure does appear, it's shallow: You can fall into it and pop right out.

The person-swallowing fissure is a superstition that predates Hollywood, though Hollywood has certainly helped to perpetuate it. Jill Stevens, an educator at the Center for Earthquake Research and Information at Memphis State University, says the most common question she's asked by children is still, "Is the ground going to open up and swallow me?"

She theorizes: "We have a basic fear of the earth moving beneath us. It's our feeling of stability that has suddenly been removed. What do we fear most? That we're going to fall into a deep hole."

There's an additional reason for our fear. During an earthquake, the smell of sulfur sometimes fills the air, released from organic matter buried beneath the ground. And you know what sulfur means: Fire and brimstone. *Hell*.

Why does no one ever strike oil that's not quite ripe?

Your laserlike mind instantly perceives what a great question this is. Oil is the result of dead dinosaurs and primordial swamp ferns and deceased microscopic plankton, right? And this stuff became oil because it was buried for millions of years, right? So why doesn't anyone strike a patch that needs just one or two more eons until it's ready? Why don't they hit the stuff when it's still a little green?

You cretins, the answer is obvious. The organic stuff is originally dispersed over a wide area of subterranean rock, called source rock. It gradually turns to oil when exposed to heat and high pressure, then slowly migrates through fissures and crevices and pores in the rock. As the oil is lighter than the water that saturates the rock, it tends to float up toward the surface. The weight of all that rock also squeezes it upward to regions of less pressure. Eventually, the oil hits an impermeable layer of rock and is trapped. It collects in the reservoir rock. That's an oil field.

So wrap your noggin around this: We can't hit premature oil because it doesn't puddle down there in the rock until it's ripe.

The big question is, how much credibility can we assign to the famous story of a man named Jed, a poor mountaineer who barely kept his family fed? You know how one day he was shooting at some food, and up through the ground came a-bubblin' crude? Black gold? Texas tea? Well, that's utter nonsense. Oil doesn't shoot out of the ground like that, it just leaks serenely. In rare cases it will pool and form a tar pit like the ones in Los Angeles.

This should be a cautionary tale: Never, never take your geophysical knowledge from TV sitcoms.

Why can't we create ozone in factories and spray it into the atmosphere, to replenish the ozone layer?

As you know, the human race is in the middle of two distinct global experiments designed to see what will happen if we drastically alter the atmosphere of the entire planet.

First, by using certain aerosol sprays and cooling systems we are spewing nasty molecules called chlorofluorocarbons (CFCs) into the atmosphere. These destroy the ozone layer, which is nature's version of sunblock. Without any ozone protection, life as we know it would be destroyed.

Second, as a species we have a bad habit of burning things, like tanks of gasoline and entire tropical rain forests, and this increases the carbon dioxide in the air, which somehow causes more of the sun's heat to be trapped, which melts the polar ice caps, which causes the sea level to rise, until finally Miami Beach disappears from the map and *everyone* drowns in Bangladesh.

Naturally, the first thing an intelligent person should ask is, "Which catastrophe should I worry about more?" It's a tough call. The ozone problem has the nasty characteristic of possibly threatening Life Itself. The greenhouse effect, on the other hand, probably doesn't pose an extinction threat. It would merely destroy our civilization.

Taking everything into account, we probably have to give the nod to carbon dioxide as the gas more worthy of extreme concern, simply because it will be harder to break the habit of burning things than to break the habit of using CFCs.

In both cases, it would be nice if there were a technological quick fix. Like maybe we could replenish ozone by manufacturing it in laboratories and spraying it toward the sky. A great idea? Actually, it's like Wile E. Coyote trying to catch the Road Runner by wearing rocket-powered roller skates. It'll never work. True, a scientist can make ozone in a lab. Ozone is nothing fancy, just three oxygen atoms glued together. (By "glued" we are using a figure of speech. The actual adhesive is chewing gum.) There's no theoretical reason the stuff couldn't be launched into the atmosphere. There are common-sense problems, though.

John Gille, a physicist at the National Center for Atmospheric Research in Boulder, Colorado, says, "You can make it, but it takes a fair amount of energy, and to put any appreciable quantity in the atmosphere would take more energy and cost more than is practical."

The fact is, lots of ozone can be destroyed by just a very few of those chlorofluorocarbons. A single aerosol spray can might be able to wipe out a full day's production at our mythical ozone factory. "One chlorine atom can be responsible for the destruction of, say, 100,000 ozone molecules," says Gille.

The cheaper, easier solution is low-tech: Stop producing CFCs. An international treaty could halt CFC production around the world before the end of the decade.

Now, is there a high-tech solution to the greenhouse effect? John Martin of Moss Landing Marine Laboratories in California says we should think about dumping huge supplies of iron in the southern ocean near Antarctica. The iron might make phytoplankton, a type of algae, grow like mad, and if so suck carbon dioxide right out of the air. This is called the Geritol Solution to global warming.

"This is based on very rough calculations," he told us. "It's essentially an *idea*."

And possibly a bad one. Most scientists think the biosphere is too complicated, too sensitive, too mysterious to be treated like a bowl of chili that just needs a little more cayenne pepper.

John Firor, a physicist at the National Center for Atmospheric Research, says of Martin's plan, "I think it's the worst sort of technological messing around. . . . It might shift the whole food chain for the whole ocean."

So forget high-tech. Earth's ill health really requires preventive medicine, a sharp cutback in the steady diet of toxins, rather than a quick high-tech cure through some kind of fancy global chemotherapy. Firor says, "All these wild high-tech ideas about how to stop the heating ignore the fact that we already know how to stop the heating, and it's technologically easy. And that's to stop burning so much fossil fuel."

Technologically easy, for sure. But sociologically? Most Americans feel about their cars the way some folks feel about their guns: They'll give them up when they're pried from their cold, dead fingers.

Why hasn't continental drift thrown Stonehenge out of whack as a celestial calendar?

Perhaps a better question is: Why do we insist on asking questions that no one could possibly care about? We respond indignantly: This is actually a brilliant query because it dares to take two distinctly boring disciplines—geology and astronomy—and knit them together into a single stultifying tapestry.

You recall that Stonehenge is a bunch of big slabs of rock on one of those lonely plains in England. It makes you think of Druids, and though you don't know exactly what Druids are, you imagine them wearing hooded robes and behaving in a manner that is distressingly grave. You also know that the slabs are arranged like the Greek letter pi, with two vertical slabs supporting one horizontal slab—this was the ancient version of Lincoln Logs. You may even know that the formation is oriented according to the summer solstice, so that it functions kind of like a big calendar, letting you know when summer has arrived and it's time to go to the beach house.

Meanwhile, there is the plate tectonics situation. This is where the continents are constantly shifting and sliding and subducting and subverting, rearranging themselves, and, over a very long period of time, "North America" turns into "Lebanon." (If you catch our drift.)

Put these two phenomena together and you have to wonder: Shouldn't Stonehenge be wrong by now? As a calendar, isn't it a tad . . . unreliable?

The answer is no and yes: Stonehenge really *is* out of astronomical whack, but it's not because of continental drift.

The continents move at sub-turtle speed. The Eurasian plate is sliding away from the North American plate, roughly toward the east, at two to four centimeters a year. Over the course of several thousand years that will result in several dozen meters of movement, which seems like a lot, but because it is moving toward the east it doesn't mess up the alignment with the sun. To do that, the Eurasian plate would have to move toward the north or south, or, better yet, rotate, so that Stonehenge moves clockwise or counterclockwise.

What has thrown Stonehenge out of line is the change in the tilt of Earth's axis and other wobbles in the planet's orbit around the sun. These are much more dramatic than continental drift. Earth is a bit more tilted now than it was when Stonehenge was built—a change in the "obliquity of the ecliptic," to speak fancily.

We called the authority on Stonehenge—*the* authority—Richard John Copland Atkinson, professor emeritus of archaeology at University College in Cardiff, Wales, and he told us that, from a perspective within the center of Stonehenge, the position of the summer solstice sunrise has moved east by about two diameters of the sun. It was aligned originally in about 2100 B.C., he said.

Who built the darn thing, anyway? What about these theories that it was constructed by or for ancient astronauts from outer space?

"Rubbish. Absolute rubbish," Atkinson said. "All one can say is that it must have been built by people living in Britain."

Were they Druids?

"Good heavens, no. The Druids didn't exist until 1,500 years after Stonehenge was already a ruin."

So presumably even the Druids thought the place was kind of weird.

Why are there no Eskimos in Antarctica?

When we asked this question of a top Antarctica scientist, he said, "Because the Eskimos live in the Arctic." Which is the exact, scientific answer! We felt momentarily ashamed for using "Eskimo" as though it were the generic name for "someone who lives in an insanely cold place."

So, to rephrase: Why aren't there native Antarcticans? Why aren't there any aboriginal peoples who hunt penguins?

We figured there were two possible answers:

1. Humans couldn't get there.
2. They got there but it was too cold and nasty.

The first answer, we learned, is the right one—though the second answer explains why no one has set up homesteads down there in recent years despite the abundance of free land.

A look at a globe reveals that Antarctica is extremely isolated, surrounded by a vast ocean. The closest Antarctica comes to the extreme tip of South America is about six hundred miles, and the waters in those latitudes are notoriously treacherous. Most importantly, Antarctica has a buffer of sea ice. This floating ice pack made Antarctica undiscoverable during the Age of Discovery. You have to remember that the Niña, Pinta, Santa Maria, and most of the exploratory ships in the centuries thereafter were puny little wooden contraptions that your average Fort Lauderdale yachtsman wouldn't dare set foot in.

The existence of Antarctica was predicted as far back as the time of the ancient Greeks, who knew the world was a sphere and believed that a southern land mass had to exist to balance the continents of the northern hemisphere. The people with the best chance to find Antarctica were probably the Polynesians, masterful navigators who boldly explored the South Pacific. One Polynesian by the name of Ui-te-Rangiora led an expedition by canoe into the southern seas in about A.D. 650, according to island legends. The first person known to penetrate the Antarctic Circle was the famed British sailor Captain James Cook, but he managed to circumnavigate the entire continent in 1774 without seeing land—leading many to conclude that it just wasn't there.

Sealers—you know, people who kill seals—were the next wave of explorers. Gradually, they visited the southern islands that are close to the continent. It's debatable who actually first saw or landed on Antarctica itself; there are several claimants in the years 1819 and 1820.

But it's not a place you'd want to set up housekeeping. The Arctic region of North America, where the Eskimos live, is relatively benign in comparison. The obvious problem with Antarctica is that it is covered with a massive ice sheet that's more than two miles thick in places. Air slides down off the high elevations of the ice pack, pulled by gravity, and creates hurricane-force winds along the coast. There is only one plant native to the entire place, plus some lichens, fungi, and algae. No caribou. No polar bears.

Nanook of the North would have taken one look at the place and said, "Live here? And give up the comforts of home?"

Why are there two high tides a day, rather than one?

Being a not-totally-dense person, you know the tides are caused by the moon. You cling like a drowning person to this thin fiber of knowledge.

Regrettably, if you visualize the situation, you realize that it doesn't make any sense. Imagine the earth and the moon facing one another across a void of a quarter of a million miles. The moon is pulling on the earth, right? The ocean is bulging up a little, right? And the earth is spinning, right? So now ask yourself why a given piece of ocean shouldn't bulge up only once every twenty-four hours (when the moon passes overhead), rather than twice.

Scratch your noggin on that.

Of course, the Why staff knows the answer. We know because, moments ago, in a profound state of panic and confusion, we called the esteemed physicist Charles Misner of the University of Maryland. (He's especially esteemed for being reachable from the Why bunker with a local telephone call, which, as far as we're concerned, makes him the New Einstein.) He solved the mystery, to wit:

Gravity is pulling Earth and the moon toward one another. But you may have noticed that they never smash together and disintegrate in a tragic spray of planetary detritus. This is because they are also subject to an outward centrifugal force, created as they go winging through space in orbit around a point between them (the idea that the moon orbits the earth is not precisely correct). The gravity and the centrifugal force cancel each other out, which is why the earth and the moon are always approximately the same distance apart.

But hold on. While this neat little balancing act may be true for the *center* of the earth, it's not quite true for the *edges* of the planet, the surface, where the oceans are. The side facing the moon is about four thousand miles closer to the moon than is the earth's core, and so the surface feels a greater gravitational tug. It bulges toward the moon. That's your first high tide.

Now shift to the other side of the planet, the side farthest from the moon. It's not affected by the moon's gravitational field as much as the center of the planet or the moon-facing side, and simultaneously it is subject to greater centrifugal force, because it's moving at greater speed in the earth/moon orbit (in much the same way that the outer edge of a record album moves faster than any of the inner grooves). So it bulges away from the moon. There's your second high tide.

That said, these bulges are pretty wimpy out there in the middle of the big blue sea. The tides we notice are magnified by the shallow waters of the coast and by unusual coastal configurations. The Chesapeake Bay has a tide that can be measured in mere inches, while Maine has a ten-foot tide and the Bay of Fundy has a nauseating thirty-foot tide. (This may be one reason why, when you ask someone where he or she is from, the answer is never "The Bay of Fundy.")

Footnote: This explanation was not an unqualified success. Everyone hated it.

For example, Toby R., a physics teacher in Orlando, Florida, wrote, "Just because someone is a journalist doesn't qualify them to explain physical, medical, legal, chemical, economic, and political phenomena."

He is correct. We aren't "qualified" to explain anything (except, perhaps, chemical phenomena). But we are forced to plunge ahead, giving it our best shot, because "experts" are the worst explainers of all—almost invariably incomprehensible, humorless, and, often as not, just as wrong.

Case in point: Toby R. We hate to do this to the Tobester,

but he included a separate page with the heading "How I would have explained it." Here's his attempt, in full:

"On the side of the planet closest to the moon, the moon's gravity pulls the water up, hence one of the high tides. The moon is normally opposite the sun, so the usual effect is that the moon pulls on one side of the planet and the sun pulls on the other, causing two bulges. This is not always the case, though, so the tides are really a much more complicated phenomenon."

A dazzling effort! One picky objection: If the moon were, in fact, "normally opposite the sun," there would "normally" be a full moon outside all the time, which there is not; hence the answer is preposterous. But maybe there is always a full moon in Orlando. Some kind of Disney gimmick.

(Toby, by the way, told us by phone that he didn't like

his explanation much either. Still, he said, his version was better than ours, "even though it's wrong.")

Now let's hear from James Weidener of Miami, a professional surveyor and mapper who came up with an explanation for why some places have just one high tide:

"Tides that rise and fall twice daily are known as semi-diurnal, and they are predominant in the world. Even though there are two high tides, they are seldom equal. The range of such tides is primarily controlled by 'phase inequality,' with tides at the new and full moon being 'spring tides' and those at quadrature being 'neap tides.'

"Diurnal tides (one high and one low per day) are also common and are caused by 'diurnal inequality'—the result of the varying declination of the sun and moon. The declination changes from 18½ degrees to 28½ degrees, and back, over an 18.6-year period called the regression of the moon's nodes."

To which we respond: *Neap* tides?

The moon's *nodes*?

We quit.

OUTER SPACE AND BEYOND

Why doesn't a black hole somewhere get so big and powerful that it eventually goes SKLURRP! And sucks the entire galaxy, including the planet Earth, into its dreadful maw?

It's easy to imagine that black holes are sort of like the sharks of outer space, roaming around, devouring everything—stars, plants, old automobiles, tin cans, etc. There have been reports that there may be a black hole at the center of the galaxy with a mass of as many as a million stars. Now, let's be honest: Doesn't that set off alarm bells? Don't you want to know if that thing is safe?

The answer, we've learned, is that black holes are surprisingly benign. In fact, they're almost cute. You see, a black hole isn't really a sucking machine. Sure, stuff can fall into a black hole and never return, but we should remember that the only force at work is gravity, and gravity is basically harmless, something we cope with all the time without any dire problems. Hold your arm out to one side, and keep it there for a few seconds. Feel that gentle tug? That's gravity. It's weak!

Consider what would happen to us here on Earth if, magically, the sun suddenly became a black hole: nothing.

The sun's gravity would remain the same. There'd be only one major difference: It'd be dark outside. And cold. Life would end. But otherwise, no problem.

The fact is, we have totally misconstrued black holes. Their significance is not their power, it's their size. They're small. That's what makes them special. The stuff that used to constitute an entire star can be crushed into an incredibly dense pebble. Gravity is stronger the closer you get to an object, and because a black hole is so small you can, in effect, get closer to its mass than you could if all that mass were spread out in something the size of a planet or a star.

It doesn't matter to us, out here in the suburbs of the galaxy, what causes the gravitational field that we inhabit.

It's the same to us whether the gravitational pull comes from a million individual stars floating around the center of the galaxy, or from a single black hole with the collected mass of a million stars.

The only thing you don't want to do is get close to a black hole. When you get too close, the gravity becomes so strong that not even light can escape. This is the "event horizon," beyond which is darkness, torment, the gnashing of teeth, and the inconsolable wailing of the damned, *who knows*?, we can't see in there so we're just guessing. So the bottom line is, fear not the black hole—but if you're walking down the sidewalk and a total stranger pulls out a little dark object and says to you, "Here, hold this," keep in mind that it might be the compressed matter of a collapsed star. Just keep walking.

Why does the universe have so much empty space? Why isn't there more stuff in it?

We could answer that space has to be mostly vacant or else it wouldn't be *space*. But that would be dumb.

There is actually a genuine puzzle here: The universe needn't be such a thin gruel. You could pack loads more moons and planets and stars and galaxies into it without fear of overcrowding. As it is, the universe is ridiculously empty. How empty is it? It takes four years for a beam of light to travel, at 186,000 miles per second, between our sun and the nearest star, a trip even duller than crossing Kansas on Interstate 70. Or consider this: If two galaxies drift together, chances are that none of the stars will collide.

You numbers freaks will want the precise statistic: The average density of space, including all the stars, is only one-tenth of one-billionth of yet another billionth of a *trillionth* of a gram of matter per cubic centimeter. That comes out to a few lonely atoms per household.

The answer to our question is also the answer to a seemingly unrelated mystery: Why do we live in a universe filled with matter rather than antimatter? You see, in your basic atom, electrons have a negative charge and protons have a positive charge, but there's no reason it couldn't be the other way around. There could be positive electrons and negative protons. In fact, scientists have created in the laboratory small amounts of this "antimatter." It quickly disappears in a flash of energy when it touches real, red-blooded matter. It's the most volatile stuff ever invented. If Earth collided with even a small patch of antimatter, Texas would go rocketing through Australia.

It won't happen. Antimatter doesn't seem to occur much in nature—not anymore. Here's why: Most cosmologists believe that the universe began as a dense knot of energy, which suddenly "exploded" and rapidly expanded. Within that first second of existence, both matter and antimatter were formed in roughly equal amounts, but there was just a tad more matter. Then, a fraction of a second later, the newly created matter and antimatter annihilated each other, converting back to energy. All that was left was a few dribbles of matter, about one-billionth of the original supply.

So the rest of space was null and void.

Why doesn't space, which is a vacuum, suck all the air off our planet?

Just the other day we thought we had invented the perfect no-moving-parts, no-fuel-required spaceship launcher: a tube a hundred miles high and a few yards wide. Okay, so it would be hard to build. But that's why they have engineers. It's just a big metal tube; that can't be *too* tricky.

The open-ended top would be above the atmosphere. The bottom would be at ground level, sealed off. If you opened the valve at the bottom, the entire tube would act like a vacuum cleaner hose as air rushed upward toward the void of space. You could put an astronaut at the bottom, throw a switch, and VROOSH! you'd have an instant satellite.

Brilliant? No, idiotic. The air in the tube would just sit there, as does the air on the planet. Gravity is holding it in place. Now, it's certainly true that a vacuum cleaner is more powerful than gravity, or else the dirt would never come up off your floor. The planet's atmosphere is designed brilliantly, however, because there's no single point at which space begins. The atmosphere is sort of phased out over the distance of about a hundred miles. This means that there is never a place where there is a vacuum side by side with a pressurized zone. So there's no suction. Gravity, though weak, is just strong enough to make the air molecules settle around the planet.

Now then, what if we pumped out our no-moving-parts spaceship launcher to create a true vacuum inside, with no air, then put our vessel at the bottom? (Obviously, we've lost a lot of our energy saving by having to do the pumping, but let's play along.) As air rushed into the tube, it would lift the vessel toward space, but then stop, far below the top of the tube.

This is because the air that's lifting the vessel will undergo a decrease in density as it gets farther away from the earth's center of gravity—it's the same thing that happens to the air on top of mountains. Eventually the pressure of the rising column of air is unable to push the heavy spaceship upward, and the craft falls back to the ground, crushing the hapless experimenters.

Why can't a really fast jet take off from a runway and fly into space, so we don't have to horse around with these dangerous rockets?

Nothing prevents a jet from aiming straight up and heading toward space. But it would conk out eventually. Jet engines breathe air. That's why you can get sucked into them if you stand too close and are having

a *really* bad day. The oxygen is needed for combustion. There's no oxygen in space.

A space plane may yet be built, though. It would have to have huge air intakes for the jets, to capture the dispersed molecules high in the atmosphere. Once the plane reached twenty-two times the speed of sound, at about forty miles above the ground, it would then switch to rocket power, using tanks of liquid oxygen, for the final boost to Mach 24 and low Earth orbit. (While there is no real edge to space—no altitude at which the atmosphere suddenly dissipates—traditionally space is said to begin a hundred miles up.) The space plane would also have to be constructed of light, super-strong materials that could withstand the heat caused by moving so fast, particularly on reentry into the atmosphere.

Now let's deal with a tangentially related question that we heard recently:

Why doesn't the space shuttle get stuck in the vacuum of space, where there's nothing to push against when it wants to come back to Earth?

Our first guess was that there's a teensy bit of atmosphere up there, even though it's 140 miles above the surface of the planet. But that's not it. The answer is: The shuttle pushes against itself, sort of. The orbital maneuvering system thrusters on the space shuttle don't have to push against anything other than their own housing.

"For every force there's an equal and opposite force," says Keith Hudkins, chief of the Orbiter Division of NASA headquarters. "It's just action and reaction. Newton. Newton's law." But of course.

When the shuttle has to return to Earth, a series of reaction control system thrusters are fired, and the shuttle rolls into a tail-first position. Then the orbital maneuvering system thrusters do their job. The thrusters (powered by the combustion of monomethyl hydrazine upon mixture with nitrogen tetroxide, in case you were curious) are bell-shaped, with the narrow portion toward the front of the craft, creating more pressure in that direction and causing the shuttle to go "forward"—though in this instance it is already zooming along tail-first, so it just slows down. With less speed, the shuttle simply falls out of orbit.

Why is there something rather than nothing?

Go outside. What do you see? An entire world of wonder! Why is it here? Why does *anything* exist? Even if you assume that the Creation was of divine origin, why is there a Creator? Wouldn't "nothingness" be more logical?

We called up the famous philosopher Robert Nozick, and he said that, yes, he could handle this one. (We like to think of Nozick as the Brooks Robinson of philosophers, always flying horizontally through the air to backhand a sizzling intellectual liner.) Nozick cited his book *Philosophical Explanations*, in which the something-rather-than-nothing issue is explicitly addressed. Unfortunately, for low-wattage types like us, Nozick's writing is pretty impenetrable, with lines like, "Nothing explains itself; there is no X and Y such that X explains Y and Y explains X; and for all X, Y, Z, if X explains Y and Y explains Z then X explains Z."

(How does one respond to such a statement? You say confidently, "Yep, there's no gainsaying the obvious.")

We'll just have to answer the question the best we can, which is to offer one morsel of conjecture: Nothing does not exist because Nothing *cannot* exist. Your question is prejudiced, you see, in that it presumes that Nothing is a more natural condition than Something, that there is a greater onus to explain Something than there would be to explain Nothing.

But ask yourself: Is Nothing a natural state? What does "Nothing" mean? When you picture Nothing in your head you probably see a large, dark void—but would that be Nothing? Actually, it would be something—call it Not Much—because, as you picture it, it has dimensions, including a time dimension. It has a *presence*. But the pure, unadulterated Nothing should have no characteristics! It would not "exist" in the way that Something exists.

And chew on this mystery: How could a nonexistent thing turn into Something?

"If ever nothing was the natural state then something could never have arisen. But there is something. So nothingness is not the natural state; if there is a natural state, it is somethingness," Nozick writes.

(As for the catchall "God" answer, Nozick told us, "That's not much of an explanatory theory.")

Seeking further insight, we spoke to Sidney Coleman, a revered theoretical physicist at Harvard, someone who thinks about pretty far-out stuff, like whether our universe is connected to innumerable others through "wormholes." (Sounds right, doesn't it?) He pointed out that our statement that Something could not emerge from Nothing is pretty stupid, because "emerge" is nonsensical in this context. "Emerge" implies casuality, which requires a dimension of time, but everything we know about the universe suggests that long ago it was in a condition in which there was no time.

"You go back and back and back and after a while you find you can't go any further back, not because you hit a barrier, but because 'back' ceases to have any meaning," Coleman says.

This is, admittedly, a dense subject. (Uproariously funny physicist joke.) See, the scientists think they can trace the history of the universe almost all the way back to Time Zero, when the infinitely dense and hot universe suddenly began to expand and cool, a moment known as the Big Bang. But it's impossible to draw a time line that includes Time Zero.

The reason is that time and space do not exist *independently* of objects, but are merely dimensions that *describe* those objects and how they move about.

Unfortunately, there is this annoying theory of quantum mechanics, which says that no distance can be shorter than something called the "Planck length," and no period of time can be briefer than "Planck time." (Length and time are related, you know, because they're part of the same thing, the "space–time continuum.")

These are the rules. And when we look back in time, we see, early on, a universe that was no larger than the Planck length—a universe so small it had no "time" dimension.

What this really means is that *the universe has always existed*. It had no beginning. Contrary to popular belief and to some recent press reports, the Big Bang does not define "the beginning of time." Time can be *finite but unbounded*, just like spatial dimensions (remember that the surface of the earth is finite in two dimensions but lacks a boundary).

The initial moment after the Big Bang is, nonetheless, sometimes expressed in terms of a fraction of a second, but "there might have been thirty billion years before that," says Coleman.

He doesn't really mean "before." If there is no time, there can be no "before." So the question of what happened before the Big Bang is a bit like asking how tall a year is.

Besides, there could be a larger "universe" in which ours is but a local event. And that larger mega-universe might be perched on the fingernail of a giant named Zar-Moo. And . . . hey, when did it get to be three in the morning?

A HURRICANE STORY

HOMESTEAD, FLA.

When the winds died, the people found themselves in a state of nature, side by side with beasts. They moved along the roofless ruins of their homes. There were no rules anymore, no laws, and time itself had reverted to an elemental rhythm: the suffocating predawn humidity, the pitiless midday sun, the soaking cloudbursts, the night that brought a darkness blacker than anyone could have imagined. The people had to learn everything all over again, the basic procedures of human existence: how to eat, how to sleep, how to go to the bathroom when you no longer have a bathroom, how to find fuel, how to protect the tribe from invaders. The reinvention of civilization would not be easy.

On the road that leads to the Everglades there are three families living under a single large tent, waiting for the looters to come. So far there have only been baboons. The baboons escaped from a research facility destroyed by Hurricane Andrew. When the first ape showed up, the men got out their guns and fired warning shots. They threw trash cans and made loud noises. The creature wouldn't leave. It looked hungry, and nasty—it wasn't going to go away until it got food. In the contest of man versus ape, the smaller-brained primate had no chance.

"It was the Chinese assault rifle, wasn't it, that Mikey was carrying around?" says one of the Debbies.

"It was the shotgun," says another one of the Debbies.

There are four women here, and they are all named Debbie. *There are no rules anymore.* The tent was put up by Vietnam veterans who came to the rescue on their Harleys. Two flags fly overhead, one American, one Confederate. The people spend the day waiting for whatever it is that is supposed to happen now that civilization has come to an end. At least they now have supplies: Beers and sodas are in the coolers, and a few iridescent red pickled sausages float in a gallon jar.

One of the men, Don Lindsey, is wearing a shirt on his head. "My last clean dirty shirt," he says. A pearl-handled revolver juts from the pocket where some men carry a wallet. He keeps his squirrel gun, "a Jed Clampett special," nearby in case the looters come. "We have an arsenal," says one of the Debbies.

George Koci walks out to the cucumber field where they buried the baboon. A simple wooden cross marks the spot. Koci says they asked a passing police officer what to do, and he said to go ahead and shoot it. They felt pretty bad about it anyway.

"We didn't want to do it," he says. "He looked so innocent-looking."

What happened to South Dade could happen to anyone, anywhere, either in the obvious manner of a hurricane or in some subtler form, some personal hurricane, a health disaster, a spiritual catastrophe, a financial cataclysm. There is no moral to this story, but there is a question: What will you do when your storm comes?

You can run. You can fight. You can be a giver or be a taker. You can lose all sense of yourself and totally disintegrate or you can achieve a mental clarity, an inner peace, a resolve.

I spoke to dozens of hurricane victims, and no one seemed more indomitable than Mary Ann Ballard, age seventy-seven. She lives in a house built in 1908 in the Redlands, an area of avocado groves, plant nurseries, and pine woods, an area where the streets have lovely names like Silver Palm Drive and Farm Life Road. There is nothing lovely here anymore. Ballard lost her own avocado groves, suffered damage to her house, and suddenly has no income. Her only insurance is her circle of family and friends. She had spent fifteen years resurrecting a historic village in Goulds, a stop on Henry Flagler's railroad line to Key West. She turned abandoned buildings into antique galleries and artisan shops, and called it Cauley Square. The two-story main building is now one story; the building marked Tea Room is now on its side, as though someone booted it over.

"This is no worse than the bombing of London, the bombing of Hamburg. I intend to rebuild. I think Americans are ingenious, clever, courageous, and I think we're unsinkable, especially Southerners," she said. "Them that stay and rebuild will be infinitely strengthened by this. The easy thing to do is pack up and leave."

Her husband of fifty-two years, Major General Robert Ballard, died in April. He loved to look out the windows and see the royal palms everywhere, more than 150 of them hiding their home from the rest of the world. Only 23 of the palms survived the hurricane.

She said: "We all go through fire. Sometimes it's emotional and no one sees it. This is obvious, and so you get sympathy. I have a deep philosophy that everyone suffers in some terrible way in their lifetime, and that is the test." And she says, "I hope before I die, I pass this test."

The storm struck the mainland shortly before 5 A.M. on August 24, 1992, with 141 mph sustained winds. The National Hurricane Center in Coral Gables registered gusts as high as 164 mph before its measuring instruments were blown off the roof. On the Saffir-Simpson scale it was a Category 4 storm, one notch below the ultimate level of violence. The meteorologists say it was a "dry" storm, and fast, and unusually small for a hurricane—merely forty miles wide, beady-eyed. The victims say it was an unusually large tornado.

The tales of terror and heroism down here are so common that they all start to blend together, a single near-death experience. People recall the glow on the horizon as the transformers blew up. The first sign that this would not be just another hard blow came when the rain shot horizontally through the cracks around the front door. A home's entrance became its weak link, buckling as the winds topped a hundred miles an hour; once the storm got inside, the roof would blow, the house literally bursting, like something that shouldn't have been put in the microwave. And such noise! The storm roared so loudly it drowned out the snapping of huge trees and the playful rearrangement of parked cars. In a few short hours, South Dade lost not only $20 billion or so in property, but all its shade as well.

Jack Kephart, sixty-seven, felt his room collapsing, and went to the room of another tenant in his building, Peter Johnson, forty-two. Dade County is famous for racial tension, but the older white man and the younger black man, mere acquaintances, huddled together in that little room. When the roof fell and they were buried in the rubble they called out each other's names, and said, "Hang in there," simple but sincere instructions. Johnson says: "We were down in the rubble praying. The rubble protected us with a bit of shelter, even though we were rained on." A week after the storm, it's all so matter-of-fact. But he feels good about what is happening within the community, how it is spiritually strong even if the infrastructure is gone. "The various ethnic groups all came together. It wasn't about social differences, or nationality; it was about survival, the basic necessities of life."

Everyone has a story. In fact, there's almost a glut of heroism. At one point I found myself actually yawning while a man told how he had managed to save his kids by leading them from his collapsing house over and around downed power lines, to a safer house during the brief calm as the eye of the storm passed overhead. People tell of putting mattresses on their heads, of hiding in closets, of packing the children into the cabinets beneath the kitchen sink. "I was using myself as a wedge between the floor and the ceiling," says *Miami Herald* reporter Don Van Natta, who had been trapped in a collapsing motel room minutes after promising, as the eye passed, to file a story for the next edition.

This disaster cannot be captured by a photograph, a newsreel, or even the most adjective-laden paragraph. You have to drive it. It seems impossible that no one recognized the extent of the damage for several days. We have become accustomed to instant, precise, twenty-four-hour, satellite-bounced information, and the initial read on Hurricane Andrew was that it wasn't so bad, a mere eight-foot storm surge. The latest estimate is that fifteen people died during the storm itself. The Dan Rathers of journalism barely looked over the scene before taking off for Louisiana, to hoist their microphones in the air and catch Andrew's next howl.

Not even the locals knew at first. Maybe one reason is that Dade County is a big place and the southern portions do not significantly overlap, culturally, with the heart of Miami. Most Miamians live north of the severely damaged areas. Places like Homestead and Florida City are road-trip distance, places you would go for an adventure, an airboat ride, a taste of alligator meat, the reassuring sight of endless bean fields.

Every Miamian probably knew someone who lost his or her house, maybe several people, but most Miamians just lost trees, at worst. The storm passed through on a Monday morning, but not until midweek was it clear that the homeless numbered over 200,000, that the damage would be in the tens of billions, that this kind of property damage hasn't been seen in the mainland United States since the San Francisco earthquake of 1906.

You could argue that Hurricane Andrew destroyed the most authentic part of Dade County. South Dade was never concocted for the entertainment of tourists. It never caught on to the pastel rage of the "Miami Vice" years. There are no shiny banks, few Cigarette boats and Ferraris. Visitors would stay at a motel or at Grandma Newton's Bed and Breakfast (which now lies across the street in a heap— Grandma survived under a table in a shed out back).

You would go through Homestead and Florida City to get to the Florida Keys or Everglades National Park, but you probably wouldn't stop unless you had an affection for warehouses filled with tomatoes, or wanted to go to the kind of bar where everyone has a tattoo, or had a hankering for some of the Mexican food at El Toro Taco, famous for chile con queso. Or you might go just for the expansiveness of the terrain, the vast horizon, the thunderheads rising like mountains out of the Everglades.

"There was a tremendous serenity about the Redlands," says Ballard. "Wherever there are acres and acres of trees and a house or two, there is a tremendous peacefulness."

Now the Redlands are defoliated, and to the south, in Homestead and Florida City, there are just miles and miles of rubble, trash, punched-out buildings, lines of sunburned people, and an occupation army of 20,000 troops. On rural roads you see soldiers marching around in red berets, going who knows where.

It is a horrible scene, tragic, and yet it is also a little boy's fantasy, the militarizing of daily life. Choppers everywhere! Real soldiers in uniform! School postponed until September 14!

Kids whiz around on bikes. On Wednesday the boys and girls at the Everglades Labor Camp, once home to thousands of migrant farmworkers, wheeled around the ruins of their neighborhood, helping the animal control officers round up stray dogs. Their masters gone, the dogs had started running in packs in the evening.

The emergence of civilization took more than a week, and it required the harnessing of technology. This was the second stage of the emergence from the state of nature, after the food had been gathered and the shelter built. Paul Bailey, for example, reinvented the shower. The West Kendall salesman, whose house was gutted by the storm, put a nozzle on a bilge pump, hooked it up to the boat's battery, dropped the pump into a trash basket full of water, squatted naked by the boat, and scrubbed down. Not a pretty sight, but, he says, "it's wonderful, it's what I look forward to at the end of the day."

There is an exhilaration in the wake of a catastrophe. People can feel themselves passing the test. They are living simply, but living large. You learn who you are. You can smell yourself. You bunker down in the ruins of your life and say, "Here, I make a stand."

Olin McKenzie doesn't seem to want it to end. One day he was a dentist, the next, a frontiersman. He lives in the affluent Pinecrest neighborhood, about a half mile north of where the ten-mile-wide "eye wall" passed like the blade of a lawn mower; that distance is the difference between those who lost their homes and those who merely lost trees, windows, cars, boats, electricity, water.

"We've been camping. We've been spending twenty hours a day *living*—getting the daily requirements for life, your food, your fuel," he says.

He and his family bathed in the swimming pool. McKenzie rigged up a generator, then scrounged up generators for a half dozen other families, and soon he was the Generator Man, the guy everyone would go to for survival tips. He could go to a hotel, sleep in AC, eat in fine restaurants, but it wouldn't be right—he's the Generator Man!

His friend Dave Barry spent the first few days after the storm chain-sawing downed trees, precisely the kind of thing he would normally have paid someone else to do. "In South Florida we pay men to do our yard, do our pool, everything, and I have this bizarre profession of writing humor columns," Barry says. "I know this last week I felt really honest."

He and his wife, Beth, and their son, Robby, gave me a flashlight tour of their backyard, where once had stood a veritable tropical hammock.

"The operative word around here is 'gone.' People keep saying, remember the so-and-so? Gone!" said Beth.

"Here's our power pole," said Dave. "Gone!"

Beth: "We had here a beautiful queen palm, a very valuable tree."

"Gone!" they shouted as one voice.

The subtropical ecosystem of South Florida will rebound. Hurricanes are encoded into the biological design of the peninsula; the native species know how to absorb the blow. The task now is for the humans to prove they are similarly adaptable.

Perhaps the can-do exuberance is just a phase, a denial reaction. It may give way to fatigue, anger, and disillusionment once the national spotlight is gone. Things change daily, if not hourly. Baking heat turns to thunderous rain; shock becomes serenity, serenity becomes despair. The people camped out in their roofless homes will have to get out, eventually. Those who desperately wished their damaged homes could be saved may change their minds when they realize that it will never be the same, that the doors will never hang right, that the yards will never look the same, that the resale possibilities have all but vanished. The people who dug the bay bottom muck and the dead fish out of their living rooms—they have to pray for a total loss or they're stuck with the thing the rest of their lives.

A stage in human civilization is the spreading of stories. When a disaster strikes, the stories come in the form of wild, crazy, horrifying rumors.

That there are two thousand people living in the Everglades, illegal aliens afraid of deportation!

That the government is covering up the number of dead—eighty people crushed in one building alone!

That as the hurricane approached, authorities dug trenches at the landfill. Mass graves to bury the dead!

And the classic: That thousands of AIDS-infected monkeys, from a medical research facility, are roaming the streets!

The last was not totally false. There were a lot of animals on the loose—simian, bovine, canine—but they weren't vectors for disease, they were just in the same situation as everyone else, homeless and hungry.

I saw two heifers and a steer walking single-file down a suburban street. Two boys on all-terrain vehicles were buzzing around them. The steer, confused, tried to mount one of the heifers. *There are no rules anymore.*

I stopped by Monkey Jungle. Trashed, naturally. A lush paradise reduced to sticks. Bill Puckett, who runs the St. Augustine Alligator Farm tourist attraction, came down to help clean things up. He showed me around, saying, "The unique thing about the Monkey Jungle is that the people are in the cage and the monkeys run free." But the cage in which we were walking was torn, ripped up. Monkeys were all around us, waiting for something. Since the storm, both the humans and the monkeys run free.

The U.S. military dresses the same whether it is storming a foreign country or passing out water to storm victims. The standard outfit is the battle dress uniform, or BDU, and even the way the sleeves can be rolled up is covered by regulations (it must be *just so*). Undershirts are required, and boots, and long pants, everything camouflage green even though there are no leaves for thirty miles. "Comfort doesn't enter the equation," an officer tells me, rolling up his sleeves. "The Army cares abut versatility." Panama, Kuwait, South Florida—the BDU goes everywhere.

The hurricane relief effort was initially as disastrous as the storm itself. People had nothing to eat or drink for days; some were literally trapped in their homes, cut off from the outside world. The emergence of capitalism, another step in the story of civilization, was an ugly sight at first: Trucks rolled in selling ice for five bucks a bag, and $500 generators were hawked for $1,500 each (all were snapped up—supply and demand).

Local officials demanded to know where the cavalry was on this one, and soon enough, disaster relief became almost a national preoccupation. Americans are so big-hearted they are going to beat this town into the ground with disaster relief. Trucks of food have already been turned away; the radio says more trucks are on the way, from all over America, a convoy of humanitarianism and (let it be said) self-promotion. That smell in the air down here: Bodies? No, food, rotting. There are piles of clothing on the roadside, boxes and boxes of clothes strewed all over the ground, heavy stuff you could never wear in this heat anyway. In some places you can't tell the hurricane damage from the relief damage. Socialism means well, but it's not always efficient.

The real problem is, disasters can't be repaired with charity, and disaster victims can't be rescued by the cavalry. They are ultimately on their own: They have to reclaim a role in society, something other than "hurricane victim."

I went into one of the many disaster relief headquarters, inside Champagne's, a Homestead disco. A generator filled the room with a dull rumbling. More unsettling was the light, an orange glow, with spots of light roaming the walls—yes, reflections off the mirrored ball twirling over the dance floor, where newly homeless people ate free sandwiches and waited to be processed.

Sharon Fields, forty-two, had lost her house, so she came here to get relief. But she didn't know what kind of relief was being offered, or if she was eligible, or if it was really a good idea to take it. She was told to take a number. "Everything is a line!" she said. She turned to her daughter: "I can't take much more. Some people can roll with the punches. I can't."

She waited fifteen minutes and then Sharon Davis, an employee of the Federal Emergency Management Agency, came for her. Davis had a form marked Disaster Assistance Registration/Application, and a separate form filled with warnings and stipulations. Davis went into a monotonal explanation of the various types of benefits available, the caveats, the exceptions, and finally Fields said: "I don't know where I fit in. My insurance papers mean nothing to me. I am frazzled! I want to get out of here!"

Could she take the form home? No, said Davis. Fields asked Davis several questions, and each time, Davis left the table to find out the answer from a supervisor. Eventually

Fields decided to forgo the relief for the moment—it was impossible to figure out. The final stage of civilization: We get confused by the forms.

Before she left, Fields said what everyone says: Some people have it worse. She pointed to her son-in-law. "He's a repossession man. All his car dealerships are gone. Gone!"

On the trail of the Human Spirit one finds contradictions. A gutted motel on U.S. 1 in Homestead has the spray-painted greeting ENTER AND DIE (whatever happened to NO VACANCY?). The enthusiastic gunplay, the postapocalyptic fear of marauders, the squinty-eyed survivalism hardly paint a picture of Norman Rockwell community togetherness. On the other hand, there are good samaritans everywhere, people willing to drop everything to go to South Dade and help in any way possible. All that corny stuff that President Bush said about the American Spirit—it's a fact!

One afternoon while looking over a relief station I ran into an old friend, Paula Harper, an art history professor at the University of Miami. "There's not many calls right now for art history professors," she said. I asked her to say something cosmic about what it all means, the grand lesson of the disaster. She said: "I can't take quite that broad a perspective at the moment. What we were doing was putting all the cans marked 'meat' in one pile and all the cans marked 'tuna' in another pile."

So let that be the cosmic lesson. There comes a day in your life when you simply have to separate the meat cans from the tuna cans.

FLOTSAM AND JETSAM

(Or, questions of above-average miscellaneity.)

Why don't seeds die, even though they have no sustenance and are sealed inside a packet on a rack at the garden shop?

Seeds, whether they be dustlike begonia seeds or mighty coconuts, possess in common the ability to postpone life until, like Frankenstein's monster, they suddenly spring up off the slab and start wreaking havoc. In gardens throughout America there are men and women who kneel in the dirt and shake their clawlike hands at the sky, screaming I HAVE CREATED LIIIIIIIIIIFE. Gardening: hobby or horror movie?

Supposedly grain seeds found in Egyptian pyramids have germinated after thousands of years of storage. Weed seeds found on the sunken Spanish galleon *Atocha* have sprouted after 350 years in salt water. Doesn't this violate some sort of physical law? Like Newton's third corollary to the law of conservation of vegetables? (Or whatever.)

Seeds are, in fact, alive, even when they appear to be dry and dead. They're just *calm*. Seeds are like tiny plants rolled up in a ball and suffering from a severe case of the common coma.

There are even tiny leaves encased in the fruity part, sometimes. In a bean, for example, the green leaf bud is encased in white, pulpy seed leaves called cotyledons, which store all the food the bean needs while it is dormant. (Our advice is that you remember "cotyledon" and use it whenever you need a multisyllabic word with a scientific sound to it. If your child asks you what the biggest dinosaur was, say, "The Cotyledon." If you want to feign a hand injury, say, "I broke a small bone, one of my cotyledons." If you want to play golf instead of going to work, call in sick and tell your boss, "My doctor says I shouldn't drive while I'm taking Cotyledon.")

The reason the food doesn't get used up is that the bean—or any seed, really—is totally chilled out, its metabolism nearly nonexistent. But if the seed gets too warm or wet it will bolt upright, start getting big ideas, and suddenly blow all its energy before it has even hit pay dirt.

So if you want to keep those seeds in limbo successfully, it's best to keep 'em cool and dry—unless it's a coconut, which you might consider using for a piña colada.

Why do hospital gowns seem to be designed for maximum humiliation?

In civilized society, one of the general rules we abide by is: You have private parts. But a hospital is not part of civilized society. You check your dignity at the door. The hospital, in fact, wants you to be mortified, because this makes you all the more pliant and submissive.

The mortification starts when you are forced to undress completely, underwear and all, and put on a flimsy, non-heat-retaining garment that ties in back and seems de-

326 ■ WHY THINGS ARE (VOLUME II): The Big Picture

signed for emergency orifice checks. If the hospital provides no slippers, you will have to wear your street shoes. What a sight you make: your gown, your peekaboo butt, your wingtips.

Of course, your attending physician is also a mere "resident" or "intern," meaning "a person who does not sleep and may accidentally inject you with Drāno," and who ignores you for several hours except to occasionally ask in a loud voice that everyone in the hospital can hear, "YOU'RE THE RECTAL, RIGHT?"

Well, if it's any solace, we've found out why the hospital gowns are so ridiculous. They're *meant* to be flimsy because that requires less fabric and costs the hospital less. It's the awful truth! Why do they open in back? Well, it's either that or the front. Choose your humiliation.

Kathy Bennett, spokeswoman for ATD-American Co., a hospital supplies manufacturer in Wyncote, Pennsylvania, says there are all kinds of gowns that hospitals can buy, and some do cover the patient fully. There is, for example, the "3-Armhole Wrap-Around All Purpose Gown," which, according to the ATD catalogue, is the "Ultimate in Modesty." But the cheapest gown is the "Center Back," meaning the one that ties in the center of your back with no overlapping fabric.

"The ones that open in the back are the most economical. That's because there's the least to them," says Bennett.

After recounting her own hospital experiences—including being forced to wear high heels with a flimsy gown—Bennett comments that perhaps citizens should learn to become smarter consumers of hospital services.

"If patients started patronizing hospitals that offered more coverage, you'd better believe that the other hospitals would come around," she says.

So call your local hospital and ask if it uses "Overlapping Back" gowns, and if so, are they the ones with the four-inch overlap or the eight-inch overlap. The heaviest gowns are made of "California weight," to meet the standards of that state. But regulations vary from state to state and institution to institution.

"The lowest standards, I would imagine, are for nursing homes and jails," Bennett notes.

Why are orchestra conductors considered so wonderful even though all they do is wave their arms in the air?

The musicians do all the work and yet the guy with the little baton gets all the credit! For all we know, that man with the white hair can't even play "Chopsticks" on a piano, and thinks a cello is a funny type of guitar. Who needs him?

Actually, he (or she, though the shes are fairly few and far between) is essential. His first duty is to hire and fire the band. Then he has to be the coach. He is classical music's answer to Don Shula.

"Ninety-five percent of the activity takes place in the rehearsals, saying this is not right, that's too fast, this is too slow," says Raymond Barr, head of music history at the University of Miami. "A good orchestra can play almost without a conductor, if it's well rehearsed. But to be well rehearsed, it has to have a conductor." (Remember that a football team has only eleven people trying to behave synchronously on the playing field at a given moment, but a major symphony orchestra will have no fewer than sixty musicians playing together.)

Used to be there weren't any conductors. We're going back to the 1700s, when orchestras played only in front of royalty and nobility. The composer was in charge of everything. It was improper to turn one's back on the rich folk, so no one could get up and conduct the musicians the way it's done now. Instead, the first violinist sat in front, keeping time with his bow. Only after the French Revolution did public concert halls become common, and composers began doubling as conductors, or, to use the more economical German term, *obergeneralmusikdirektors*. (That must look great on a business card. Unlike, say, "Staff Writer.")

Nowadays a lot of conductors do no composing at all.

And whether they even know what they're doing is sometimes questionable. In many cases a modern orchestra conductor merely "jets around the world and then picks up a baton and fakes his way through a rehearsal," says Milton Babbitt, the famed composer and Princeton music professor emeritus.

"The people who conduct the big orchestras in general are show biz. . . . The big-time conductors with their enormous salaries simply do not belong to the world of contemporary musical thought," Babbitt told us, and though he spoke over the telephone we had no doubt that he was gesticulating dramatically.

Why are there no ambidextrous baseball pitchers who "switch-pitch"?

Baseball is full of tricky hitters who can bat from either side of the plate. But where are the switch-pitchers?

Think of the implications: The batter plans to bat left-handed against what he thinks is a right-handed pitcher. (Because of the geometry of baseball and the nature of how a curve ball moves, it's easier to hit from the side of the plate opposite the pitcher's throwing arm.) But just as the pitcher seems to be ready to wind up, he suddenly switches the ball to his left hand. The batter, a switch-hitter, then jumps to the other side of the plate. The pitcher jerks around and starts to throw right-handed, the batter leaps, etc.

Fantasy? Not quite. According to baseball historian Lloyd Johnson, switch-pitching occurred several times in the 1880s. The first known instance was when Tony Mullane of Louisville baffled Baltimore by switch-pitching in a game in 1882. In 1884, Larry Corcoran of Chicago was the only pitcher left on the staff in a long game. He had a sore right arm. He pitched with his left and, uh, didn't do so hot, is what we hear. In 1888, Louisville's Ice Box Chamberlain was leading Kansas City 18–6, so he pitched the eighth and ninth innings left-handed.

Next came Paul Richards of Muskogee in a minor league game in 1928, and, in the most recent case on record, Bert "Campy" Campaneris pitched both left-handed and right-handed for Daytona Beach in the Florida State League in 1962.

But these are basically one-time stunts. There's a practical problem: Pitching effectively, with major league competence, is a complex skill. It's hard enough with one arm. With two, it is nearly impossible. That wipes out all but a few of the most ambidextrous players.

Moreover, it would be hard to keep both arms "warm," as athletes put it. Let's say you pitched with your right arm against five consecutive right-handed batters. Your left arm wouldn't be loose enough to throw a fastball ninety miles an hour.

Finally, what about the glove? Baseball prohibits a player from having more than one glove (the rule was passed a few years ago after catcher Clay Dalrymple of the Philadelphia Phillies kept a fielder's glove Velcroed to the back of his belt for making plays on runners sliding into the plate).

Journeyman pitcher Greg Harris is ambidextrous and has been vowing for years to switch-pitch. He even has a trick glove that can be twisted around to serve either the right or left hand. But no coach has let him do it. And Marty Springstead, major league baseball supervisor of umpires, says the glove probably wouldn't meet the exacting regulations of the rulebook.

Why is the Super Bowl usually such a lousy game?

Of the first twenty-six Super Bowls, only six have been decided by less than a touchdown. You could count the really great games on one hand. Why is the Super Bowl so often a Super Bore?

R.T.

Some possible answers:

1. The Super Bowl is not really much different from most football games, but we want it to be superior in order to justify all the hype. Or, in other words, "How many good football games are there during the course of a season?" asks Seymour Siwoff, president of the Elias Sports Bureau.

The problem with this explanation is that a back-of-the-envelope calculation shows the average margin of victory in the Super Bowl, since it started in 1967, has been nearly sixteen points. Just for a rough comparison, we looked at the first two weeks of the 1991 regular season. Of twenty-eight games, eleven were decided by less than a touchdown and the average victory margin was eight points. So this is a lousy answer.

2. Choking. "I think the Super Bowl represents the NFL's choking price," theorizes Jerry Magee, longtime sports-writer for the *San Diego Union-Tribune*. (Choking price is a gambler's term.) "When teams get behind in the Super

Bowl they tend to panic. We saw that in the game between the Redskins and the Bills [won by Washington, 37–24]. The Bills clearly panicked." He adds, "A lot of guys can play golf great for a buck and a quarter, but if they're playing for ten bucks they can't play worth a damn."

3. The bell curve of talent. It's lonely out on the margin. The list of truly great teams in any year is usually only one or two names long, and it's unusual for two superior teams to arise in *separate conferences* and make it through the playoff games to a Super Bowl showdown. Instead, you usually have a clear favorite, a dominating team. And guess what: It wins. Upsets, Joe Namath and the Jets notwithstanding, have been a Super Bowl rarity.

4. Chance. Numbers distribute themselves in quirky patterns that contain no larger significance. The next twenty-six Super Bowls may be unusually close. And if not, the commercials are still awesome.

Why is the Air Force just now getting around to building the B-1 and the B-2 even though it has already built the B-29, the B-52, etc.?

In 1962 the Pentagon decided that the numbers on bombers and fighter planes were getting too high—into the three digits, in the case of fighters—and started over from zero. So the B-1 we read about in the paper is not the first B-1. There was a B-1 designed back in 1926, and also a B-2. (The B-2, today, is more commonly known as a Stealth bomber.)

Amazingly, there seem to be a number of people in the military whose job it is to decide what number to give an airplane. This awesome task is handled by the Engineering Services Group of the Engineering Documents Division of the Aeronautical Systems Division at Wright-Patterson Air Force Base in Dayton, Ohio.

Shorty Hess, an equipment specialist in that division, says he and his colleagues normally recommend that the

332 ■ WHY THINGS ARE (VOLUME II): The Big Picture

plane be assigned the next highest number. Simple enough. That would mean that the new fighter for the Air Force should be the F-24. But wait! The Pentagon brass, for reasons unclear, decided to call it the F-117A—so much for getting rid of big numbers. Government bureaucracy is like that, and in the case of the Pentagon moguls, there's no war going on, so *bureaucracy is all they have left*.

Why can't we clean up oil slicks by burning them?

We can. Sometimes. In fact, they tried that with the huge spill from the *Exxon Valdez* in Alaska. It didn't work. The trick is, you have to start the fire soon after the spill, when the lighter, more volatile parts of the crude oil have yet to evaporate. Crude oil contains an assortment of hydrocarbon molecules, ranging from propane and butane to heavy, sludgy stuff that is basically asphalt. The lighter elements are what will burn on top of the ocean.

Flicking one's Bic over oil spills "is a time-honored process," says Exxon spokesman Amos Plante. One reason you don't see the technique used more often is that you have to make sure there aren't any boats around, like grounded tankers, that might go up in flames. The other reason is that it makes an appalling pall of black smoke. You can just imagine what your basic major oil company thinks when it sees that it has not only polluted the ocean but also the atmosphere: Another public relations nightmare!

Why are there twenty-four hours in a day?

You're thinking: Because there *are* twenty-four hours in a day. (This is why you don't get to be on the Why staff.)

The Egyptians determined that twelve major constellations rise in the sky during the night. This was, obviously, back when there was no TV and people had nothing to do but wander in the dark. So the Egyptians divided the night into twelve segments, what we now call hours. Despite their pyramid skills, however, they were so daft they didn't think to make the hours of equal length. That came later.

They also had a peculiar system for daytime: They decided there were ten daylight hours—the decimal system is popular in every culture because you can count with your fingers—and then, since it seemed kind of weird having twelve night hours and only ten day hours, they slyly added an additional "twilight" hour to either end of the daytime, bringing the total number of hours to twenty-four.

Then they made the hours "equinoctial," which is an extremely fancy way of saying they all lasted sixty minutes. But now you want to know why there are sixty minutes in an hour. That's because 60 is a special number: divisible by 1, 2, 3, 4, 5, 6, 10, 12, 15, 20, 30. Very impressive! Plus, you can do funky things with 60, like make a clock face in which a one-twelfth turn means both five minutes and one hour.

Why do certain colors "go together" while others "clash"?

We are experts in this subject because we once rented a furnished apartment with a mandarin orange couch and a pinkish-red shag carpet, a combination that invariably incited guests to long discussions of Color Theory.

The three aspects of color are easily memorized:

1. Hue. This refers to the extremely scientific fact that different colors are nothing more than light waves of different wavelengths, in the visible portion of the spectrum. Pink and red are of the same hue but look different because of:

2. Saturation. If you dilute red—that is, add gray—you get pink. Saturation means how pure the color is. This should not be confused with:

3. Value, sometimes called "brilliance." This is a measure of how light or dark the color is—literally, how reflective it is of light.

When two colors "clash," it is often because they are close to each other in hue, saturation, or value. Red doesn't go with orange because they are adjacent on the spectrum. But a red rose surrounded by green leaves looks great, because green is distant from red on the spectrum, and the colors are therefore "complementary." Navy blue doesn't go with black because they are too similar in value. And deep red doesn't go with a slightly lighter red, because they are nearly identically saturated.

Designers possess a "color wheel" that puts all the colors in a circle. They usually pick color combos from opposite sides of the wheel. Why are opposites attractive? To some extent, it's cultural. Nature does not dictate that green looks good with red, but we think it does. Or take purple and yellow. They are different hues, but together they look garish. This is because we're trained, from childhood, to think purple-and-yellow is a loud, unpleasant, revolting combination. (Which is why many teenagers and several radical French designers are now using lots of purple and yellow.)

That said, there may be a certain artistic sensibility that goes beyond culture. You could argue that psychedelic patterns and clashing colors are inherently less pleasing than simple, understated designs in which one color dominates and complementary colors are used as highlights.

That's because profusion begats confusion, whereas simplicity spawns serendipity. Designers therefore rarely mix colors in equal proportion, preferring to have one dominant color making up at least 70 percent of the composition, with a subordinate and perhaps tertiary color making up the rest.

Explains Leatrice Eisman, director of the Pantone Color Institute in Woodland Hills, California, "If a woman has a dress and it's divided down the center with one solid stripe, and she has black on one side and red on the other, it's a very boring kind of look; it's very staid. Whereas if you move that line over and make it asymmetrical, and the red becomes dominant, then you have what I call the aha! syndrome. You look at it and you say, 'Now I get the message of that garment.' "

Okay, so maybe those of us who are severely fashion impaired still find the message a bit cryptic. Our best fashion advice is: Stick to black. It travels anywhere. Never goes out of fashion. Wear it and people might think that you are someone.

Why is the cloverleaf-shaped suit in a deck of cards called "clubs," instead of "clovers"?

This is a case of multiculturalism gone too far.

The design that we call "clubs" is, in fact, a cloverleaf. The clover design is taken from French playing cards. The French word for a clover is *trefle* and appropriately enough, when the French play cards, they call clubs *trefles*.

The English, though, got a trifle mixed up. The mistake occurred back in Renaissance times: They adopted the French cloverleaf design, but instead of calling it a clover they called it a club, because "clubs" was the name of one of the suits on Spanish cards in those days. The word "club" is an exact translation of the Spanish word "basto" and the Italian word "bastone," according to the *Barnhart Dictionary of Etymology*. Even on some new Spanish and Mexican playing cards today there is an illustration of a club.

Now, you ask, what kind of club was on these old Spanish cards? A wooden object? Or something like Studio 54? The answer is that it's something with which you would whonk someone else over the head. A cudgel.

We confirmed this with Bernice De Somer, director of the Chicago Playing Card Collectors, who has actually seen some of these cards. They feature wooden clubs, she says, like those used by "the cave people."

(Note: We later got some Spanish playing cards in the mail from a helpful reader. Sure enough: The King was carrying a club big enough to brain an elephant.)

Why aren't racehorses getting any faster, the way humans are, even though horses, not humans, are carefully bred for speed?

First, today's betting tip: Never put money on a horse with the name "Glue Boy."

Now, back to breeding. The mystery is this: It doesn't work. Horse breeding is kind of like alchemy—it's more hocus-pocus than science.

Take the 1989 Breeders' Cup. Two great horses, Sunday Silence and Easy Goer, strained and grunted for a mile and a quarter and finished almost as close as they started out. Sunday Silence won by a neck. The time: About three seconds slower than the record for that distance, set in 1977 at Santa Anita Park in Arcadia, California, by some creature named Double Discount.

The fastest a horse has ever run a quarter-mile is 20.8 seconds. That was Big Racket back in February 1945. The record for two and a half miles was set by Miss Grillo in 1948. The three-mile best is still claimed by Farragut from 1941.

You could argue the point. Some tracks, like Santa Anita, are faster than others. And the quarter-mile, two-and-a-half-mile, and three-mile races are obsolete. But the general trend is that horses aren't getting *significantly* faster. Compare that to human beings: Florence Griffith Joyner set the 100-meter and 200-meter speed records for women in 1988. The best mile ever by a man was by Steve Cram in 1985. Most of the track records have been set in the past decade.

Does this mean that thoroughbreds are not that thoroughly bred? Neigh, say the experts. (And to think this is professional humor writing.) The top times haven't changed much, but speeds *on the whole*—including all those 90-to-1 long shots—have improved. "The average horse these days runs very close to the speeds only the great horses used to run," says Jeff Seder of Equine Biomechanics, a Philadelphia company that gathers data and advises horse breeders.

So why haven't the top speeds changed much? There are several possible answers:

1. The ability to run fast is not genetically simple, as Colin Tudge noted in a 1989 article in *New Scientist*. So the chances that it will be passed on from one generation to another are slim. Speed is a "polymorphic trait" depending on such factors as muscle density, length of stride, efficiency of the blood to process oxygen, and intangibles like courage and pride. The more variables there are, the harder it is for a trait, including speed, to be inherited. This is also true of humans, which is why the children of great athletes are rarely great athletes themselves.

2. Breeders deliberately limit their horses' effectiveness. Because racing is a sport—and a high-stakes business—horses aren't bred the same way that, say, bulls or pigs are. A good bull will have his semen dispersed by artificial insemination to innumerable cows, but horses are allowed to breed only in the old-fashioned, romantic way, to avoid flooding the market. The owners charge a hefty price for such a fling. This limited edition approach limits the chances of producing a champion colt. Even a great horse like Secretariat needs a lot of chances: Of all his offspring, only one, Risen Star, won numerous stakes.

3. Breeders are dumb, sometimes. We are told by breeding expert Paul Mostert, a professor of mathematics at the University of Kansas, that the horse community has suffered from some rather unscientific thoughts over the years, such as the idea that a little dose of these genes and a little dose of those genes will result in a genetically perfect horse. For instance, a breeder might try to combine the genes of a great sprinter with the genes of a great long-distance horse. The result: A horse destined to become dog chow.

There's no reason to think that genes stack up on top of each other rather than cancel each other out. "You can't just mix up horses like you do a batch of pancakes," Mostert says.

4. Horses are retiring before they're physically mature. A lot of the old speed records were set by five-year-olds. But now horses race at a younger age, starting at age two, and are more likely to get hurt (perhaps because physical soundness is not sufficiently emphasized in breeding). They're put out to stud while they're still adolescent.

5. Horses have hit their genetic peak already. Breeding has been around for centuries and horses can't get faster indefinitely. At some point a species runs into a wall. Why are humans more successful at improving their times? Because humans are more adaptable than horses. They're more easily trained, more clever, able to master complex new techniques. And have such great new sneakers!

DEAR "WHY THINGS ARE"

(The public demands answers—
and still doesn't understand that
we only do Why questions.)

As you may know, this book grows out of a weekly column that is researched and manufactured at the Why Things Are International Command Bunker, a fifteen-acre underground micro-city originally constructed by the Pentagon as the operations center for the prosecution of prolonged nuclear war. With the Cold War over, the military sold the facility at auction, and we made the purchase with a portion of the proceeds from our first book.

As part of a process of opening up to public scrutiny, we now permit tourists to view certain activities within the bunker through large plate-glass windows, like those used at seaquariums. Footprints are painted on the floor to show visitors where they are permitted to stand. No photographs are allowed, but a few out-of-focus postcards are on sale in the gift shop.

The bunker has a number of unusual design features. There are no clocks, only a huge pendulum in the center of the room, by which researchers synchronize their own personal wrist-pendulums; intrabunker communication is effected by small slips of paper sucked through vacuum tubes; beneath each researcher's chair is a trapdoor leading to a pool stocked with man-eating sharks (because one can never be too complacent about errors).

But surely the most dramatic sight, even more compelling than the geysers of blood from a researcher who has made a spelling mistake, is the daily mail delivery. Letters are delivered on pallets hauled into the bunker with fork-lifts, then sorted by topic (Big Bang Revisionism, Sex Habits of Ancient Greeks, Why Drive On Parkway But Park On Driveway, How Come Men Got Nipples, etc.). Eventually the Why staff plans not only to write back to our correspondents but also to pay them each a personal visit, possibly over a long weekend. Until then, the letters pile up, higher and higher, a monument to human curiosity.

We have an extremely strict policy of never answering non-Why questions, except when we are "in the mood." Here, then, are some of those format-busting or merely bird-brained questions we rescued from the oblivion of The Pile. Many of the questions are like this one from Fred K., of Royal Oak, Michigan:

How high above San Francisco would a beacon light have to be in order to be seen when one is standing on Virginia's coast at sea level using a high-powered telescope?

Dear Fred: The answer is some number. You need to contact nerds of a higher order. Call NASA.

Jim H. of Detroit sends us a record-breaking list of twenty-five questions, including:

The expansion joints on freeway bridge girders look like two meshed S-shapes pinned together with large bolts. The S-shapes appear to be oriented so that if the bolts fail most of the bridge will pancake on the road below. Why is this?

Dear Jim: You dolt, those aren't S-shapes, those are 5s!

Timothy W. of Arlington, Virginia, writes:

If, when you raise your right arm while looking into a mirror, the person in the mirror raises their left, then why aren't they standing on their head?

Dear Tim: We get this question constantly, and it makes us want to do something rash, like eat a beer bottle. Trust us: A standard, flat mirror doesn't switch anything. It merely *reflects*. In your brain, though, you imagine a switch: You see your image, pretend that the image is, in fact, *you*, and then you get flustered because the part in your hair is on the wrong side. Just repeat to yourself: *The man in the mirror is not real.*

Rita R. of South Daytona Beach asks:

Why is it that when we open our eyes we see instantly, but when our eyes are closed we do not see the back of our eyelids?

Dear Rita: The bulb inside switches off when you shut your eyes. This design is modeled after the refrigerator.

Bill C., of Summerland Key, Florida, writes:

It's raining very hard and I do not have a raincoat or an umbrella. My car is parked two blocks away. Should I walk, which will expose me to the rain for a longer period of time, or should I run and intercept more rain drops with my rapid forward movement?

Dear Bill: Let's not waste any time getting to the obvious answer. RUN, FOOL.

That said, there are some surprising subtleties to this. We asked Robert Park, a University of Maryland physicist, to figure out the relationship between your speed of travel and how wet you get. He made some assumptions, to make the calculations easier, starting with: You're a rectangle. You have a flat top, flat front, flat back, etc. Also, the rain is falling straight down.

His conclusion is rather amazing: You can walk in slow motion or run like Carl Lewis and it won't affect how wet your front side gets. Your tie, for example, will soak up exactly the same amount of water regardless of your speed.

Why? Because as you go faster, your front side intercepts more rain, but you also shorten the duration of your journey, and these two factors cancel each other out precisely.

So why run? Because your top side will be drier. A lot drier. The amount of rain that falls on your head, Park says, is *inversely proportional to the square of your velocity.* (You have to love the way physicists always manage to use the square of things.)

Though we are incredibly appreciative of Park's efforts, we do need to acknowledge one nitpick: In real life, your front side probably does get a bit wetter if you walk slowly through the rain, because there is water that dribbles from your head down onto your front. See, people are not, in fact, rectangular. Though we've known a lot of squares in our day.

Lucia W. of Troy, Michigan, sent a letter of desperation, asking if we knew the technical name for the pound sign on a telephone.

Dear Lucia: We are told by AT&T Bell Labs that it is, as you suspect, the "octothorp," although there is some question as to whether there's an *e* on the end. The word is rather controversial. Western Electric, the former AT&T subsidiary that manufactured telephones, complained in 1973 that the word "octothorp" was a contrivance of unknown origin, and that the real name for the button is "the number sign."

Frankly, we think it should be called "the tic-tac-toe button."

Len D. of Wheaton, Maryland, asks:

What shape would a match flame make on the space shuttle?

He made a guess: Spherical. He was right. A match flame points upward only in the presence of gravity. The flame heats the air, which expands and rises, creating an updraft that stretches the flame. Without gravity, there's no such air flow.

But lighting a match is not something that you'd actually want to *do* on the shuttle, says Brad Carpenter, a scientist at NASA who specializes in microgravity. Although the match wouldn't burn with much intensity (because the lack of air flow inhibits the amount of oxygen getting to the flame), the soot might damage instruments, and if anything went wrong, "there's no fire escape."

A certain Mrs. Richards, a teacher at South Middle School in Belleville, Michigan, sends us a conundrum and demands an explanation:

A man climbed up on the roof, then he jumped off. Q: Where was he when he jumped? A: On the roof? No, he was on the roof before he jumped. A: In the air? No, he was in the air after he jumped.

This is, on the surface, just a semantics issue. Mrs. Richards is concerned that the word "jump" refers solely to the precise moment when the man loses contact with the roof. But a jump is a complex sequence of events that starts when he's on the roof (her first possible answer) and ends when he's in the air (the second possibility). Recommendation: Say "He jumped from the roof."

Lurking beneath this question is a puzzle that has been around for a couple of millenniums. Mrs. Richards is perhaps confused by the idea that an infinitely reducible series of steps can add up to a finite result. This is Zeno's paradox. Zeno of Elea, a Greek philosopher who lived about 2,500 years ago, said that it ought to be impossible to walk across the room, much less climb a ladder and jump off the roof. He gave as an example a race between Achilles and a tortoise.

He said, imagine that Achilles runs ten times as fast as the tortoise. But the tortoise has a head start of ten feet. The race begins. At some point Achilles will reach the ten-foot mark, but—here's the problem—he won't have caught the tortoise, because it would have moved forward another foot. Right? So, without pause, Achilles keeps zooming forward, but when he reaches the eleven-foot mark he still is trailing, because by that time the tortoise will have inched forward a little bit more, to a little over eleven feet and one inch in front of the starting point. Zeno argues that Achilles, in fact, can *never* catch the tortoise, because there always is another little gradation, ever smaller and smaller, between the man and the creature.

The Greeks were so perplexed by this that they began to dread the concept of the infinite. (Isn't that called zenophobia?) Since then, mathematicians have calmed down and realized that when something gets infinitely small—in this case, the distance between Achilles and the tortoise—it reaches zero. It may be true that, as Zeno said, there are infinite divisions within a finite distance, but the distance itself *is still finite*. That's why it's possible to walk to the other side of the room, notwithstanding the infinite gradations along the way. And that's also why there are an infinite number of points on a line, even though it may be merely a foot wide.

Zeno's paradox is thus a psychological problem, not a mathematical one. Psychologically, we find it hard to conceive that an infinite series of steps would have a finite result.

This just goes to show that if you think too hard, you'll get nowhere in life.

S.A.H. of Penfield, New York, asks:

If I were to drill a hole through the center of the earth

(pole to pole) and then dropped a baseball in the hole, would the ball stop at the center?

Dear S.A.: Nope.

Let's say, for the sake of argument, that we drill this hole and put in place a frictionless tube. Okay, sure, there's no such thing as a frictionless tube, but we can pretend. We'll also stipulate that the inside of the tube is a perfect vacuum. Thus, there's nothing to rob any energy from our plummeting baseball.

We drop the baseball at ankle level into the tube. Then we wait.

An hour passes.

We wait some more.

After exactly 84.4 minutes, the ball will reappear at our feet. This is a true fact.

The precise moment that we notice the ball, it will start to drop away from us again. Then it will reappear a second time after another 84.4 minutes. This process will repeat itself into eternity.

The 84.4 minutes is, obviously, a special number. It's called the Schuler period, after a physicist named Max Schuler, who first worked out the equations. (Most great physicists are named Max.) What happens is that the moment you drop the ball, it starts accelerating toward the center of the earth. At the center it hits maximum velocity, a speed of about 18,000 miles an hour, estimates our trusted source, Chuck Counselman of the Massachusetts Institute of Technology. The ball then starts slowing down, and finally stops "falling" the moment it reaches the other side of the earth. Then it starts back our way, zooming by the center, until it returns to its starting position at our feet.

That is not the last time we come across the Schuler period. Let's say we build a shorter tube, one that doesn't go straight through the center of the planet, but instead goes from New York to London. The tube would therefore not represent the diameter but rather a "chord" (surely you remember these geometry terms). We drop the ball. It falls somewhat more slowly this time, because it is not heading straight toward the center of the earth's mass. It reappears at our feet after . . . 84.4 minutes. The distance was shorter, but the acceleration wasn't as great, and these variables cancel out each other.

Now let's say we stand on an open prairie and hurl the baseball on the horizontal plane with such incredible velocity that it goes into a perfect head-high orbit around the planet. (Scientists actually use the term "rooftop satellite" to describe such an object; once again, for simplicity's sake, we'll pretend there's no atmospheric drag.) We would eventually be able to turn around, lift a mitt, and catch the ball as it arrived from the opposite direction. How long would this orbit last? You got it: 84.4 minutes. That dang number is everywhere!

There is a lesson here, and try to wrap your soggy brain around it: An object in orbit, whether it is a baseball or a space shuttle or a communications satellite, is actually falling the entire time. Astronauts can attest to this: The sensation they feel of weightlessness is really the sensation of free fall. So just as a baseball "falls" through the center of the earth, so too can it fall *around* the planet in what we'd call an orbit.

As for throwing a baseball around the earth, that's obviously impossible. Though maybe Nolan Ryan should give it a try.

A question that pops up frequently in journalism circles is:

Does the Christian Science Monitor *provide health care benefits to employees?*

In case this is too obscure, please understand that Christian Scientists don't believe in using medicine or medical intervention. So naturally, journalists, who tend to be a fairly sickly species, are concerned that if they were to work for the *Monitor* they might have to try to pray themselves healthy.

The answer is: Yes, the *Monitor* offers health benefits, since some *Monitor* employees aren't Christian Scientists. The paper gives its employees a choice of either a standard medical insurance program or a Christian Science treatment program provided by the Mother Church.

"The healing prayer of practitioners is generally recognized [by insurance companies] today as a legitimate and effective method of treatment for disease, sickness, or injury," says W. Michael Born, a church spokesman. Thus, he said, even if you don't work for the *Monitor* or any other Christian Science office, your existing insurance would probably reimburse the cost of "scientific prayer treatment."

And best of all: No needles.

Seth K. of Silver Spring, Maryland, writes:

What do classical DJs do while the music is playing?

Dear Seth: We turned your question over to Robert Aubry Davis, a classical music DJ at WETA-FM in Washington, D.C. He said he tapes interviews, writes to record companies to get free CDs, answers letters, and stays plenty busy. He adds, though, "There are classical DJs or broadcasters who literally are glued to the board, don't move, and think about what they're going to say for forty-five minutes until the end of the Brahms piano quartet." And some cuts are even longer: "They can be as long as Mahler's Third or Gliere's Third, each of which is over an hour and a half."

Charles F. of Detroit writes,

Is it in essence true that there are two dimensions below us and dimensions to infinity beyond the third dimension?

Dear Chuck: You should have paid attention to Rod Serling, who summarized the situation perfectly: "There is a fifth dimension, beyond that which is known to man. It is the middle ground between light and shadow, between science and superstition, and it lies between the pit of man's fears and the summit of his knowledge. This is the dimension of the imagination. It is an area which we call The Twilight Zone."

What Serling didn't say is that there may be as many as

ten or even twenty-six dimensions. That's the word from theoretical physicists. A theoretical physicist is paid to think up dumb stuff like that. If you corner one of these geniuses and ask the obvious question about the phantom dimensions—where are they?—you'll probably be told that they are very small and curled up and aren't "flat" like the dimensions we experience. (Ah, *that* old excuse.) Essentially, these extra dimensions are just mathematical inventions.

In our own experience, there are exactly four dimensions. We see three of them, and have a psychological perception of the fourth (time). Einstein realized that space and time are inseparable, that time does not have some independent reality but rather is merely a dimension by which we can describe the coordinates of an object (i.e., we can say that Michael Jordan is ten feet off the ground at longitude 88 west and latitude 42 north at 8:30 P.M.—four coordinates).

In Stephen Hawking's book *A Brief History of Time* (universally owned but not actually read), he gives a terrific summary of why our universe *must* be four "flat" dimensions. In a world with more than three spatial dimensions, gravity would be different—it would fluctuate more dramatically as distances between objects varied (in our universe it decreases quite dependably by the square of the distance between objects). This would in turn prevent matter from cohering into nice, stable solar systems capable of supporting life.

Moreover, living creatures probably need at least three spatial dimensions, because otherwise blood and nutrients couldn't circulate. If you draw a person on paper, showing food entering at one end and waste exiting at the other, you'll see the problem: Your two-dimensional person is in two pieces, bisected by the gastrointestinal passageway. How could you live if you were literally cut in half?

This doesn't mean 2-D or 10-D universes don't exist somewhere out there. But they would probably remain lifeless. In fact, a 4-D universe like ours might be rare, but these are the only kind of universes in which there are living creatures who count dimensions.

Vernon F. of Lake Mary, Florida, asks:

If the pilot of a military airplane flying at five hundred miles an hour fires his gun's bullets at five hundred miles an hour velocity, would the bullets just drop out of the barrel? If he fires them from a turret backward, would the bullets just drop out?

Vern, in your first example, the bullets would travel at a thousand miles an hour relative to the ground (500 plus 500), and five hundred miles an hour relative to the plane. Your second guess is correct, insofar as the bullet would appear, from the ground, to fall out of the barrel. But most bullets go faster than five hundred miles an hour, so you're not likely to see this happen. Also, keep in mind that the days of the Red Baron are over, and fighter jets aren't twittering around going *rat-tat-tat* anymore; they prefer to use missiles, which sound more like FWEEEESSSH . . . FOOM!

Harvey K. of Arlington, Virginia, asks:

Why don't we feel the Earth's spin around its axis?

Dear Harvey: As a kid you probably learned that gravity saves us from the centrifugal force of the Earth's spin, which supposedly would otherwise send us winging off into space. That's a stretcher. The planet isn't really spinning very fast. Sure, if you're standing at the equator you're whizzing along at about a thousand miles an hour, but the planet is so big that it takes twenty-four of these hours to make a single revolution, which is extremely tame compared to your basic puke-inducing carnival ride.

Moreover, the planet is flat. Sort of. Go outside sometime. It looks flat. The earth is so big that the surface curves gently, imperceptibly. This is important, says Tina Kaarsberg, a physicist at the American Physical Society in Washington, D.C. The gentle curvature means that as the earth spins, we change the direction of our motion through space *very slowly*.

Think of it this way: You're driving down the interstate. Your speed is constant, your direction is straight—and so your body barely registers any motion at all. When you come to a sharp curve to the left, however, your body lurches right. If the curve is gentle, you feel essentially nothing. The earth has that kind of gentle curve, and thus gives us a smooth, nondizzying ride. It's the Lincoln Town Car of planets.

Speaking of winging off into space, Doug E. of Miami asks:

What happens to bodies that float off into space? Preservation or eventual rot?

Dear Doug: Our sources say that you wouldn't rot, because the bacteria wouldn't last that long. But you would gradually erode. The solar wind—atomic particles ejected by storms on the sun—would eat away at your frozen carcass. And you'd also get cratered by dust and other microasteroids moving at high speed. Fortunately, your bones and connective tissues would probably prevent you from being actually shattered.

John T., of Winter Springs, Florida, asks:

When I meet the Grim Reaper, will my new heart pacemaker still keep my heart beating on and on, for eternity?

Dear John: It'll try. A pacemaker battery can last up to eight years, according to Joe Klingensmith, quality assurance manager at Biocontrol Technology Inc. (By the way, some of the firm's pacemakers are nuclear-powered, and the Nuclear Regulatory Commission requires the company to recover them after the patient is deceased.) Unless the pacemaker is "explanted," as Klingensmith puts it, it will continue to pace away even if you are declared brain-dead. Once you die, though, the electrolytes in your blood aren't replenished, and the pacemaker quickly loses its ability to make the heart muscle contract. Thus you needn't worry about your casket making noise, like some twist on Edgar Allan Poe's "The Tell-Tale Heart."

Jim A. of Washington, D.C., asks:

Why can't we move faster than the speed of light?

Jim, experiments have confirmed that it would take an infinite amount of energy to accelerate any object to the speed of light. (Okay, so "experiments have confirmed" sounds lame; if you want something better, find the kind of book that has footnotes.)

Even something as tiny and fast as an electron doesn't quite reach the speed of light. Your phone calls, which run on electricity, do not even operate at the speed of light, contrary to popular belief.

The reason a photon (the unit of light) goes faster than an electron is that a photon is pure energy. It would have *no mass at all* if it ever came to rest. A photon is like a packet of nothingness moving really fast. For something to go faster than the speed of light (i.e. faster than a photon), it would have to be a packet of less-than-nothingness.

Tom N. of Spotsylvania, Virginia, asks:

Why is it possible to go east forever, round and round the globe, yet it's not possible to go north forever?

Disturbing question. Think: If you go north, you eventually hit the North Pole, and then have no choice but to go south. But going east, you never suddenly find yourself having to go west.

There's a good reason for this. It's because there's no East Pole. Earth has only two poles, the terminal points of the planet's rotational axis. When we say we are going "north," we mean we are moving toward one of these poles. Eventually we will get there, and thus, by definition, we can go north no more.

In contrast, when we say we are going "east," our reference point is less obvious; "east" might be best defined as the direction of Earth's rotation. Because there's no East Pole that you can ever reach, your eastward journey never ends. This is what the Zen masters teach.

A correspondent in Alexandria, Virginia, writes:

Last night before I fell asleep I thought of two really great questions. But now I can't remember what those questions were. Now my question is, Why do we forget things?

We referred your question to Dan Alkon, chief of the Neural Systems Laboratory for the National Institutes of Health, and he said ... uh, let's see ... darn, where are those notes ... oh yes, he said that you're probably dying. Not really! (Yet another humor diversion while we collect our thoughts.) He said that basically you have way too many perceptions constantly bombarding you, and thus too many new memories getting stored in your brain, to allow you to retrace your steps and find one specific memory that you filed last night. That question of yours is buried under the clutter of your cranial desk.

"What you really have to do is find a new path, and you can't do that on purpose at the spur of the moment," he said. In other words, chill out. It'll come to you. But then you'll probably forget it again. Whenever we come up with good Why questions we always jot them down immediately, without fail, on little pieces of paper.

Which are around here somewhere . . .

• • •

A final thought. In general, there are two complaints leveled against our weekly column: We don't know what we're talking about, and no one cares about our questions anyway. As for the first, we can assure you that omniscience doesn't come easily to us—it takes several hours of work every week and often two or three phone calls, possibly even some reading.

It's the second criticism that hurts us deeply and makes us consider getting out of the Why business once and for all, insanely lucrative though it may be. A recent critic wrote that the questions we pick "are of little or no concern to your subscribers," and added, "Somewhere along the line, [the Why staff] went from giving us relevant, practical information, and then meandered into the realm of conjecture."

Dear Mr. Critic: When did we *ever* provide "practical information"? Find us the date of that column so we can root it out from our records and burn it. Facts may be useful, but conjecture is beautiful.

Yes, many of our topics may be of little or no concern to some of our readers, and we wish it were otherwise, but we're not going to start doing "market research" as a way of giving our material a wider appeal. We aren't manufacturing a McColumn.

That burst of defensiveness aside, let's deal with a question this hurtful critic sent our way:

Is it still possible to find a TV set that is manufactured in our country by a company that is not owned by a foreign nation?

You're outta luck. "American-made" products are rapidly becoming extinct, except in the dreams of consumers and the rhetoric of politicians. We called a major electronics store and were told that it stocks twelve different brands of televisions: GE, JVC, Magnavox, Mitsubishi, Panasonic, Philco, Quasar, RCA, Sharp, Sony, Toshiba, and Zenith. You would think that surely there's an American TV in there somewhere, but the labels are deceiving. The televisions with GE and RCA labels are made by a French company, Thomson Electronics. Philco and Magnavox televisions are made by a Netherlands company. Zenith is an American company, but it makes most of its televisions in Mexico. The exception, until recently, was a twenty-seven-inch top-of-the-line model made in Springfield, Missouri, but Zenith announced in November 1991 that it was shutting down the Springfield factory and moving the assembly operation to Mexico.

So what should you do? Joel Joseph, chairman of the Made In The USA Foundation, in Bethesda, Maryland, suggests buying a television that is at least partially assembled in the United States. We are informed that this includes some Magnavox, RCA, Mitsubishi, and Sony televisions. So our "practical information" for those who want to buy an American television is: Read a book instead.

INDEX

ABOUT THE AUTHOR

Joel Achenbach was born in 1960 in Gainesville, Fla. After graduating from Princeton University he spent eight years as a reporter for *The Miami Herald*. Since 1990 he has worked for the Style section of *The Washington Post*, writing feature stories and the weekly column "Why Things Are," which is syndicated nationally by The Washington Post Writers Group. His commentaries appear regularly on National Public Radio's "Morning Edition."